The Parliaments of Early Modern Europe

MICHAEL A.R. GRAVES

Longman

An imprint of **Pearson Education**

Harlow, England · London · New York · Reading, Massachusetts · San Francisco
Toronto · Don Mills, Ontario · Sydney · Tokyo · Singapore · Hong Kong · Seoul
Taipei · Cape Town · Madrid · Mexico City · Amsterdam · Munich · Paris · Milan

Pearson Education Limited

Head Office:
Edinburgh Gate
Harlow
Essex CM20 2JE
Tel: +44 (0)1279 623623
Fax: +44 (0)1279 431059

London Office:
128 Long Acre
London WC2E 9AN
Tel: +44 (0)20 7447 2000
Fax: +44 (0)20 7240 5771
Website: www.business-minds.com

First published in Great Britain in 2001

ISBN 0 582 30587 X

British Library Cataloguing-in-Publication Data
A CIP catalogue record for this book can be obtained from the British Library

Library of Congress Cataloging-in-Publication Data
A catalog record for this book can be obtained from the Library of Congress

10 9 8 7 6 5 4 3 2 1
05 04 03 02 01

Typeset by 7 in 11.5/13pt Van Dijck
Produced by Pearson Education Asia Pte Ltd
Printed in Malaysia,

The Publishers' policy is to use paper manufactured from sustainable forests.

Contents

List of Abbreviations

APH	*Acta Poloniae Historica*
AHR	*American Historical Review*
BIHR	*Bulletin of the Institute of Historical Research*
HJ	*Historical Journal*
PER	*Parliaments, Estates and Representation*
P&P	*Past and Present*
SHR	*Scottish Historical Review*
TRHS	*Transactions of the Royal Historical Society*

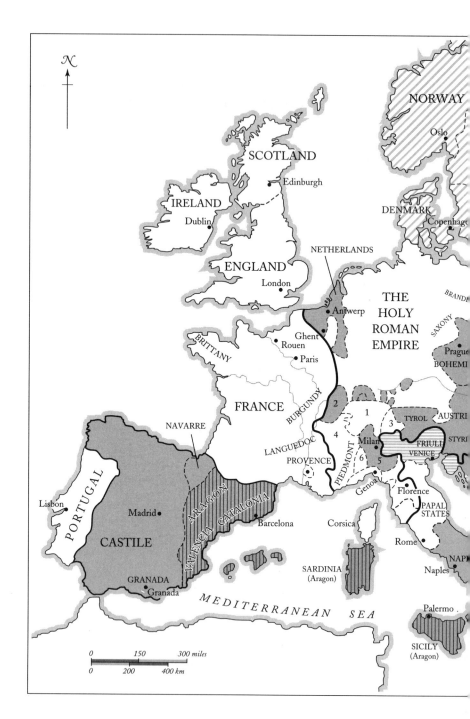

Europe in the early sixteenth century

Introduction

THE PURPOSE of this volume is to examine the fortunes of representative assemblies during a critical period in their history. The institution of parliament is central to modern political history, and not only in Europe which is the particular concern of this study. It was also very important in most parts of early modern catholic Christian Europe. As meetings between the ruler and his socio-political elite, representative assemblies were not only political fora, in which he sought advice and his subjects aired grievances, but also occasions on which *auxilium* (aid), especially in the form of taxes, was given to him and laws were enacted on a wide range of political, religious, social and economic concerns. As we proceed, however, such a statement will need qualification. Perhaps the only two constants in early modern European parliamentary history are variety in kind and variability over time. Assemblies, variously identified as parliaments, diets or estates, had titles which differed from one country, region or locality to another. They also differed widely in the time, rate and nature of their development, their structure and composition, functions and authority, and their relations with the ruler.

Any study of European parliaments must encompass and, where possible, explain such diversity. It also needs to put to rest common misconceptions about their historical development. The parliamentary tradition on the European continent is very old and not a relatively recent phenomenon triggered by political idealism and the French Revolution at the end of the eighteenth century. In particular, it should be emphasised that, in age at least, the English representative assembly was not the 'mother-of-parliaments'. When it came into existence as an identifiable parliament, it was younger than the assembly of Leon and just one of a number of institutions emerging in the thirteenth century in parts of the Spanish peninsula, Sicily, Germany and elsewhere. Furthermore, at least until the seventeenth century, some continental assemblies, such as the Cortes of Aragon, Catalonia and Valencia, the Sicilian *Parlamento* and the Polish *Sejm*, wielded more authority, possessed stronger safeguards and enjoyed greater privileges and liberties than their English counterpart.

Medieval and early modern Europe were governed by princes, the most important (though not all) of whom were kings and queens. In the past many of the national histories of those centuries have been written as regnal studies with the monarch as the focus. This has been particularly true of the early modern royal constellation of rising, ambitious and seemingly successful 'autocratic' rulers: for example, the England of Henry VIII and Elizabeth, Philip II's Spain, the reign of Frederick III of Denmark or Karl XII of Sweden and of course the Sun King, Louis XIV, in France. However, recent research is demonstrating that, behind the glittering images and pretentious façades of even the most autocratic, successful and powerful monarchies, rulers still operated a decentralised system of government, albeit less decentralised than in medieval Europe. Even as late as the seventeenth century much regional and local power remained in the hands of socio-political territorial elites, commercial cities, bureacracies and other corporate groups, all of whom possessed considerable autonomy of action.[1]

European parliaments were occasions when, for a variety of reasons, rulers met with representatives of these power-groups, who in turn represented a wide range of social, political, sectional and local interests. It is true that there was no standardised pattern of representation. In France no clergy sat in the provincial estates of Normandy, whilst nobles did not attend the assembly in Auvergne. In contrast, noble domination excluded all other social orders and corporate bodies from the Polish national assembly, the *Sejm*. And, as a further ingredient in the pot-pourri, there was peasant representation in the Tyrol, West Friesland, Sweden and (until 1627) Denmark. Diversity is the essence of European parliamentary history. Nevertheless representative assemblies were, no matter what form they took, a 'coming together' of rulers and subjects, of governments and communities. Therefore a study of them enables us to examine early modern Christian Europe through their interaction.

This is one of the specific purposes and objectives of this volume. Indeed, no meaningful study of representative assemblies is possible unless they are examined as an integral part of both the contemporary political structure and their socio-political context. They were called to assist the ruler, but their meetings were also occasions for airing discontent and giving voice to grievances. They gave public expression to problems and alerted the government as to what was going on, or going wrong, out there in the various parts of the kingdom. In other words, a parliament was a mirror which reflected the current issues, problems and stresses in the wider community. Charles I of England became painfully aware of this when he met his last assembly, the Long Parliament, in 1640. Of course, an examination of that English crisis – or indeed of any crown–parliament confrontation – in isolation does not provide a European dimension. That dimension is provided partly by the comparative framework of this study, but also by the due consideration of 'external forces', which often impacted on relations between ruler and subjects, king and parliaments. The politics, diplomacy and military burdens of the Thirty Years' War (1618–48), for example, had an important, even crucial, effect on the fortunes of assemblies in those countries caught up in the conflict. Developments in national, regional and even local representative institutions often become meaningful only if they are examined within the broader contemporary European context.

Although this is not intended to be a narrow, technical, institutional study, due attention will be given to institutional characteristics such as organisation, structure, functions and membership. Such characteristics were vital to the historical role of representative assemblies: to their relative efficiency and productivity; to their ability to support the ruler with aid and counsel and, at the same time, to represent both specific interests and those of the wider community; and above all to their capacity to protect such interests, even to survive, in the hostile political climate of early modern Europe. The last of these is the central concern of this study. The early modern period was an age of revitalised, aspiring, strong and in some cases even autocratic kingship and eventually, in some countries, of absolute monarchy. As ambitious rulers jettisoned medieval ideals of moral obligation, consensus and power-sharing in pursuit of more effective and authoritarian government, they targeted obstacles to the fulfilment of their long-term policies. Prominent amongst the obstacles were representative assemblies, in which those medieval ideals were entrenched and which often included the social orders and corporate groups most threatened by expansive monarchy. Some princes sought to subordinate them, manipulate them, or simply leave them in abeyance. In response, European assemblies became, in varying degrees, the watchdogs of privilege and power-sharing and the champions of localism, regionalism and the community-at-large, especially the community's right of consent to taxation. Characteristically the story of their fortunes and fates is one of rich diversity. In Castile, Denmark, France, Ireland, Naples, Piedmont, Scotland and some German principalities parliaments declined or disappeared. But in the elective monarchies of the Holy Roman Empire and Poland, the new Dutch state of the United Provinces, Sweden and (from the 1640s) England royal authority was restricted or eclipsed as the power of parliaments grew. It is the prime purpose of this study to trace and explain the divergent experiences of assemblies in the often turbulent political and religious transformation of early modern Europe.

Note

1   E.g. H.M. Scott, ed., *The European Nobilities in the Seventeenth and Eighteenth Centuries* 2 vols (London, 1995).

PART ONE

The Parliamentary Story

I

The Origin and Growth of European Parliaments until the Fifteenth Century

R EPRESENTATIVE ASSEMBLIES were not a dramatic innovation when they appeared on the European scene between the twelfth and fifteenth centuries. They were regional or national expressions of representation, which had for a long time been practised in central, local and ecclesiastical government and corporate bodies. Such assemblies were also the product of (1) an established socio-political system, based on lordship and vassalage and existing in much of western Europe, and (2) the principles which it embodied, in particular the legacy of Roman jurisprudence and the evolving corpus of the catholic Church's canon law. Just as important and perhaps even more so, because they were ongoing, relentless and often urgent, were the practical needs and priorities of the ruler and the ruled.

Lordship and vassalage

The development of a system of lordship and vassalage, resting on mutual loyalty and benefits, was essentially a Germanic phenomenon. It spread from the kingdom of the Franks into Germany, England and other, but not all, parts of Europe. In Spain and some of the countries of central, eastern and Scandinavian Europe feudalism evolved in a variety of ways or did not develop as fully, or even at all.[1] In its fullest form, especially in the Germanic territories, vassals had the obligation to support their lord with advice and aid, especially military assistance. This accorded with an older Germanic tradition whereby warriors had assembled *en masse* and provided the same services to their rulers.[2] The gatherings of kings and their vassals, however, do not bear any relationship to later representative institutions. They were meetings of great men. On the one hand there was the king who, as overlord, gave protection and rewards to his faithful vassals. On the other there were the vassals, who were the recipients of grants of land (fiefs) and other benefits from him or his royal predecessors. With their own vassals they rendered military assistance and, from the power-bases of their fiefs, they were in effective control of the administration of justice and the maintenance of law and order in the localities.

Although such assemblies were not representative of the community as a whole, but only meetings of great men, they had, in common with later representative institutions, the two functions and responsibilities of *consilium* (advice) and *auxilium* (aid). Furthermore, just as those who attended later parliaments thought in terms not only of obligations but also of rights – the right to be consulted, to question royal policies, to safeguard interests and even extend privileges – so, centuries before, vassals gradually extended their role and priorities at meetings with the king.[3] This is a significant link between these early gatherings and representative assemblies, because many of the vassals' descendants were to sit in the emerging parliaments as members of the privileged clerical and noble estates.

Roman and canon law

Nevertheless notions of representation had no place in such gatherings of great men. They derived from the two bodies of inherited Roman law and the developing canon law of the Church which, in time, were to pervade Europe. By the fourteenth century, when many of Europe's parliaments took shape, two legal principles upheld by both Roman and canon law had become widely accepted by governors and governed. They were *plena potestas* (full power) and *quod omnes tangit, ab omnibus approbetur* (what touches all shall be approved by all). The first of these, derived from Roman law, concerned the authority given to a lawyer who was representing his client in court. This could be and was extended to corporate representation. So full power of attorney was given by the members of a corporate body to those who represented their interests in court. In the course of time this was further extended to national concerns which touched the entire community. The king would summon representatives of the community to assemble, bearing full powers to act in its name and to make decisions which were binding upon it. This did not occur until the emergence of parliaments in the thirteenth century. Long before then however, canon lawyers had adapted this principle of Roman law in order to serve the needs of the catholic Church, which abounded in corporate bodies. During the twelfth century it was employed not only in ecclesiastical courts, but also in assemblies of religious orders and, by the pope, in Church councils. The final step was its adoption and adaptation by secular rulers. It enabled them to consult and seek the assistance, not only of great men, but also of prosperous cities and towns (with a considerable tax potential), corporations and new, emerging social groups: knights in England, lesser nobles in Aragon and Poland, and even free peasantry.[4]

The second principle, *quod omnes tangit*, was also taken from Roman law and adapted, first into canon law and then, by thirteenth-century canon lawyers, to secular needs. It was originally a legal principle which ensured that the rights of individuals and corporate groups were protected in the courts. This was achieved by the requirement that the consent of all individuals or of the majority of a corporation to a legal decision was necessary. The adoption of a majority vote in a parliamentary election or in a parliamentary division was a secular application of this principle. The extension of it from ecclesiastical to secular institutions was an acknowledgement that rulers were bound by law, custom and the rights and privileges of subjects. Between the thirteenth and sixteenth centuries *quod omnes tangit* became a constitutional commonplace, cited, quoted, set forth in parliamentary summons, or used as a justification for the existence of representative assemblies.

Limited power and growing needs

Such legal principles, however, do not of themselves explain why, in practice, medieval rulers chose to reach out from meetings with the powerful and privileged in order to consult, deliberate and reach decisions with representatives of a wider community.[5] It may be explained by the fact that the medieval prince 'was a leader, not a master . . . [H]e relied on the conscious and willing collaboration of his subjects as the most effective and easiest instrument of success'. So, Marongiu argues, it was hard political facts about a prince's limited power, his need and his dependence which promoted 'the doctrine of collaboration and consent'.[6] This may have been given further impetus by the pressing needs of princes in a Europe characterised by prolonged internal political rivalries, inter-state wars and conflict between the temporal power and the papacy: for example the Anglo-Scottish wars from the end of the thirteenth century, recurrent struggles between emperor and pope and the Hundred Years' War between England and France. Advice, the provision of justice and order, and especially military assistance and financial aid became frequent and often sustained royal needs. This would have encouraged princes to reach out beyond the gathering of vassals, in order to tap new and growing urban wealth and to enlist the active support of new emergent social groups.

The concept of community

However, Brian Tierney finds the 'administrative convenience' of representative assemblies, as a means of satisfying princely needs, an unsatisfactory explanation for their emergence. Koenigsberger offers a persuasive additional element 'inherent in the very idea of representation: a feeling of community in the whole of a given political structure'. Such community consciousness extended beyond the narrow limits of feudal vassals to encompass cities and towns, professional interests (especially lawyers) and corporate bodies, particularly those engaged in trade. It was not something which, at that early stage, could be defined as national awareness. Nor, on the other hand, was it simply an expression of protective parochial or sectional interest at a national level. However, it did denote a shift, indeed a broadening from the older feudal focus to the wider horizons of the kingdom.[7] Historians have and will continue to debate the relative importance of the part which, not only this 'feeling of community' but also feudal gatherings, the legacy of Roman law, the development of canon law in catholic Christendom and pressing royal needs all played in the emergence of European representative institutions. But it is probable that they were all of some, albeit varying, significance, as princes sought advice and consent within a framework of accepted custom and given law.

The political context of early modern parliaments

Two legacies from the ancient world of the Roman empire had an important part to play in the development of representative institutions.

One was Roman law, which, as we have seen, included the principles of *plena potestas* and *quod omnes tangit*. These, however, figured only as maxims of private law. It was the achievement of canon lawyers of the medieval catholic Church to apply them also in the field of constitutional law.[8] This brings us to the other legacy, which, in the first instance, can be traced back to the conversion of Emperor Constantine (306–37) to Christianity. Until then it had been an often unpopular minority religion and one subjected to intermittent persecution. It now became the official established Church of the empire. It was, however, a divided Church, which eventually would split into a western catholic Church, based on the see of Rome, and an eastern Greek Church centred on Constantinople (Byzantium), the city named after its founder, Emperor Constantine. The rise of an institutionalised Church in western Europe, which is the area of our particular concern, led to serious problems and conflicts over the respective roles and authority of Church and state. There was a positive side, however, to the Church's assertion of independence from secular control from the tenth–eleventh centuries onwards. As, in Tierney's words, it 'began to reshape its own laws . . . [f]or centuries the leaders of the church . . . considered the problems of right order within a Christian society; and, in doing so, they created an array of ideas and procedures that were eventually assimilated into the theory and practice of Western constitutional government'.[9] It was within this receptive climate of ideas and jurisprudence that the parliaments of western Europe emerged and developed from the late thirteenth century onwards.

The importance of the two legacies of law and Church in the origins of parliaments was considerable. Apart from that, however, the Roman world from which they derived had long since vanished by the time such assemblies began to appear. The long and complex process of economic decline, the barbarian invasions and (in the fourth and fifth centuries) the political break-up of the ancient Roman empire does not concern us here. Emperor Justinian (527–565) failed in his unrealistic attempt to revive the old empire by reconquering the west from his eastern capital, Byzantium.[10] In the seventh and early eighth centuries Muslim conquerors from the east overwhelmed Arabia (including territories belonging to Byzantium), north Africa and Spain. Their expansion into western Europe was halted only by their defeat at the hands of Charles Martel, king of the Franks, in 732 when they invaded France. The Franks, one of the Germanic barbarian peoples who invaded and, in the fifth century, settled in the western part of the Roman empire, emerged as the major force there. At the end of the fifth century the Frankish king Clovis, and therefore the Franks, was received into the catholic Church. His Merovingian dynasty ruled the Franks until 751 when it was succeeded by the Carolingians. Under the Carolingian dynasty Church and state became mutually involved in both ecclesiastical and secular government and the system of feudal lordship and vassalage, as it spread to Germany and other parts of Christian Europe. In 800 the greatest of the Carolingians, Charlemagne, was crowned emperor by Pope Leo III. However one interprets the symbolism and significance of the occasion, it certainly appeared to regenerate the Christian Roman Empire. It also affirmed and reinforced the involvement of Carolingian rulers and popes in the affairs of each other's domain. But, as the new emperor received his title and crown from the pope, it also symbolised the subordination of his kingdom to the Church.[11] Both feudal developments and what were to become the longlasting thorny issues of the authority of Church and state, and of the relationship between them, were to be important at various stages in the origins and history of parliaments.

Family conflicts amongst Charlemagne's descendants over the Carolingian inheritance, successive partitions, and the raids and invasions by Vikings, Muslims, Arabs and Hungarians in the ninth and tenth centuries resulted in the disintegration of the western empire. But out of the chaos and collapse in western Europe there gradually emerged the successor states of France and the Germanic Empire.[12] Expansion eastwards in the following centuries extended the area of Germanic control to Austria, Styria and Bohemia and, at times, of imperial overlordship of Poland. To the west there emerged feudal monarchies in England and France. Anglo-Saxon kings, Viking conquerors in the early eleventh century and Duke William of Normandy (from 1066) provided a tradition of strong institutionalised monarchy in a relatively unified English kingdom (though not in the rest of Britain). In France the expansion of royal authority and of territory directly under the control of the king, not of his vassals, was a much slower and more prolonged process, especially as some of those vassals commanded greater resources and territory. Nevertheless, such a process did occur, especially under the kings of the thirteenth and early fourteenth centuries. Meanwhile, south of the Pyrenees, which separated France from the Spanish peninsula, Christian principalities, such as Leon and Castile, Aragon and Catalonia, continued to survive north of the Muslim caliphate. From the mid-eleventh century onwards the Christians began to move southward against the Muslims in a crusade known as the *Reconquista*. In the thirteenth century the kingdoms of Portugal, Leon-Castile and Aragon (united with Catalonia in 1137 and now in possession of Valencia) had, with the exception of Granada, reconquered the peninsula. The Crown of Aragon further extended its territory into the Mediterranean with the acquisition of Sicily (1282) and Sardinia (in the fourteenth century).[13]

In all of these states, which emerged, stabilised and expanded in the centuries following the break-up of the Carolingian empire, parliaments came into existence, especially in the thirteenth and fourteenth centuries. The new states of western Europe were legatees of both the Roman empire and Christian communities. As such they were, as we have seen, susceptible to the influence of Roman legal principles to which canonists gave a constitutional dimension. Furthermore, in the feudal monarchies the meetings of rulers with their vassals helped to develop the concepts of royal responsibility, consent and the rights as well as duties of at least the greater subjects.

Why parliaments came into existence

Such ideas, concepts and legal principles help to explain the nature of medieval representative assemblies when they came into existence, but they do not explain why they did so. Most monarchs of the central and later middle ages had urgent – often military – needs. They were sometimes defensive, but often expansionist and aggressive: the monarchs' geographical extension of royal authority in France in the thirteenth and fourteenth centuries, the eastward expansion of Germanic emperors, the *Reconquista* conducted by the Christian kingdoms of northern Spain and the prolonged Anglo-French conflict of the fourteenth and fifteenth centuries are just a few examples. Such circumstances led them to seek the advice, assistance and consent not only of important individuals, but of corporate bodies which, in some sense, represented the wider community. And they were encouraged to do so by the development of community consciousness. This was a variable development. Not all monarchies were enthusiastic about consultation with assemblies. Charles VI of France (1380–1422) was advised 'that no great assemblies of nobles or of *communes* take place in your kingdom', whilst his successor Charles VII was reputedly hostile to the representative idea.[14]

Nevertheless, in most of the states of Christian Europe there was, from the late twelfth century, a move from the non-representative meetings of kings and great subjects to a more representative institution.

Just as the catholic Church had translated the principles of representation and consent from private into constitutional law, so it provided a working example of those principles. This was expressed in the ecclesiastical national synods and councils held for centuries before the emergence of secular assemblies summoned by kings. This is not to suggest that they constituted some kind of model on which secular assemblies were consciously based. Such assemblies, however, especially in the religious orders such as the Dominican friars, were precursors. And it *may* be significant that many of the medieval monarchs' ministers, councillors and bureaucrats were recruited from an educated clergy. They had knowledge, perhaps personal experience, of Church assemblies, whilst canonists in public office would have been acquainted with the constitutional application of *plena potestas* and *quod omnes tangit*.[15] We cannot be sure of the precise nature of the link between Church practice, the involvement of the clergy in secular government and the emergence of parliaments. Nevertheless it was in ecclesiastical assemblies, not meetings of kings and vassals, that the idea of representation was expressed in a practical way. From there, as Koenigsberger writes, 'it was a logical step to extend the idea of representation to secular institutions. It became convenient for rulers to summon not only individual magnates but representatives of rich cities and powerful ecclesiastical corporations.'[16]

Where and when did such parliaments emerge in catholic Christian Europe?

The earliest known assemblies were in the Spanish peninsula: in Leon in the later twelfth century and in Castile in the early thirteenth. The first known council of Leon, to which the king summoned not only prominent ecclesiastics and lords but also 'chosen' citizens from the chief cities, was held in 1188. This first recorded Cortes (parliament) was probably called involuntarily by a new king, Alfonso IX, under pressure from clergy, nobility and urban communities. Its proceedings resulted in a kind of constitutional agreement by which, in the future, the assembly would give the king honest counsel and he, in return, would act in accordance with the advice of bishops, nobles and 'wise men'. Thereafter the information on further meetings of the Cortes of Leon is very patchy. Then in the mid-thirteenth century the kingdoms of Leon and Castile were united. Until that time there is no evidence that Castilian assemblies of secular lords and churchmen were afforced by elected and participating representatives of cities and towns. When, however, the union of the two kingdoms resulted in a single Cortes, it consisted of three estates, including elected urban representatives, the *procuradores*, whose role was to grow in importance. Furthermore, they represented an expanding kingdom as the *Reconquista* made progress southwards against Islam.

During the thirteenth century, Cortes developed also in the eastern Christian kingdoms of the Spanish peninsula. In 1137 dynastic marriage united Aragon and the richer commercial Catalonia and in the 1230s King James I of Aragon-Catalonia conquered Valencia. In the federation of these three states, known as the Crown of Aragon, each one developed and retained its own parliament. Although they sometimes assembled simultaneously in one city, such as Monzon, and even met in joint sessions, particularism proved to be stronger than political union in the crown. As we shall see, their structure and organisation varied, but they shared several common features: their relations with the king constituted a legal compact with mutual obligations; they had extensive powers, including legislation and control of the grant of taxes; they were reinforced by a range of privileges, which the Castilian Cortes lacked, and by certain procedures and institutions which protected the rights and liberties of both assemblies and subjects.[17]

The Cortes of the Crown of Aragon came into being slowly and undramatically in the thirteenth and early fourteenth centuries. At an assembly of clerics, nobles and urban representatives in Catalonia in 1283, Peter III guaranteed the rights and privileges of his subjects, promised no new laws without the assembly's assent and declared that he would call annual meetings. Some historians view this as the instant at which the Corts of Catalonia were born. Thomas Bisson, however, persuasively argues that 'it would be truer to interpret this event as a fulfilment of institutional growth. Almost every element of the procedure and the programme of 1283 . . . had its precedents in Catalonia.' Furthermore, 1283 was not the curtain-raiser to dramatic development. Bisson concludes that, whilst the Cortes had 'achieved objective institutional identity' early in the next century, they 'were still in gestation'.[18] This is equally true in Aragon, where assemblies gradually assumed a parliamentary form, as urban representatives joined meetings of nobles during the thirteenth century. But the contractual relationship between king and subjects, 'upon which the basic principles of Aragonese parliamentarism were founded', was not achieved until 1348.[19] As for the Valencian Cortes, created after King James I had conquered the territory, their emergence has been dated at various points between the 1230s and the early fourteenth century.

In the thirteenth and fourteenth centuries the Aragonese federation, especially Catalonia, expanded its Mediterranean trade, political influence and, with the acquisition of Sicily and Sardinia, its possessions. In 1282 a Sicilian assembly, which for the first time included urban representatives, voluntarily offered the crown of Sicily to King Peter III of Aragon, in order to be rid of oppressive and financially burdensome Angevin rule. By 1296 it was well established in a contractual relationship with the monarchy.[20] As assemblies of the Aragonese Crown the Sicilian *Parlamento* (whose development as an assembly antedates 1282) and the later Sardinian *Stamento* both acquired many of the attributes of the Aragonese-Catalan Cortes. So representative institutions spread across the Spanish peninsula and into the western Mediterranean. In the fourteenth and early fifteenth centuries assemblies, based on fealty, *auxilium*, and decisions requiring the approval of all and binding on all, developed also in Portugal and Navarre. Although the Spanish peninsula was to be united under Habsburg rule in the sixteenth century, the component parts of this 'composite monarchy' would retain their political diversity, liberties and law. They also had and would retain separate loyalties and identity – as Aragonese, Catalans or Castilians, rather than as Spaniards. Love of *patria* (country) meant loyalty to Valencia, Portugal or Navarre rather than to Spain. Particularism resulted in the emergence of separate medieval assemblies. And it would ensure their continuation, despite a growing sense of being Spanish, which was evident from the sixteenth century.[21]

Particularism was also a political characteristic north of the Pyrenees. In France, however, there were several other circumstances which inhibited the growth of an effective general assembly for the kingdom as a whole. Some of the vassals of the French feudal monarchy, such as the dukes of Burgundy and Aquitaine and the count of Champagne, governed more extensive territories and possessed greater resources and military capacity than the king himself. Furthermore, from the mid-twelfth century, when King Henry II of England (1154–89), duke of Normandy and count of Anjou and Maine, acquired Aquitaine by marriage, his territory and power overshadowed those of the French monarchy. Such territories lay outside the effective feudal lordship of French kings.

Nevertheless they did call general assemblies of those feudal vassals and ecclesiastics who, no matter how tenuously or inconstantly, acknowledged royal overlordship. During and after the reign of Louis IX ('Saint Louis', 1226–70) representatives of towns were summoned, especially for advice on economic or financial matters. This did not, however, result in either frequent meetings or assemblies which represented the whole kingdom. Much was under English control, and French kings, such as Philip IV, Philip V and Charles IV (1285–1328), often preferred to consult with nobles, ecclesiastics and townsmen, from areas under their lordship, in two separate assemblies: for *Langue d'Oil* (the northern provinces) and *Langue d'Oc* (southern France). There were various reasons for this preference: the size of France; poor communications; the lack of a national community consciousness, which meant that members from central and distant, northern and southern provinces were unlikely to work in co-operation with each other; and royal concern that a 'national' assembly might exert greater pressure on the king, in terms of grievances and demands. Perhaps the most serious obstacle to the establishment of an effective general representative assembly was a common royal attitude: an unwillingness to allow the constraints on authority and involvement in policy which were implicit in the acceptance of the principle *quod omnes tangit*. As Marongiu points out, there is nothing in the admittedly slender evidence to prove that, in the early fourteenth century, 'the kingdom of France possessed a representative body, with definite and recognisable attributes and a deliberative power more or less accepted in public law'.[22]

Nor did this situation fundamentally change in the long term. Marongiu effectively sums up the history of French general assemblies as 'not so much the history of an institution as of single episodes and moments of history'.[23] French kings much preferred to seek *auxilium* and to hear grievances in the more communicative and productive sessions of the provincial 'estates' [assemblies]. Such assemblies developed throughout the French kingdom. They neither flourished nor lasted in central France, where royal authority was strong and effective, but elsewhere they grew in political confidence and muscle as an expression of provincial political identity. They appeared in the south, for example, in Languedoc, Provence and Dauphiné, in the east –

Burgundy – and in the English sphere of control in Normandy, Maine, Anjou, Poitou and Guyenne. By 1400 they had become constitutional fixtures, protecting local liberties and negotiating with the king's officials for an equitable sum whenever he sought taxation. There were inevitable variations: in the frequency of their meetings, their composition and powers. They did, however, have two common denominators. First, as Myers argues, 'it was not the Estates General that mattered as part of the normal machinery of government and as representative of the interests of powerful social groups; it was the provincial Estates that counted'. Secondly, 'particularism' was the paramount common characteristic.[24]

Across the English Channel particularism did not present the same kind of problem to another feudal monarchy, which ruled the kingdom of England. Medieval English monarchs were blessed with the benefits and advantages accruing from Duke William's conquest of England in 1066. With one more or less uniform system of administration and common law, the local identity of shire communities did not confront English kings with the administrative difficulties, political problems and constitutional obstacles which hedged in the French monarchy. Furthermore, the unified nature of the kingdom encouraged the growth of a conscious sense of the wider community. Therefore it is ironic that the English Parliament was not the result of a natural extension from a feudal *concilium* to a broader representative institution, in which the king sought the advice and assistance of that wider community. Instead it was, in the first instance, the product of baronial opposition to King Henry III in 1258–65. In 1264 Simon de Montfort, leader of the baronial movement, attempted to drum up community support when he summoned borough representatives and the sub-noble rural class of 'knights of the shire' to an assembly. De Montfort lost the struggle when he was killed in battle in the following year. Henry III, his son Edward I and their successors continued to call rural knights and urban burgesses to assemblies. It made political sense and it was expedient to do so. After all it was the numerous knights and burgesses rather than the few nobles who administered the county communities, maintained order and adjudicated in their courts. Nevertheless Edward I, who did so much to develop the institution of parliament, did so because he viewed it, and for much of his reign confidently used it, as an effective tool of royal government: between 1274 and 1294 he summoned it more than forty times. But frequency encourages institutional development, delineation of membership and definition of function. Furthermore, deteriorating king–parliament relations, first under Edward I from the 1290s and then under Edward II (1307–27), stimulated the growth of parliament as a critic of royal policy, defender of liberties, presenter of grievances and, finally, party to the deposition of Edward II.[25]

Parliaments developed also in England's Celtic neighbours: in the thirteenth century in Ireland and in the fourteenth century in Scotland. The great stimulus to the calling of Irish assemblies was royal financial need, especially during Edward I's wars with the Welsh, French and Scots in the later thirteenth century. He looked to Ireland as one of the providers for his expensive policies and, as a consequence, the grant of parliamentary subsidies became an established practice. It was a classic example of a representative institution based on the principles of *auxilium, quod omnes tangit* and *plena potestas.* The practice of parliamentary taxation was 'based firmly on the principle of consent and the accepted obligation of every freeman to help the king in his necessity, with elected representatives having full power to bind their communities to whatever was agreed in parliament'.[26] However, as so often elsewhere, afforced meetings of the royal council were slow to evolve into what were recognisably parliaments. It is not certain that elected representatives from the counties were called before 1297 or members from cities and towns before 1299–1300. Under Edward I of England (1272–1307) legislation was clearly a parliamentary function, but grants of parliamentary taxation with the assent of elected representatives became frequent and important only in the course of the fourteenth century.

Although an institution styled 'Parliament' is recorded in Scotland as early as the 1230s, it was no more than a gathering of temporal and ecclesiastical lords. Until the fourteenth century they alone were regarded as comprising the community of the realm. Urban representatives had been present to ratify a treaty in 1296, but only during the fourteenth century did 'commissioners' from royal boroughs become a constituent part of what had been until then rather a *curia* or council of the king and his feudal vassals. Once again, regular urban representation was the consequence of royal financial necessity. Nevertheless, in comparison with the other British assemblies the Scottish Parliament was a late 'arrival'. The existence of an alternative institution, the general council (later known as the convention), may have played a part in this. Whilst general councils, unlike parliaments, had no judicial functions or powers, they both exercised legislative and taxing authority. Furthermore, it was easier and quicker for the king to summon, 'on short notice by royal letters', a general council. More than two centuries later, between 1580 and 1600, Scottish government summoned forty-nine councils, but only eleven parliaments. It should be added that, whatever is written about the parliament of Scotland now may require modification or revision in the near future. For much of the twentieth century the work and publications of R.S. Rait and, to a lesser extent, C.S. Terry, formed our views about Scottish assemblies. They adopted the English Parliament as a model against which the Scottish assembly was measured, found wanting, and dismissed as 'feeble and imperfect'. Recent research and revitalised interest in the parliament of Scotland, as a subject of study in its own right and without reference to an English constitutional yardstick, are rapidly increasing our knowledge and understanding and altering our perception of it.[27]

In contrast to the single national assemblies which, with the exception of the English-controlled principality of Wales, emerged in the component states of the British Isles, there were the Low Countries (or Netherlands). These were, until the fourteenth and fifteenth centuries, a cluster of largely independent counties, duchies and ecclesiastical principalities, and some of them, especially Flanders, Brabant and Holland, were becoming highly urbanised societies with growing industrial and commercial wealth. Financial necessity on the part of rulers, such as the counts of Flanders and dukes of Brabant, encouraged the growth of assemblies in which the representatives of wealthy urban communities were significant and sometimes predominant. Rulers were invoking the recognised principle of *auxilium*. At the same time financial demands and, in particular, attempts by Flanders' feudal overlord, the French king, to assert direct control over it during the thirteenth century, caused assemblies to assert themselves. Flemish counts solicited their parliaments' support and involved them in the business of government. Other assemblies defended liberties, especially consent to taxation. So they in turn were invoking the principle of *quod omnes tangit*. The most dramatic example is to be found in Brabant where, in 1356, the 'estates' or parliament extracted from the new duke a charter, known as the *joyeuse entrée*. It is an innocuous, indeed warm and affectionate term, referring as it does to the 'joyous entry' of the new duke to his regal place. It was, however, also an oath which he and his successors had to swear on accession. It required them to promise observance of the charter: in particular, acceptance of the assembly's consent to war, taxation and – the most important contemporary economic concern – the minting and devaluation of the coinage. During the fourteenth and fifteenth centuries, however, the dukes of Burgundy, in a piecemeal process, acquired the Low Countries. It was then that, as we shall see, the dukes promoted a general assembly, representing all the principalities under Burgundian control, as a means of creating a unified state.[28]

In contrast to the western states of catholic Christendom, the development of parliaments in central, eastern and northern Europe was a slower process, whilst in Italy it was a story of considerable variety. The political structure and climate of Italian city states in Lombardy and Tuscany, with their direct citizen involvement or, in the case of Venice, with its oligarchic domination, had no place for representative assemblies. As they extended their authority geographically and acquired subject territories there was no point in inviting constitutional resistance by summoning representatives from them to a general assembly. Likewise Rome, capital of an authoritarian papacy, was no breeding ground of representative institutions.

It is true that in several northern Italian states – Montferrat, Friuli and Piedmont – parliaments did emerge during the fourteenth century. As was so often the case, their development and history were influenced, even determined, by succession disputes within the ruling house or the intervention of external forces, especially more powerful neighbours. In Montferrat the assembly profited from such succession struggles and asserted a contractual relationship with its new ruling marquis in 1379. Friuli's prince was an ecclesiastic, the patriarch of Aquileia. Therefore it was not afflicted with dynastic succession disputes. Fourteenth-century patriarchs, however, were weakened by external threats, especially from Venice. There were also lengthy vacancies when patriarchs died. In such circumstances the assembly became vitally important because it provided stability and continuity, money and the means of defence. In contrast, the Piedmontese parliament developed without either the problems of dynastic infighting or a major threat from aggressive neighbours. But the dukes' modest financial resources made them financially dependent. This in turn allowed the growth of parliamentary initiative and assertiveness. Yet, as we shall see, in the end the Piedmontese parliament shared with the others the common problem of external forces. It was French aggression which triggered the events leading to its extinction in 1560. In similar fashion Friuli's incorporation into the Venetian Republic emasculated parliament, whilst in Montferrat the work of centralising princes, followed by military occupation and annexation by its neighbours, terminated the life of the assembly in 1533.[29]

Southern Italy lacked vigorous parliamentary institutions. When King Alfonso V of Aragon (1416–58) conquered the kingdom of Naples, it still had no effective representative assembly. This was largely the consequence of the attitudes and policies of its earlier Angevin rulers. When, at the end of the thirteenth century, Aragon acquired Sicily from Charles of Anjou by war, he was left only with the mainland kingdom of Naples. The monarchy was under pressure, especially from its papal over-lord, to call assemblies, consult them and seek their consent to taxes. This pressure was reinforced by a papal decree of 1285 which limited the occasions on which taxes could be sought and the amounts to be taken. Furthermore, an assembly of 1290 required that it should meet twice a year. Angevin rulers, however, took little notice of such intended constraints. Assemblies, which consisted of members of the baronage but not of the clergy and rarely of the cities, were not representative of the community. They did not meet often and, when they did, it was usually for some special occasion. They also varied in composition. Kings promulgated laws and levied taxes without seeking prior consent from such assemblies. It was not until the fifteenth-century Aragonese conquest that they began to acquire some of the functional, structural and constitutional characteristics of representative institutions.[30]

Italy's northern neighbours included Switzerland and Germany. The development of the Swiss Confederation was a lengthy, complicated process between 1291 and the sixteenth century. Problems of direct communication with the wider community, due to size or physical geography, were a common reason for the growth of representative assemblies. The Alpine location of Swiss cantons, however, had an adverse effect. Swiss towns acquired oligarchic merchant regimes. Although rural cantons, controlled by the peasantry, held their own assemblies, the federal parliament or *Bundestag* which emerged had little authority and was hedged in with restraints. The cantons, to a large extent isolated one from another, had neither consciousness of a wider community nor a desire for one. Their priorities were preservation of local identity, privileges and self-government.

Italy's other northern neighbour, Germany, was, like Switzerland, a state with a federal structure. But here the similarity ends. Whereas the Swiss Confederation had no single ruler, Germany was by far the largest component part of the Holy Roman Empire, governed by an imperial head. Indeed, the Swiss created their state by breaking away from the Empire and, after two centuries of struggle, securing imperial recognition in 1499. This was just one example of imperial decline from the mid-thirteenth century onwards. The emperor's authority and direct control deteriorated within Germany too. German princes and wealthy commercial cities asserted autonomous power in their territories. This received official acknowledgement in 1356 when Emperor Charles IV named three archbishops and four temporal princes of Bavaria, Brandenburg, the Rhine Palatinate and Saxony, as the electors of emperors in the future. Although, from the thirteenth century onwards, the chosen emperor was normally a member of the Habsburg family, it did not provide him with the security of an hereditary succession. He was, after all, beholden to seven men for his place. He enjoyed great prestige, but little authority in internal affairs. Only in the Habsburg hereditary lands, centred on Austria in south-east Germany, did he exercise effective political control.

The long process of diminishing imperial authority and growing political fragmentation contributed to the growth of German assemblies and the time-framework in which that growth occurred. From the thirteenth century the imperial *Reichstag* developed as the essence of particularism. The chief stimulus for its growth lay not with the emperor but rather with the seven electors, the lay and ecclesiastical princes and the 'free' (autonomous) imperial cities who sat there and whose prime concern was the protection of their territorial autonomy from imperial interference. He could not levy taxes without its consent, nor could he hope to manipulate the membership in his own interest. It is questionable, however, whether this can be regarded as a representative assembly. Princes and imperial cities were imperial vassals and so were members of a feudal gathering rather than of a parliament.[31]

Assemblies (*Landtage*), in which the free imperial cities had no place, also evolved in the principalities, although they tended to be among the later parliamentary 'arrivals' in Europe. Political instability was common. Sometimes it was the result of war by aggressive princes, but frequently it was the consequence of dynastic disputes over the succession or the partition of lands amongst heirs. So it was, for example, in Hesse in central Germany, where brothers fought over division of the territory. The Hessian assembly, which first met in 1387, grew in importance as it attempted to arbitrate over such recurring disputes. In Upper and

Lower Bavaria, a duchy in southern Germany, assemblies of nobles and towns, later afforced by the clergy, emerged between 1347 and the end of the century. They opposed the political struggles and sometimes military conflicts between members of the ruling Wittelsbach family. By the 1390s they had extracted the right of resistance from the ruling dukes and, as family conflicts worsened in the next century, there emerged one national body, the *Landschaft*. It expressed the consciousness of the wider community and represented the privileges, interests and security of that community. The story is repeated in Saxony, situated to the east of Hesse. From the mid-fourteenth century the ruling house of Wettin was obliged to seek financial assistance from the nobility, clergy and wealthy towns. Partitions, actual or intended, involved members of the three estates as arbiters. By 1438 an assembly, representing the entire principality, granted a tax which was to be administered by it and the terms of which were strictly defined. In the following decades taxes were granted under the same controls, whilst the parliament even intervened to prevent a partition.

In contrast to such principalities as Hesse, Bavaria and Saxony, the medieval county (later duchy) of Württemberg was characterised by internal political and social stability and no significant external threats. This may explain why the Württemberg Diet did not emerge until the mid-fifteenth century and why, when it did so, it had, in F.L. Carsten's words, only 'limited powers' and a 'modest role'.[32]

The commoner Germanic relationship between weak and unstable royal government on the one hand and the emergence of a strong parliamentary assembly on the other, seen already in Hesse, Bavaria and Saxony, was repeated elsewhere, not only in central but also in eastern and northern Europe. Frequent dynastic changes in fourteenth-century Brandenburg played a part in the growth of its *Landtag*. Whilst strong monarchy encouraged the growth of the Bohemian *Sněm* in the fourteenth century, it was once again royal weakness and a contested crown which later extended its activity. And, in similar fashion, the Hungarian Diet became a strong representative institution only as a consequence of the long succession crisis of 1437–57, although it had come into existence in the previous century. To the east, in Poland, the development of representative assemblies and the steady growth of noble power went hand-in-hand, at the expense of royal authority. The development of provincial 'meetings' or *colloquia* in the thirteenth century, the growth of provincial parliaments (*sejmiki*) and a national diet (*Sejm*) in the fourteenth all marked stages in the rise of noble power and the decline of royal authority. From the accession of Wladislaw Jagiello in 1386, the Polish monarch was elected by the *Sejm*. Candidates had to make concessions or agree to power-limitations including, in 1493, a noble-dominated bicameral *Sejm*.

Like their counterparts in Poland and many of the German principalities, the Danish *Rigsdag* and Swedish *Riksdag* were relatively late developers and beneficiaries of royal weakness. In Denmark King Christian I, who like his predecessors was under constant pressure from his nobles, called the first representative parliament in 1468. It consisted of townsmen and free peasantry as well as nobles, instead of the customary aristocratic assembly. At that time Sweden was united to Denmark and Norway in the Union of Kalmar, which lasted from 1397 to 1523. In the 1520s Sweden broke away from the Union, in which it occupied a subordinate place, and in 1523 a national assembly (*Riksdag*) of nobles, clergy, representatives of towns, miners and peasants recognised the Swedish rebel leader Gustav Vasa as King Gustav I. The *Riksdag* was not a new institution, but from this point it would develop as the national assembly of an independent state.

Structure and membership of medieval parliaments

Medieval society in most of Christian Europe was based upon estates or social orders and corporate bodies and it was characterised by a structure of privilege, liberties and inequality. Three estates evolved: the nobility, often as a feudal order; the great clergy, both as prominent members of that most privileged of corporate bodies, the Church, and also as feudal vassals; and urban oligarchs and merchants, who sought trading privileges for their companies and corporate rights, liberties and degrees of self-government for their cities and towns. When medieval kings required advice and assistance, it was natural to turn to the first estate of clergy and the second, noble, estate. These were the men who wielded great local authority, who, in many cases, had very extensive regional power-bases, and who were often bonded with the monarch through the feudal oath. As clergy and nobles acquired an awareness of belonging to an estate, there developed a collective or corporate sense of estate coherence. So it became politically sensible, even necessary, for rulers to consult such powerful, privileged bodies and seek their help in 'restricted' assemblies. It was also expedient to enlarge assemblies by the inclusion of the third estate, consisting usually of rich cities and towns, or at least representatives of them, because they provided an important and growing source of tax revenue. So the basis and structure of medieval assemblies were usually the 'three estates'. Emile Lousse explained the composition and chief concerns of such parliaments:

> une assemblée politique composée de représentants de l'ordre ou des ordres politiquement privilégiés . . . instituée pour veiller au maintien des privilèges des ordres, des corps et des individus ainsi qu'à la défense des droits fondamentaux de ce pays et d'autre part, pour rendre au prince les services stipulés dans les chartes comme contre partie des droits reconnus et des privilèges concédés par lui.[33]

The simplistic picture of parliaments composed of three estates, however, bears little relation to reality. Of course there were the classic three-chamber assemblies, in which the 'three estates' of clergy, nobility and urban representatives sat separately. These existed in the medieval French Estates-general and the Castilian Cortes. However, representation of the third estate varied. It extended to members of the free taxpaying peasantry in the Tyrol, Friesland and Sweden. The Church tended to be represented by its upper clergy, the prelates, but clerical proctors attended English parliaments until part-way through the fourteenth century, whilst lower clergy disappeared from Irish assemblies only in Henry VIII's reign. There were also variations in the organisational structure of representative institutions. The Aragonese Cortes had four chambers, whilst, at the other end of the spectrum, there was the unicameral Scottish Parliament. It might be argued that these, and all the variations in between, still accommodated the concept of estates as the structural basis of both society and parliaments. Although two of Aragon's four chambers consisted of *ricos-hombres* and *caballeros*, greater and lesser nobility, the overall structure of its Cortes consisted of the traditional three estates. Whilst Scotland's Parliament was, in contrast, unicameral, the term 'estates' was frequently used by the mid-fourteenth century to describe an assembly consisting of clergy, nobles and burgesses, all of whom sat together. That is not surprising, perhaps because of the 'auld' anti-English alliance between Scotland and France, where the 'three-estates' concept was firmly established. French usage may well have been influential. This concept was, to some extent, in competition with the idea that Scottish parliaments represented 'the community of the realm'. However, Julian Goodare has shown that by the sixteenth century 'the three estates had long been entrenched as the constituent parts of Parliament' and recognised as such by contemporaries.[34]

There were, therefore, many variations in the structure, organisation and composition of medieval European representative assemblies, as they emerged and developed during the thirteenth–fifteenth centuries. One assembly, the English Parliament, has been treated as an unusual, even unique exception to this general European process. In its early stages it followed the normal pattern of development: afforced conciliar meetings consisting of the king's advisers, clergy, nobles and urban representatives. Then the representation of the wider community of the 'third estate' or 'commons' was enlarged to include not only citizens and burgesses, but also knights of the shire. These were elected from and by the numerous sub-noble landed gentry, who performed a vital role in administration and justice in the counties. During the reigns of Edward I and Edward II (1272–1327) and beyond, the presence of representatives of cities, towns and counties was not automatic and not deemed to be necessary.[35] With the passage of time, however, they came to be regarded as an integral part of parliaments. Then, during the fourteenth century, and certainly by 1332, knights, citizens and burgesses began to sit apart from the great ecclesiastics (bishops, abbots and priors) and nobles. Instead of separating and occupying different venues, the estates of lords spiritual (upper clergy) and lords temporal (nobility) continued to sit together and with the king's councillors, judges and law officers. Meanwhile the elected deputies of the lower clergy ceased to sit in parliaments and attended the provincial convocations of the Church.

These developments amounted to a significant change in the structure and composition of the English Parliament. They might also seem to mark it off as an exception and contrast to the estates model of continental assemblies. Certainly, as Koenigsberger has pointed out, historians have often emphasised and exaggerated these differences. He argues realistically that such changes should be treated in the context of a European parliamentary tapestry of rich diversity. There was no estate model from which England was a deviant. Rather, there were 'many variations in the development of representative institutions in medieval Europe'.[36] Noble dominance, for example, could threaten the parliamentary role of other estates and even displace them, as eventually happened in the Polish *Sejm*, Hungarian Diet and Bohemian *Sněm*. In contrast, the nobles of Württemberg withdrew from the Diet not long after its mid-fifteenth-century emergence. The Brabant assembly had three estates, but very few members turned up anyway.[37] Denmark's four estates included free peasantry. Differences and alterations in the structure and membership of parliaments had much more to do with political realities than with adherence to or non-observance of a concept of estates. In any case the essence of a parliament lay in its functions, rather than in the precise way in which the community was represented.

The functions of medieval parliaments

As we have already seen, parliaments were initiated from above, not below, as rulers sought not approval but advice on royal policies and important decisions, as well as *auxilium*, especially taxation. External threats and prolonged wars, such as the Hundred Years' War between England and France (1350s–1450s), often made taxation, which did require consent, the chief reason for summoning an assembly. As expanded versions of the monarch's council, early parliaments also displayed some of its curial characteristics. It was in this respect that many saw the benefits and advantages of parliaments. It was there that they could raise matters of justice, present petitions, voice grievances, and secure the recognition, confirmation and extension of social and territorial privileges, liberties and immunities. This is illustrated by the presence of common law judges and royal law officers in the English 'High Court of Parliament' and, especially during the first century of its existence, by the submission of many petitions for consideration and the hearing of pleas. The dispensing of justice was also an important function of other assemblies, such as the Scottish and Irish parliaments, the Aragonese Cortes, the Polish *Sejm* and the Friuli parliament.[38]

Gradually, however, legislation, rather than judicial process or parliamentary consultation, sought solutions to grievances, private and commons' petitions and 'urgent and weighty affairs'. Indeed law-making became an important function of many medieval parliaments; not only in England but also, for example, in Aragon, where the basis of government was contractual and the king could secure new laws only with the consent of the Cortes. Both the Catalan Corts and Valencian

Cortes enjoyed and retained the same legislative authority. In contrast, the Castilian assembly lost that power early on and thereafter it could only petition for new laws to be enacted by the crown. To the north, across the Pyrenees, fourteenth-century French kings did not require representatives to come to the Estates-general with *plena potestas* (full power) because they and their subjects 'regarded central assemblies as a vehicle for counsel rather than consent'. A central assembly might advise that, for example, war subsidies were necessary, but they would be negotiated at the local level.[39] Similarly, French kings made laws independently of the 'national' parliament.

Castile and France were to be the major powers of early modern Europe. Nevertheless, European parliamentary developments should not be judged in terms of their parliamentary record. Many medieval representative institutions, in the British Isles, the Low Countries, Germany, central Europe, Poland and Scandinavia, acquired control or at least a major role in law-making. Some monarchs, it is true, retained a residual authority to issue edicts or ordinances without parliamentary consultation or approval. That was desirable and in the interest of good government, when parliaments met irregularly or infrequently. It should not be seen as some kind of *threat* to parliamentary authority any more than parliamentary assent to new laws was a *challenge* to royal prerogative power. It is true that, whilst rulers summoned parliaments for their own purposes, the estates developed their own agendas. This, as Emile Lousse explains, was designed to protect fundamental rights and social and territorial privileges.[40] Sometimes there was a clash of priorities, leading to confrontation and, when they were in a weak position, rulers might lose. Succession disputes, the widespread incidence of partible inheritance in Germany and, in contrast, fifteenth- and sixteenth-century attempts to impose an artificial political unity on the linguistic, ethnic, economic and socio-political diversity of the Low Countries all increased the potential for such confrontations. The medieval estates of Hesse, Saxony and Bavaria sought the continued unity of their territories, sometimes acting as arbiters in succession disputes, but also imposing conditions and restraints upon the ruler of the moment.[41] The duchy of Brabant too was afflicted with succession crises – seven between 1248 and 1430 – and the estates intervened in the interest of stability. It was during one of these crises that they extracted from the duke the *joyeuse entrée*.[42]

These were very real relationship crises, but they were the product of specific circumstances and were usually resolved. They should not be seen as episodes in interminable contests for power between rulers and representative assemblies. As they developed, medieval parliaments served the individual and mutual interests of all participating parties. To most governments most of the time their ongoing benefits far outweighed the occasional inconvenience, disadvantage or crisis which occurred. One particular benefit, additional to those already discussed, was of special importance because of the relatively primitive and certainly slow nature of communications. G.R. Elton described the English Parliament as a vital 'point of contact', between the ruler and the governing class, between the centre and the localities. That was true not only of England but in all European countries, particularly those in which the temporal and spiritual elites were represented.[43]

So the emergence and development of representative institutions was a common medieval European experience. But, as we have seen, that is where consistency and uniformity end. A range of variables – for example, in political and social structure; the impact of codes of law and theories of social organisation; internal stability; external threats – all contributed to a kaleidoscope rather than a pattern of change. Furthermore, by, let us say, the mid-fifteenth century they varied considerably in age and some were embryonic. Yet, before the major, even dramatic changes of late medieval and Renaissance Europe, one can make a general distinction between inherently weak assemblies and those which had acquired specific institutional strengths and checks on royal government. National assemblies of large divergent kingdoms, such as Castile or France, where parochialism or provincialism was the key to loyalty, were not popular. The French Estates-general, for example, could not look to a national community of interests. Also its membership was too narrow and exclusive, it was functionally weak and its meetings were too intermittent. In some smaller kingdoms too, however, assemblies were inherently weakened by circumstances, structural weaknesses or the members' simple lack of foresight or interest. Scotland, with the option of general councils or conventions, was such a case.[44] Furthermore, from 1367 members of parliament appointed a committee 'of articles' to remain and transact the business of the session. Then, 'owing to the inconvenience of the season and the dearness of provisions', the rest went home. In other words, most members abdicated their parliamentary responsibility.[45]

In contrast some parliaments developed impressive institutional strengths. Although English knights and burgesses individually came to parliament with *plena potestas*, collectively they constituted a strong assembly, capable of resisting royal coercion. Members of many continental assemblies were armed only with limited mandates and in some cases, as in Castile, delegates had to consult with those who had elected them before committing themselves to a public stance on particular matters placed before them. In some of the German *Landtage*, French provincial assemblies and especially in the Cortes of Aragon, Catalonia and Valencia, standing parliamentary committees controlled the collection of taxes. They also constituted permanent watchdog committees, keeping an eye on royal activity which might infringe their communities' liberties. A unanimous vote (*nemine discrepante*) was required in all four of the Aragonese Cortes' *brazos* (houses), and in the noble estates of Catalonia and Valencia.[46] Nor did the catalogue of Aragonese safeguards end there. The office of *Justicia*, held by an Aragonese noble, kept constant vigil in the protection of the privileges and liberties of the kingdom. And, one might add here, the oath of allegiance supposedly sworn to each new king was conditional and contractual: 'We who are worth as much as you . . . [accepted him as sovereign lord if he observed their laws and liberties but] if not, not'. Although this was probably a post-medieval invention, it accords with both the traditional Aragonese position and the contractual nature of their coronation oath: they must obey the king, but he must respect their fundamental liberties. European parliaments, whose origins were grounded on relatively common attributes of Roman and canon law, royal necessity and community consciousness, had diversified in many ways by the fifteenth century. They were, in consequence, more or less well-equipped to cope with the challenges of the next 250 years.

Notes

1   It could also merge with existing systems. The early medieval law of Scotland, for example, was a mixture of 'native customary law and feudal principles drawn from Anglo-Norman sources'. W. Ferguson, 'Introduction', in C. Jones, ed., *The Scots and Parliament* (Edinburgh, 1996), p. 5.

2   H.G. Koenigsberger, 'Parliaments and estates', in R.W. Davis, ed., *The Origins of Modern Freedom in the West* (Stanford, CA, 1995), pp. 138–40.

3   Ibid., pp. 140–1.

4   B. Tierney, 'Freedom and the medieval church', in Davis, ed., *Origins of Modern Freedom*, pp. 85–6; G. Post, 'Roman law and early representation in Spain and Italy, 1150–1250' *Speculum* 18 (1943), pp. 211–12, 215–17; G. Post, '*Plena potestas* and consent in medieval assemblies, 1150–1325', in J. Quasten and S. Kuttner, eds, *Traditio* I (1943), pp. 356, 359–61, 364–70.

5   Tierney, 'Freedom and the medieval church', pp. 86–8.

6   A. Marongiu, *Medieval Parliaments. A Comparative Study* (London, 1968), pp. 33–4.

7   Tierney, 'Freedom and the medieval church', p. 84; Koenigsberger, 'Parliaments and estates', pp. 144–6.

8   Tierney, 'Freedom and the medieval church', pp. 85–7.

9   Ibid., p. 64.

10 To his credit, however, Justinian was responsible for the codification of Roman law, the *Corpus Juris Civilis*. It was studied by medieval lawyers, who thus had access to the maxims *plena potestas* and *quod omnes tangit*, though still as an aspect of private law.

11 R.H.C. Davis, *A History of Medieval Europe* (2nd edn, London, 1995), pp. 128–42.

12 There was also a growing separateness from the eastern Latin empire of Byzantium, the power and territory of which diminished during the central and later middle ages, until it fell to the Turks in 1453.

13 J.H. Elliott, *Imperial Spain, 1469–1716* (London, 1969), pp. 14–15; C. Brooke, *Europe in the Central Middle Ages, 962–1154* (2nd edn, London, 1987), pp. 45–6, 314–19.

14 P. S. Lewis, 'The failure of the French medieval estates' *P&P* 23 (Nov. 1962), pp. 6–7.

15 Marongiu, *Medieval Parliaments*, pp. 37–41; O. Hintze, 'The preconditions of representative government', in F. Gilbert, ed., *The Historical Essays of Otto Hintze* (Oxford, 1975), pp. 318–21.

16 H.G. Koenigsberger, *Medieval Europe, 400–1500* (London, 1987), pp. 300–1.

17 Marongiu, *Medieval Parliaments*, pp. 61–4; A.R. Myers, *Parliaments and Estates of Europe to 1789* (London, 1975), pp. 59–65.

18 T.N. Bisson, 'The origin of the Corts of Catalonia' *PER* 16 (1996), pp. 31–5, 40, 43–5; Marongiu describes Peter III's action as 'the basis, indeed the birth certificate, of the Catalan parliament'. Marongiu, *Medieval Parliaments*, pp. 67–9; Myers, *Parliaments*, p. 64.

19 X. Gil, 'Crown and Cortes in early modern Aragon: reassessing revisionisms' *PER* 13, 2 (Dec. 1993), p. 111.

20 Marongiu dates this process in Sicily from the very end of the fourteenth century. Marongiu, *Medieval Parliaments*, p. 160; Koenigsberger, 'Parliaments and estates', p. 145.

21 See M.J. Rodriguez-Salgado, 'Christians, civilised and Spanish: multiple identities in sixteenth-century Spain' *TRHS*, 6th ser., 8 (1998), pp. 233–7.

22 Marongiu, *Medieval Parliaments*, p. 100.

23 Ibid., p. 103.

24 Myers, *Parliaments*, p. 73.

25 Koenigsberger, 'Parliaments and estates', pp. 148–50; G.L. Harriss, 'The formation of Parliament, 1272–1377', in R.G. Davies and J.H. Denton, eds, *The English Parliament in the Middle Ages* (Philadelphia, PA, 1981), pp. 29–31.

26 A. Cosgrove, *A New History of Ireland*, Vol. II *Medieval Ireland, 1169–1534* (Oxford, 1987), pp. 196–7.

27 J. Goodare, 'The estates in the Scottish Parliament, 1286–1707', in C. Jones, ed., *The Scots and Parliament*, pp. 12–14; R.S. Rait, *The Parliaments of Scotland* (Glasgow, 1924); R.S. Rait, *The Scottish Parliament*, Historical Association (London, 1925); C.S. Terry, *The Scottish Parliament, 1603–1707* (Glasgow, 1905); W. Ferguson, 'Introduction', in C. Jones, ed., *The Scots and Parliament*, pp. 1–4; J.M. Goodare, 'Parliament and society in Scotland, 1560–1603' PhD, University of Edinburgh, 1989; G. Donaldson, *Scotland's History: Approaches and Reflections*, ed. J. Kirk (Edinburgh, 1995), p. 49.

28 H.G. Koenigsberger, 'The beginnings of the States General of the Netherlands' *PER* 8, 2 (Dec. 1988), pp. 103–5; ibid., 'Dominium regale or dominium politicum et regale: monarchies and parliaments in early modern Europe', in *Politicians and Virtuosi* (London, 1986), pp. 14–16; ibid., 'Parliaments and estates', pp. 145–6.

29 H.G. Koenigsberger, 'The Italian parliaments from their origins to the end of the 18th century', in *Politicians and Virtuosi*, pp. 27–61; Marongiu, *Medieval Parliaments*, pp. 177–206.

30 Marongiu, *Medieval Parliaments*, pp. 148–55; Koenigsberger, 'Italian parliaments', pp. 44–5; Myers, *Parliaments*, p. 94.

31 Koenigsberger, 'Parliaments and estates', pp. 170–1.

32 L. Carsten, *Princes and Parliaments in Germany* (Oxford, 1959), pp. 1–6, 149–50, 192–3, 196–7, 352–3.

33 Emile Lousse, cit.; J. Rogister, 'Some new directions in the historiography of state assemblies and parliaments in early and late modern Europe' *PER* 16 (1996), pp. 2–3.

34 Goodare, 'Estates in the Scottish Parliament', pp. 11–17.

35 H.G. Richardson and G.O. Sayles, *The English Parliament in the Middle Ages* (London, 1981), XXVI, p. 7.

36 Koenigsberger, 'Parliaments and estates', p. 154.

37 Carsten, *Princes and Parliaments*, p. 3; E. Lousse, 'The estates of Brabant to the end of the fifteenth century: the make-up of the assembly', in P. Mack and M.C. Jacob, eds, *Politics and Culture in Early Modern Europe* (Cambridge, 1987), pp. 95–100; Myers, *Parliaments*, pp. 82–8.

38 P. Sanz, 'The cities in the Aragonese Cortes in the medieval and early modern periods' *PER* 14, 2 (Dec. 1994), pp. 104–5, 107; Rait, *Parliaments of Scotland*, pp. 452–63; Marongiu, *Medieval Parliaments*, p. 182.

39 J.B. Henneman, *Royal Taxation in Fourteenth Century France. The Development of War Financing, 1322–1356* (Princeton, NJ, 1971), pp. 325–9.

40 See above, p. 26.

41 Carsten, *Princes and Parliaments*, pp. 149–50, 191–9, 352–5.

42 Koenigsberger, 'Parliaments and estates', pp. 160–1; ibid., 'Beginnings of the States General', p. 104.

43 G.R. Elton, 'Tudor government. The points of contact. I. Parliament' *TRHS*, 5th ser., 24 (1974), pp. 183–200.

44 Rait, *Parliaments of Scotland*, pp. 127–9; see above, pp. 19–20.

45 Terry, *Scottish Parliament*, pp. 103–5.

46 R.E. Giesey, *If Not, Not* (Princeton, NJ, 1968); D.R. Kelley, 'Kingship and resistance', in R.W. Davis, ed., *Origins of Modern Freedom*, pp. 244–5.

2

Parliaments in a Time of Change: Europe in the Fifteenth Century

B<small>Y THE FIFTEENTH</small> century representative institutions were entrenched in much of Christian Europe. There were, as we have seen, late-comers in German principalities, Hungary, the Low Countries, Denmark and elsewhere. In Sweden the process was even further delayed by the Union of Kalmar.[1] Nevertheless, parliaments were a characteristic of the European political system by 1500. Few territories outside central and northern Italy lacked such assemblies. So the principle of 'consent of the community' was seemingly entrenched and unquestioned. But nothing is ever static and times were changing apace. Even as the principle of *quod omnes tangit* spread to the north and eastwards it was coming under threat. However, power-flexing muscular monarchy was not as yet the common challenge to an institution which epitomised the political ideals of consent, approval, balance, co-operation and *auxilium*. Quite the contrary: in some cases it was royal authority which appeared to be in greater peril. Either way, the creation of a royal–parliamentary partnership, which embodied at least some of the initial principles and purposes of medieval government, was now in danger of being undermined. There was no simple explanation but a variety of reasons. For convenience's sake we may consider them separately. Yet at the same time we need to be aware that many of the fifteenth-century changes were interrelated and often inseparable one from another.

The core problem was clear enough. Dynasticism was the basic and enduring principle of government in most European states. It was also the ongoing and most serious threat to political stability. The continuity of a dynasty's undisputed right to rule depended upon a variety of circumstances. There were the rules regulating succession to the crown: was it automatically the eldest son? did the principle of partible inheritance operate? what place did women occupy in the order of succession? what claims might be made by collateral lines? could dynastic intermarriages provide opportunities for 'foreign' claimants?

did an elective principle allow for competing claims within the ruling family? how did the ruling family accommodate the sudden extinction of the direct line of succession? how would foreign powers attempt to exploit such a dynastic crisis for short-term political benefits or long-term imperial gains? And so on. The possibilities of a succession crisis were many, varied and always lurking in the wings. Yet no succession crisis can be considered in isolation. Each one can be understood only in relation to the current domestic and external political context in which it occurred and, in most cases, a representative institution played a part in the actual or attempted resolution of the problem.

This problem, which beset so much of Europe during the fifteenth century and beyond, was a complex one. Whilst it was, to a considerable extent, a dynastic problem generated from the top, it involved a number of quite distinct elements: the nature of royal authority in a state; the legal complexities of royal genealogy, inheritance and the right of succession; the distinctive characteristics of hereditary and elective monarchy; the role of sheer ambition and the personal search for power; and the opportunities for discomfiture, control and even absorption of ancient European rivals. These were not fifteenth-century novelties, as we have already seen. During that century, however, they were exacerbated and complemented by the simple fact that Europe was on the move in all kinds of ways: the growth of territorial conglomerates ruled, for example, by the dukes of Burgundy and by those voracious political enzymes, the Habsburgs; the emergence of Renaissance political Court cultures; the development of an autocratic *mentalité*; the intensifying need to make war and the growing frequency and cost of military operations. Parliaments had their place in these processes of change, not only because they could legitimise and re-inforce a monarch's authority as well as financially underwrite his policies, but also because they could question, criticise, keep a watchful eye on his activities (especially if they had permanent committees) and even attempt to constrain his exercise of royal power. Such European developments and their effects on the fortunes of representative institutions are considered in the following pages.

Internal circumstances: succession problems

Where peace and political stability prevailed, parliaments tended to meet less frequently and to figure less prominently. Conversely, internal instability or expensive royal military involvement tended to activate representative assemblies and bring them into political prominence. It has previously been observed, for example, that the problems associated with wars or dynastic insecurity and disputes, particularly where partible inheritance operated, contributed significantly to the growth of *Landtage* in German principalities such as Hesse, Bavaria and Saxony, whereas the assembly in the relatively stable Württemberg had less power and a smaller political role. Elective monarchies, notably in the Holy Roman Empire and Poland, were particularly advantageous for assemblies, which could hold candidates to ransom by extracting pre-election concessions.

This was particularly evident in Poland where the magnates (the greater nobility) and the *szlachta* (the lesser) steadily increased their social control, their political rights and their circumscription of the executive, money-raising and judicial authority of royal government. Although there was little love lost between magnates and *szlachta* they all worked to enlarge their privileges and powers at the elective monarchy's expense. Through the *szlachta*-dominated local assemblies, the provincial *sejmiki*, and the magnates' parliamentary citadel, the national or general *Sejm*, the Polish nobility gradually tightened its grip on state and society. In 1454, sometimes regarded as the beginning of the age of noble dominance or 'Commonwealth of Nobles', King Casimir, who was in urgent need of soldiers and war-funding, made extensive concessions. He granted the charters of Cerekwica and Nieswica, in which he limited the judicial authority of his officers and he promised no wars, troop levies, taxes or appointments to provincial offices without the consent of the assemblies. This process of consolidating noble dominance was to accelerate during the next century. Nevertheless there is a tendency to underrate the authority and effectiveness of Polish monarchs, especially the last two Jagellons.[2]

Internal circumstances: minorities

Royal minorities constituted another circumstance which weakened government, threatened stability and enhanced the place of parliaments. This might be a temporary circumstance. Whoever governed in the young ruler's name, be he a noble or even a member of the royal family, lacked the automatic allegiance which an anointed and crowned adult monarch could command. Such regency regimes were also susceptible to contests for ultimate control amongst those who managed affairs during a minority. In such circumstances the person in charge might attempt to drum up support for the regime from the governing elite and the wider community through frequent parliaments. Henry VI of England became king when he was nine months old. In his will Henry V had designated his brother Humphrey, duke of Gloucester, to manage the realm in the case of a minority. For a variety of reasons – the political insecurity of his position, conciliar rivalries and the deteriorating military situation in France – Gloucester's government had frequent recourse to parliaments. During Henry VI's fifteen-year minority (1422–37) eleven were called. It is true that the same number were called between the declaration of his majority (1437) and his deposition (1461), but it was a longer period, during which he became insane and England lost all its French possessions except Calais. A more meaningful contrast is the rule of an effective king: in the twenty-two year reign (1461–83) of Edward IV, who deposed Henry VI, only six parliaments were called; the Lancastrian Henry VII (1485–1509), who finally brought internal peace and stability to England, summoned seven in almost a quarter of a century. So parliaments receded into a less active, less frequent existence.

Yet here is a paradox. The frequency of English parliaments was not the ultimate test of their importance. During the 1450s and 1460s, when the houses of Lancaster and York, two branches of the ruling Plantagenet dynasty, were locked in a bloody contest over the succession, parliaments were financially necessary but politically unimportant. As Edward IV and Henry VII brought peace and strong government, parliaments met less often but their political and legislative significance revived. What they did when they met mattered far more than how frequently they met to do it.

Whereas the effects in England were temporary, some minorities elsewhere could and did result in significant and enduring changes, which permanently enhanced the place and power of a representative assembly. When, in 1477, Duke Charles of Burgundy was killed in battle, the States-general of the Low Countries extracted from the government of his young heiress, Mary, the *grand privilège*. Koenigsberger describes it as 'the *joyeuse entrée* of Brabant writ large and extended to the whole of the Netherlands'.[3] Obedience was to be conditional upon observance of the *grand privilège*.

However, some words of caution are necessary here. Whilst dynastic problems of various kinds tended to augment the authority and increase the active role of representative institutions, any generalisation about European parliaments is circumscribed by the usual exceptions and variations of which Scotland is a prime example (see Case Study on pages 52–3).

Changing directions

The mid-fifteenth-century English jurist, Chief Justice Sir John Fortescue, defined and discussed two sharply contrasting forms of royal government in his treatise *On the Governance of the Kingdom of England*. One was *dominium regale* (absolute or 'lordly' monarchy) and the other *dominium politicum et regale*, limited, mixed or constitutional monarchy. These he identified with French and English government respectively. The picture he drew, in England's favour of course, of the political and social consequences of these two systems of government is exaggerated and even at times a distortion of reality. But he was right about one particular feature of the English political system, described by David Sacks as 'its reliance on consent – granted in Parliament – to make laws, grant taxes, and check the potential for tyranny inherent in monarchical government [i.e. *dominium regale*]'.[4] Furthermore, Fortescue's identification of French government with his model of *dominium regale* was becoming closer to actuality in the course of his lifetime (*c.* 1394–*c.* 1474). In late fifteenth-century France the doctrine of necessity was invoked against the right of consent. This was partly the consequence of the growing needs and changing perceptions, policies, attitudes and actions, not only of French but indeed of a number of European rulers during the fifteenth and sixteenth centuries. There was a discernibly growing autocratic *mentalité*, within the context of a changing intellectual and cultural climate. Rulers were more reluctant to tolerate restrictions on their exercise of authority and there was, at the same time, a mental shift, albeit gradual, variable from place to place, undramatic and long-term, from *quod omnes tangit* to *legibus solutus* (above the law) and *principi placuit habet legis vigorem* (the prince's will has the force of the law). It all marked a stage in the development of European 'modern' states, in many of which, during the next two centuries, monarchs would be the political beneficiaries. This perception of historical change does, however, require significant modification. The French monarchy, for example, was territorially expansionist and, from the fifteenth century, it assumed theoretical powers which were gradually transformed into practice, especially at the centre. National government, however, was decentralised, fragmented, and provincial autonomy and estates continued to be strong under Renaissance kings such as Charles VIII (1483–98) and Louis XII (1498–1515).

Nevertheless a widespread autocratic tendency did exist in Europe and was strengthened by the problems, crises, even catastrophes which beset European governments in the fifteenth century. They threatened and, in some cases, ended the territorial integrity and continued independent existence of their states. Complementary to these problems were princely ambitions. According to W.M. Ormrod '[F]iscal systems owed their development to the financial pressures arising from a policy of dynastic and territorial aggrandizement.' Together crises and opportunities magnified the governments' financial needs, which could not be met from hereditary revenues or 'private' resources of rulers and led to demands for increasing taxation or 'public' revenues. These often exceeded what assemblies regarded as a legitimate and reasonable level of aid and, as a result, the traditional co-operation between ruler and estates was replaced by accumulating ill-will. As we shall see, in the long term this would threaten the vitality and even existence of some assemblies, as governments sought to make them compliant. This state of affairs was most evident where there were serious and prolonged internal crises, or external threats,[5] as in Castile and France (see Case Studies on pages 53–8).

Internal benefits but changing circumstances

The original royal impetus for the emergence of European parliaments was, as we have seen, *auxilium* and support. That, however, was only half of the parliamentary equation. In response, there were the social and geographically local and regional benefits of royal recognition and the sanction of existing and enlarged liberties and privileges. So parliaments were potentially beneficial to both kings and communities. They also provided monarchs with support from assemblies whose magnate members and representatives of cities and towns had an important role in regional and local administration. Meetings between men responsible for central and local government made parliaments a significant point of contact. And, as they usually included urban corporations, the occasion of a parliament enabled the ruler to enter into direct tax negotiations with their representatives.[6] The presence of Church representatives, usually bishops but sometimes (as in the Irish parliaments until 1537) the lesser clergy (or in the English parliaments, until 1332 or later, clerical proctors attendant on the bishops) served similar purposes.

Where peasant representation existed, it similarly enhanced parliament's value as a point of contact and further facilitated tax negotiations. Such representation was not common in Europe. Where it did exist – in northern Europe (Denmark and Sweden), Switzerland, the Tyrol and West Friesland – the representatives and those who chose them were often (but as we shall see not always) restricted to personally free, taxpaying and freeholding peasants. Certainly their presence usually contributed to the stability of the institution. Together with townsmen, they were first summoned by the weak king of Denmark in 1468, as a counterbalance to noble power. In Sweden it was a natural progression from active peasant participation in the government of largely self-governing provincial territories to representation in the national *Riksdag*. In the same way, between the thirteenth and fifteenth centuries peasant assemblies became responsible for justice and administration in the largely self-governing valley communities or 'rural republics' of Switzerland. When, in the fifteenth century, a diet (the *Tagsatzung*) was established to deal with the common concerns of rural republics and Swiss cities, peasants were duly elected by their communities. Peter Blickle has shown that, in both Sweden and Switzerland, 'Personal liberty and property ownership were advantageous but not a fundamental requirement for political representation'. The prerequisite of parliamentary representation for a peasant was 'political self-government' in an 'autonomous community'.[7] And peasant participation was secure so long as that autonomy remained intact. The greatest guarantee of its continuance was weak monarchy. Indeed the original growth of Swiss peasant representation in the *Tagsatzung* occurred as the Holy Roman Emperor's authority in Switzerland declined. The Swiss Confederation of rural republics and cities defeated successive attempts by Habsburg emperors to assert effective political control over it. By the end of the fifteenth century it was effectively independent and peasant participation was assured.

Elsewhere in that century, however, circumstances were tending to move in favour of European monarchs and against assemblies. In the course of time this would cause problems for the peasant estate in the mid-seventeenth-century Swedish *Riksdag*,[8] whilst, from 1627, the peasants would be excluded from the Danish *Rigsdag*. More immediately, increasing strains in crown–parliament relations characterised many European states in the fifteenth century. Some monarchies recovered and even enlarged their authority after prolonged periods of crisis: not only in Castile and France but also in England.[9] There, after the prolonged dynastic conflict known as the Wars of the Roses (1450s–71), Edward IV (1461–83) and the first Tudor, Henry VII (1485–1509) restored strong effective government. Monarchs might call frequent national parliaments to assist in the process of recovery, but thereafter summon them occasionally, if at all, except in time of war. After the defeat and death of Richard III at the battle of Bosworth (1485), the victorious new king, Henry VII, called the English Parliament six times in twelve years. Having established his legitimacy and authority, he called only one more in the remaining twelve years of his reign.

The fifteenth century was also marked by the changing political horizons of such rulers. In particular there was a shift in focus, from moral obligations and duty to subjects to the priority of stronger royal government. Of course any generalisation about European institutions, such as monarchy and parliaments, conceals great diversity. Against revitalised rulers in Castile, France and England, we must set Brabant, Denmark, the Swiss Confederation and the elected monarchs of Poland and the Empire. But it remains true that increasing strains in crown–parliament relations, as a result of royal ambition and diverging priorities, were a common trend. Koenigsberger sums it up neatly with a geological metaphor: 'People or states lived on a fault line; they might do so peacefully for several generations, but internal tensions would rise and, sooner or later, they would have to be resolved. This could happen through a long series of rumbles and minor adjustments, or through a sudden and violent earthquake.' As Koenigsberger goes on to explain, the resolution of such conflicts followed no predictable pattern.[10]

External circumstances

Between the late fourteenth and early sixteenth centuries wars and the mounting financial necessities of princes were dramatically increased by the growth of what are variously termed 'territorial conglomerates', 'multiple states' or 'composite monarchies'. These were accumulations of territory by princely dynasties, occasionally by war but usually by other, peaceful means. So a political agreement, the Scandinavian Union of Kalmar, brought together the three Scandinavian kingdoms of Denmark, Norway and Sweden in 1397. It was not, however, a union of equals, because it was dominated by the Danish monarchy. More frequently such conglomerates were the product of those traditional dynastic means of expansion: judicious far-sighted marriages and subsequent inheritance. Gradually, over generations and by various means, dynasties became rulers of multiple states. One of the earliest examples was the dukes of Burgundy, a branch of the French Valois dynasty. During the fourteenth and first half of the fifteenth centuries they acquired, by a classic mixture of diplomacy, marriage, bequest and the sword, Franche-Comté (the county of Burgundy), Lorraine, Luxembourg and much of the Low Countries stretching from Picardy to Holland.

In 1477, when the last duke, Charles the Bold, was killed in battle, the Burgundian multiple state fell apart. One of the principal beneficiaries was Louis XI of France, who acquired the duchy of Burgundy, Picardy, and Artois. This was just one step in the long fifteenth-century outward expansion of the French monarchy from its central domain based on Paris. By 1500 it had expelled the English from France (except for Calais) and unified most of the kingdom under its direct rule. When, in the early sixteenth century, marriage brought Brittany to the crown, the process was virtually complete. So far as the Burgundian conglomerate was concerned, however, it was not the French Valois kings but the Habsburg dynasty which was the greatest beneficiary of its break-up. The Habsburgs were peerless empire-builders by intermarriage and inheritance. From the Austrian duchies, which they acquired in the thirteenth century, they expanded their power-base in south-east Germany and, from 1440 onwards, a Habsburg was (with only one exception, Charles VII Wittelsbach in 1742) regularly elected Holy Roman Emperor until the Empire ended in 1806. The last duke of Burgundy's heiress, Mary, married Maximilian, the son of Emperor Frederick III. So her inheritance – Franche-Comté, on France's eastern border, and the rich commercial jewel of the Low Countries – passed by marriage to the Habsburgs. Their power continued to expand and their possessions to proliferate by the same dynastic means. Philip, the heir of Maximilian (who was elected emperor in 1493) and Mary of Burgundy, married Juana, the daughter of Ferdinand and Isabella of Spain. In due course Spain, its Mediterranean and New World territories, together with the Habsburg hereditary lands in the Low Countries and southeast Germany, all passed to Charles, who was the heir of Philip and Juana.

The Habsburg conglomerate was the most extensive, diverse, richest and, on paper at least, potentially the most powerful in Europe. It was also more enduring than some others, such as those of Burgundy and the Scandinavian Union of Kalmar, from which Sweden bloodily seceded in the 1520s. Nevertheless there were others: not only France, but also the three kingdoms and Mediterranean possessions of Aragon (until they were incorporated into the Habsburgs' composite monarchy); the common rule of the aristocratic 'republics' of Poland-Lithuania by one king from 1506 onwards; and the extension of English royal control over the British Isles. The English case is one which does not sit comfortably within the time-span of this chapter. The first major step in the subjugation and integration of the Celtic communities into England was taken by Edward I. He conquered the principality of Wales, shired it and built a network of castles to control it. But neither he nor his successors could subdue Scotland. Their claims to suzerainty produced 250 years of hostility, border-conflict, English incursions and Scotland's defensive 'auld alliance' with England's traditional enemy, the French. England's claim to overlordship of Ireland was equally nominal and ineffectual outside the Pale, a small east-coast area directly ruled by the English from Dublin. Not much changed until the sixteenth century. In Henry VIII's reign the rest of Wales and the marcher (= border) lordships were shired and the whole country was, in effect, integrated into the English administrative, judicial and parliamentary structure.[11] In 1541 an act of the Irish Parliament in Dublin declared Henry to be no longer overlord but king of Ireland. This had very limited practical effect on royal authority there until the Elizabethan military conquest of Ireland. By the time it was complete James VI of Scotland had, by right of inheritance, succeeded to the English throne as James I. From 1603 he was legitimate head of a composite monarchy, which encompassed the British Isles.

In most of these cases, territories – kingdoms, duchies, provinces, counties, whatever they were – which were brought together in composite states already had developed systems. Each of them therefore had different laws, rights, privileges and traditions.[12] One might add that, with few exceptions, they also had their own representative assemblies. As princes acquired new territories, they swore to recognise and observe existing liberties, privileges and immunities of localities, social orders, urban corporations and parliaments. In each of his possessions the ruler of multiple states might have a different title. Of greater importance in practical terms were the variations in his authority and the restrictions on it. So long as these diverse political realities were respected by him in each of his territories, he was unlikely to be challenged or restricted. But any serious and persistent attempt to erode or override liberties, shift the power-balance in the prince's direction or impose political uniformity throughout the composite monarchy was liable to have serious repercussions: public commotion, rebellion, or exploitative foreign intervention.[13]

By the end of the fifteenth century most territories in Christian Europe had become constituent parts of composite monarchies. That at least might seem to be a safe generalisation. However, there was no one standardised form of multiple state structure. Some composite monarchies were contiguous. The very fact of contiguity rendered it logistically easier to increase the number of constituent parts and to manage them. French kings, operating from a power-base in the Ile-de-France, expanded outwards as the English were driven from France, fiefs reverted, dynastic marriages repeated their eventual rewards, and Picardy and the Burgundian duchy were acquired after Charles the Bold's death. The very diversity of community loyalties, customs and traditions, political rights and local economies, as well as the size and geography of the French kingdom, worked in the long run against the likelihood of effective national or regional assemblies. So monarchs preferred to consult provincial assemblies in those constituent parts of the composite monarchy which had them. As this was a lengthy business, monarchs, especially when they were at war, would levy taxes first and then seek retrospective consent. In course of time parliamentary consent to emergency taxes became a mere formality and even unnecessary. On the other hand, the fiscal system was as diverse and anomalous as the political structure of the French composite monarchy. As it expanded during the fifteenth century it made concessions in order to overcome local resistance to incorporation into the French polity. Louis XI, for example, gave Guyenne a *parlement* and recognised Burgundy's right of consent to taxation. Tax exemptions to provinces, cities or social orders were commonplace; the consent of estates to ordinary, regular, annual, non-emergency taxation was necessary in many provinces; and, by the fifteenth century, the nobility was largely tax-exempt.[14] In the sixteenth

and seventeenth centuries, however, there would be many confrontations between estates and royal government, as more assertive and
needy monarchs attempted to introduce various novel taxes, especially
the *taille*[15] and the dreaded salt-tax, the *gabelle*, into previously exempt
provinces.[16]

France was not the only contiguous composite monarchy. In accordance with the agreement at Krewo in 1385 Duke Jagiello of Lithuania
was, in the following year, elected king by a gathering of Polish nobles.
So the kingdom of Poland and the grand duchy of Lithuania were united
in his person. During the next two centuries this personal union was
then transformed into a constitutional one.[17] During much of that time,
however, Poland was less a kingdom under strong royal government than
an 'aristocratic republic' in which a powerful nobility elected the king,
the greater nobles (magnates) dominated the national assembly (*Sejm*)
and the lesser nobility, the *szlachta*, controlled the regional parliaments
(the *sejmiki*). The same situation – noble dominance – prevailed in
Lithuania's sole parliament. Meanwhile, in 1454, in response to a
Prussian initiative, the Polish king incorporated Prussia into the crown.
Decades of intermittent strife followed, between the autonomous spirit
of Prussian provinces and would-be centralising Polish kings. By 1526
Prussian particularism and autonomy were consolidated, when King
Sigismund I issued the *Statuta Sigismundi*. This granted a number of noble
privileges and required two meetings each year of the Prussian *Sejm*, in
which the nobles were influential.[18]

Situated between Poland and France was what might be regarded as
another example of this particular form of state structure, the Holy
Roman Empire. Koenigsberger argues that, whilst the process was
different, the end-product was the same: 'Here was a large kingdom
which had become a kind of composite monarchy in the thirteenth
century, not by the accumulation of states and provinces under the
Crown but by the catastrophic weakening of the monarchy'.[19] By the
end of the fifteenth century the emperor had great prestige but little
imperial power. He did not even succeed in obtaining the consent of the
estates to general taxes until 1427, 1471–74 and 1495. The imperial
diet, the *Reichstag*, was dominated by the electors, those princes who
elected the emperor. The power-base of the Habsburg emperors was
their hereditary lands in south-east Germany. Elsewhere the Empire was
fragmented into a myriad of principalities, free imperial cities and
ecclesiastical territories. Particularism, a major characteristic of medieval

and early modern Europe, was also the bane of effective government and nowhere more so than in Germany. Princes used the *Reichstag* to ensure imperial non-interference in their own territories where, at the same time, some of them had to contend with their own powerful estates, as, for example, in Bavaria, Hesse and Saxony.[20] Those estates were distrustful of their own rulers, of the *Reichstag* and of the emperor. Then, in the early sixteenth century, the death of Emperor Maximilian I changed the Empire's position within the European political structure.

With the accession of Charles I to the Spanish throne in 1516, his inheritance of the Low Countries and the Habsburg hereditary lands in south-east Germany and his election as Emperor Charles V in 1519, Europe underwent a dazzling political transformation. An inexperienced, unprepossessing teenager suddenly became ruler of a multiple state structure. It incorporated the composite monarchies of Spain and its Mediterranean possessions, the Low Countries (an artificial union of provinces put together piecemeal by the Burgundian dukes) and the Holy Roman Empire. This political patchwork quilt endowed Charles with a bewildering array of titles and powers, which changed as he moved through cities, provinces, duchies, kingdoms and empire around his power-complex. Everywhere he had to treat with representative institutions, which were initially and naturally loyal, but also the articulate voices and defenders of particularist interests, liberties and privileges: the Spanish Cortes and Sicilian *Parlamento*, the provincial states and States-general in the Low Countries and the imperial *Reichstag*. Charles, however, was beset by problems which transcended such geographically narrow priorities. So many parts of his inheritance were at risk: from the French, from the Islamic threat in south-east Europe, the Mediterranean and from North Africa, and, even as he was crowned, from the beginning of the Reformation. Here too, parliaments were to loom large in Charles's rule, from the very moment of his election as emperor in 1519.

Charles's problems were exacerbated by the fact that, unlike French and Polish kings as well as previous German emperors, he did not rule over a contiguous composite monarchy. Nor did English kings. Admittedly they were small-fry compared to the Habsburgs. Nevertheless the medieval and early modern English monarchy was aggressive and expansionist. Unlike the Habsburgs it created its composite monarchy by war rather than by intermarriage and inheritance. Certainly in the eleventh and twelfth centuries England's original French possessions were the consequence either of marriage[21] or of inheritance.[22] During the next 200 years most of these were lost. When, in the fourteenth and fifteenth centuries, the English monarchy laid claim to the French crown it used war in an ultimately unsuccessful pursuit of its objective. Concurrent and, in the end, equally unsuccessful claims to suzerainty over the Scots were backed by invasions of the northern kingdom. The Welsh were subdued by military force. Pope Adrian IV's bull, *Laudabiliter*, which granted Henry II lordship of Ireland, at least afforded him some justification for its conquest. That, however, did not eventuate. Anglo-Norman warriors acquired tracts of land and established a feudal substructure, but they proved to be no more amenable to royal control than the native Irish clans. Until the later sixteenth century English overlordship (and from 1541 English kingship) was a Pale shadow outside the bridgehead centred on Dublin.

During its medieval imperialist adventures the English monarchy had to secure and retain the practical co-operation and support of the Westminster Parliament. It was there that kings sought funding for their Scottish incursions, the conquest of Wales and the invasions of France. However, Edward II's failure to seek parliamentary support against the Scots and his disastrous defeat at Bannockburn in 1314 led to baronial opposition and contributed to his removal in 1327. Elsewhere within the variable shape of the medieval English composite monarchy there was not a strong parliamentary tradition. Some of the French provinces, which, at different times, were subject to English royal authority, had active parliamentary estates. In Ireland the first known parliament met at Castledermot, county Kildare, in 1264. By 1500 about 150 parliaments had been held, usually in Dublin or some other venue within the four counties of the Pale. That is significant. These were not, in any geographical sense, 'parliaments of Ireland' or 'Irish parliaments'. In location and purpose they tended to be 'lordship parliaments'. Their first priority seems to have been to serve the interests of the king and the English administration, especially in matters of law and order.[23]

This is not, however, the whole story and to leave it there would be misleading. Certainly, like most other European assemblies, the parliaments in Ireland serviced the crown with money and new laws but, according to Steve Ellis, neither of these was the chief reason for summoning them. Parliamentary subsidies yielded little and were not worth the effort. Furthermore, as the lordship of Ireland was an English dependency, legislation enacted at Westminster also applied there. In Ellis's sample of 809 acts from the surviving parliament rolls of 1462–81 only 155 concerned the entire lordship of Ireland. All the rest were responses to private petitions and usually dealt with matters of local concern. The importance of the Irish parliament, especially in the later fifteenth century, derived rather from its handling of a large volume of administrative and judicial business. Then, in Ellis's words it 'came nearer to realising that other misleading claim of medieval parliaments, to be a court . . . [and by 1460] had become a sort of clearing house for disputes about land'. Richardson and Sayles show that an increasing number had recourse to a parliamentary remedy because of the expense, decay, impotence and corruption of the common law courts in fifteenth-century Ireland. Parliaments were performing the equitable role of the English court of chancery.

The Irish assemblies' increasing volume of business indicates that their judicial function was popular. To cope with the volume, parliaments, from the beginning of the Yorkist era in 1460, met frequently, were multi-sessional and even on occasion peripatetic. They were also of perceived value to the English administration in Dublin, because their resolution of disputes contributed to the maintenance of law and order, not only in the Pale but especially beyond. Furthermore, because of the value of parliamentary arbitration in matters of law to the wider community, representation was not confined to the Pale. Ellis has shown that, whilst the majority of the acts recorded on the surviving parliament rolls of 1462–93 deal with Palesmen's concerns, 12.5 per cent (an eighth) are about the interests of communities elsewhere. Whilst the Pale was over-represented, outlying communities also had a significant presence. Ellis concludes that the business and decisions of the late medieval parliament 'reflected the interests of the political nation in Anglo-Ireland as a whole and not merely those of the Palesmen'.[24]

As for Wales, there was no parliamentary tradition before or after Edward I's conquest of the principality.[25] When Owain Glyn Dŵr raised rebellion against Henry IV in 1400 he was proclaimed prince of Wales by a small assembly. During the course of his revolt he held several parliaments, where he canvassed for advice, presented his policy and plans for discussion and sought approval for them. By 1408 Owain had failed – and there were no more Welsh parliaments. But representative assemblies continued elsewhere in the British Isles, including the independent state of Scotland.

New perceptions and parameters

The political developments in fifteenth-century Europe paved the way for many of the momentous changes of the next 200 years: for example, the unification of France and the emergence of the Habsburg composite monarchy set the stage for a long-term struggle for supremacy within Europe. Monarchies were displaying aggressive attitudes towards those interests which rivalled them, competed with them for pre-eminence or placed constraints upon them. Such interests can be described under *three* heads: the universal, the international and the regional/local.[26] The *first* of these concerns the papal government of the Roman catholic Church. The earlier medieval pretensions of popes to universal sovereignty had crumbled by the fifteenth century. During the previous century secular rulers had asserted control over the clergy in their kingdoms. Nevertheless the clergy continued to owe a dual allegiance to pope as well as to king, whilst morals, heresy, matrimonial causes and bequests by will all fell within the jurisdiction of ecclesiastical, not royal, courts. Between 1409 and 1449 a series of Church councils sought reform, by introducing regular Church councils into the system of ecclesiastical government. The successful extension of the secular parliamentary model into the Church would have placed limits on the existing autocratic papal government. Indeed, in the late fourteenth century one secular parliament, that of the English King Richard II, enacted a statute by which any clergy guilty of praemunire – invading 'the king's regality' – could suffer indefinite imprisonment and loss of property. However, the conciliar movement failed and by 1450 the papacy had emerged intact. That was not the end of the story. The shortcomings of papal autocracy were amongst the triggers of the sixteenth-century Reformation when Scandinavian kings, German princes and others converted to protestantism; even those monarchs – for example in France, Spain and England (under Henry VIII) – who remained true to the catholic faith, asserted greater control over the Church in their kingdoms. In some cases parliaments would loom large in the process.

The *second* competitive interest, which increasingly preoccupied princes, was also one of international dimensions: rival expansionist states, which competed for precedence (even pre-eminence) or control and could threaten territorial integrity. Some rivalries, such as that between England and the 'auld alliance' of France and Scotland, were long-standing. But the one which was to dominate Europe for two centuries took shape only in the late fifteenth and early sixteenth centuries. It was then that the French monarchy extended its sovereignty throughout France and the accidents of inheritance created the Habsburg composite monster. When, in 1494, Charles VIII of France reasserted an old Angevin claim to Naples and backed it with an invading army, Italy became the first battleground in the long struggle between Europe's two superpowers. Representative assemblies were inevitably expected to fund the war-effort of the Habsburg and French Valois dynasties.

Regional and local interests constituted the *third* obstacle to assertive rulers pursuing expansive and expensive policies and objectives. Such interests encompassed the liberties, privileges and immunities of rural communities, urban corporations, merchant companies, professional bodies, social orders, especially tax-exempt nobilities (as in Castile and France), and representative institutions. On their accession rulers were expected to swear on oath that they would observe the existing laws, customs and privileges. This was normally done and often observed. The financial demands on princes, however, intensified in the later fifteenth century and escalated thereafter. The old domanial and lordship-based revenues no longer sufficed. So they were increasingly inclined to pursue taxing policies which, if successful, would enable them to tap the financial resources of their communities and fill their war chests. Of course the picture is not a simple, uniform one. Elected emperors and Polish kings, for example, were princes under pressure and in decline. Nevertheless it is true to say that, in much of Europe, the later fifteenth and early sixteenth centuries were characterised by the emergence of a number of vigorous kings who were driven by the 'fiscal imperative'. Richard Bonney argues that this fiscal imperative, the consequence of the demands of war, together with 'the longterm consequences of fiscal growth may be seen as the *primum mobile* for the development of the state'. This was, as already observed, particularly evident in the decentralised, intensely localistic composite monarchies of the Valois and Habsburgs.

Recent research has questioned, minimised, even rejected the presence of centralisation as a late medieval and early modern phenomenon. It has even been suggested that the word might in particular be removed from the French historical vocabulary of this period. The expansion of the royal bureaucracy and the creation of many *élections* (from as early as the 1350s) can really be described in no other way. It was, however, also an unsystematic process and, at the same time, much royal energy was devoted to mutually beneficial bargains, deals and compromises with provincial elites, in which the early modern nobility continued to be a prominent, even dominant force. Attempts at royal centralisation were always offset by continued dependence on *parlements*, municipal councils, provincial nobilities, noble governors and, of course, estates. Parliaments were not only the voices and defenders of the liberties, laws and customary rights of French elites and localities. They were also the points of contact between them and their monarchs as they came under increasing financial pressure in the sixteenth and seventeenth centuries. But divisions within estates and between provinces often prevented them from being effective spokesmen and encouraged royal intervention.[27]

CASE STUDIES

I Minorities and absentee rulers: Scotland

During the years 1290–92 and 1296–1306 the country experienced two interregna. Only three of the seven monarchs who then ruled Scotland between 1306 and 1488 had attained their majority before accession to the throne: Robert I (1306–29), Robert II (1371–90) and Robert III (1390–1406). Of the rest, David II (1329–71) was only five years old, James I (1406–37) twelve, James II (1437–60) seven and James III (1460–88) eight. Furthermore, David II was absent from his kingdom for nineteen years of his forty-two year reign, whilst James I was a prisoner in England for eighteen years. In such circumstances – prolonged minorities and absences – one might have expected parliaments, which were meetings of a national institution, to have become more important in the business of government. That was not the case, for a number of reasons. Although Scottish parliaments were active as a judicial and legislative body, they had no tradition as a national forum where they offered advice on policies and aired grievances. When the membership abdicated its duties and responsibilities to the committee of articles, it largely surrendered its active role in law-making. And of course there was the alternative consultative, legislative and taxing institution, the general council or convention.[28]

As Gordon Donaldson pointed out, the lack of an effective, adult, royal presence could make a difference: 'Decisions vital for the fate of the country were sometimes made by a parliament or a general council, especially during minorities when parties were delicately balanced'. Donaldson touches here upon one of the crucial characteristics of royal minorities. It was a time when rival political groupings vied for control at the centre. If one such grouping became dominant, its rivals would stay away from parliament rather than risk defeat. 'More often, especially as the king's subjects were not accustomed to take the initiative in framing policies in parliament, the decisions were made elsewhere, either by the king or by the faction in control, and any bargaining and consultation between the government and its influential subjects took place outside the parliament house.' Thus, Donaldson describes a set of political circumstances which were common to government under adult monarchs and during minorities.[29] Scottish parliaments did not assert themselves or assume political prominence at times when the kingdom was plagued by lengthy royal minorities or absences.

II Internal crisis: Castile

For much of the fifteenth century Castile was wracked by civil wars between a powerful and wealthy nobility and a crown weakened by the familiar dynastic problem of minorities and succession disputes. The Cortes could not play an effective part in resolving the conflict, which was about respective rights and powers, because of its structural and functional weaknesses. Though it had the right to petition for new laws, only the king could make them. He was obliged to apply to the assembly for a tax, the *servicio*, but he had alternative sources of revenue, above all the *alcabala* (sales tax) which had been a royal, not parliamentary tax since 1342 and was now the crown's biggest single item of revenue. Tax-exempt clergy and nobles showed little interest in the affairs of the Cortes. They were not usually called; and the *brazo* of urban representatives was left on its own to resist royal financial pressure. Further, the advisory function of parliament shifted to the royal council, where members of the clergy and nobility sat.

Matters reached a critical point in the reign of King Henry IV (1454–74). After a protracted political struggle and, in 1465–68, another civil war, the nobles imposed on him Isabella, his half-sister, as his successor. In 1469 they used parliament, which met in Madrid and

Ocaña, to carry out political reforms, by which royal power was effectively controlled by the nobility. César Olivera Serrano argues that, to some extent, it was also a noble victory over the Cortes, whose authority was, in large measure, delegated to a 'Permanent *Diputación*' of just four urban representatives (*procuradores*). Such a small number could be more easily manipulated than the full house of thirty-four. Furthermore, this quartet of members, susceptible to noble influence, continued to represent the assembly even when it was not sitting.

On the other hand, Serrano, who views Henry IV's reign as 'the most dynamic period' in the Cortes' history, regards the Madrid-Ocaña meeting as a success for it as well. The creation of the *Diputación* meant that, for the first time, the cities had a permanent, all-year-round committee which could ensure that parliamentary taxes were spent on the purposes for which they were voted. The position of *procuradores* was strengthened, as they also secured (1) the right of redress of grievances before the grant of taxes ('redress before supply') and (2) secrecy of debate, which lessened the opportunity for royal pressure and enabled members to speak more freely without fear of royal reprisal. In several significant ways, therefore, the meeting of 1469 advanced the Cortes' position in its relations with the crown.

In that same year, however, Isabella, the future queen of Castile, married Ferdinand, the future king of Aragon, Valencia and Catalonia. With his assistance she built up a network of alliances within Castile. After Henry IV's death and even during one last civil war with opposition nobles (which ended in 1479), the new queen began the task of restructuring power and restoring stability. One of her instruments in the process was the Cortes.[30] At Madrigal in 1476 it voted the largest *servicio* (tax) of the century. It also created the *Santa Hermandad*. The original, medieval *hermandades* were local, urban organisations with judicial and policing functions, but now they were placed under unified royal control with the object of restoring order and stability in the war-torn kingdom. The *Hermandad* became, in effect, a rural police force, which could also be transformed into a royal military force. At Toledo, four years later, queen and Cortes carried through further reforms, including the restructuring of the royal council and the crown's resumption of half the royal revenues which the nobility had acquired since 1464. Most significant for the Cortes' future, as we shall see in due course, was the appointment of royal officials, *corregidores*, to all the more important municipalities, including the eighteen cities which, in the future, would send *procuradores* to the assembly. The *corregidor*, who had both administrative and judicial functions, was not a local resident but a royal agent sent from the centre.[31]

Whilst they utilised the Cortes in the process of reviving royal authority, subordinating the nobility and restoring order and stability, Isabella and Ferdinand were careful to avoid dependence on it. The nobles' reforms of 1469 were not put into effect. The monarchs tended to consult the cities and towns through the *Santa Hermandad* and not the Cortes. It was only in financial matters that the Cortes was important and influential – on paper at least. The Castilian (and later the Spanish) monarch, unlike most other European rulers, had no personal patrimony in the form of estates from which he derived a substantial income. Therefore, as both a private individual and head of state, he was dependent on public funding. That might seem to place great power in the Cortes, which could withhold such revenue. Instead it became a profound moral obligation of the monarch's subjects to supply him with ample funds. In the words of I.A.A. Thompson, taxation was not so much 'an exceptional, and exceptionable, imposition as the expression of the bond between king and kingdom, a condition of the compact between them, the dowry the king received for husbanding his country, or the salary the king was paid for doing his office'.[32]

In any case, the Cortes' financial importance in the later fifteenth century was, to some extent, more apparent than real. True, the monarch was expected to apply to the Cortes for the standard tax, the *servicio*, and proposed new taxes. But the Castilian ruler had many other revenue sources available: not only the old *alcabala*, but also from the late fifteenth century the income of the great military orders, as well as a variety of customs duties, monopolies and mining revenues. As peace and order returned to Castile, the need for further Cortes diminished. Whereas four were called between 1474 and 1483, no more met for fourteen years. Then the needs of war necessitated twelve sessions between 1497 and 1516. War so often determined the rhythms of parliamentary activity and existence.[33]

III External threat: France

Whereas the Castilian monarchy faced a long *internal* crisis during the fifteenth century, that of France endured a long-standing *external* threat from England. Between the eleventh and fifteenth centuries the English controlled a large, albeit varying, proportion of the French kingdom, whilst Edward III (1327–77) and his successors launched repeated invasions in support of the English claim to the French crown. Furthermore, some of these provinces which were not under English control were quasi-autonomous, whilst, until 1435, successive powerful dukes of Burgundy, who had acquired the Netherlands by dynastic marriages, remained firmly in the English camp.

It would be misleading, indeed erroneous, to postulate a simple contrast between Castile and France: that the future development of crown–assembly relations, the divergence of royal–parliamentary priorities and the growth of friction between monarchs and parliaments were the consequences of internal crisis in one kingdom and external threat to the other. So French kings had to contend with not only the English, but also the diversity and lack of internal cohesion within their kingdom. On the other hand, France stood in classic contrast to England. Provincialism was its predominant characteristic. So there was no common administration, legal code, policing, law, free trade area or tax system. Some provinces had their own estates (parliamentary assemblies) and/or *parlements* (high courts), but others did not. Kings might call general assemblies for Languedoc (southern France) and Languedoil (central and north France), but they were reluctant to do so. In this they were in sympathy with their subjects, who did not want the upheaval, discomfort, costs and dangers of travel which these meetings involved. Language difficulties, provincial loyalties and the logistical problems involved in the staging of them in such a large kingdom reinforced these attitudes.

Several other circumstances worked against the development of effective general representative assemblies in medieval France. During the fourteenth century and especially during the Hundred Years' War (1337–1453) the French monarchy developed an extensive tax system and obtained war revenues through a variety of taxes. As the accepted function of French general parliaments was advice, when consent to taxes was sought it was to provincial and local assemblies that the king turned. Furthermore, they were the bodies which were conscious of local and regional interests and privileges and willing to defend them. So they served both the crown *and* local and regional interests. Provincialism was also characteristic of the general assemblies, but that benefited no one: the consequences were competing interests, division and lack of direction or general purpose. Although monarchs tended to exercise a degree of control over them, they derived few advantages from that. By the late fifteenth century, after the expulsion of the English and Louis XI's acquisition of the duchy of Burgundy, most of France was formally subject to his rule. That might seem a justification for general assemblies. Nominal subjection to royal headship, however, did not mean political unity. For so long before the French kings' fifteenth-century acquisitions many provinces of France had been governed by the English, Burgundian dukes or other regional rulers. Union would not sweep away provincial identity, or the diversity of laws, liberties, language and loyalties.

As the English presence in France was pressed back to Calais in the mid-fifteenth century and the needs of war became less pressing, the Estates-general sank into virtual oblivion. Charles VII called it in 1440. Thereafter it met only four times in the next 120 years: in 1468, 1484, 1560 and 1560–61. In contrast, many provinces (or *pays d'états*) had active estates at the end of the fifteenth century. Some of them were located in parts of France which had been held for long periods by English kings during the previous four centuries: such were Guyenne, Limousin and Poitou.[34] Others were in distant parts of France, remote from the seat of royal government in the Ile-de-France: for example, Languedoc, Dauphiné and Provence. As these provinces were acquired by the French crown in the course of the fifteenth century they were allowed to retain their estates – so too were Burgundy, Brittany and others. Such concessions amounted to a realistic attempt, by a relatively weak monarchy, to deal with the particularism of often geographically remote, ethnographically different and linguistically 'foreign' provinces.

However, the fact that so many provinces retained their estates, as the French monarchy extended its authority throughout France, should not be seen as a disadvantage to kings. Because national assemblies in France served little financial purpose, the most effective way to obtain a tax was to negotiate with individual provinces and, in the case of *pays d'états*, with their assemblies. There, persuasion, influence and management tended to be more profitable and less dangerous than open aggression, threats and the politics of confrontation. Poitou is a case in point. During the earlier part of the Hundred Years' War its estates regularly voted grants to its overlord, the duke of Berry: for example, 40,000 *écus* or *francs* in 1393, 1395, 1396, 1399 and 1411 and, in 1415, 50,000 *livres*. Then, in 1417, the estates pledged allegiance to the dauphin (heir to the French crown), as the new count of Poitou. Thereafter grants became more frequent: 40,000 *livres* in the spring of 1418 and 42,000 in October; the same amount in 1420. From 1422 it was regularly voting money to the king: in 1422, 1423, 1424, 1425 and 1429 (60,000 *livres* for his coronation). Taxation was not annual and tax grants by the estates were less frequent after the defeat of the English. On the other hand, the provincial assembly was faced with a typical long-term royal campaign to introduce a range of non-parliamentary taxes into Poitou: the *aides*, levied on wine and spirits (1435–38 and from 1454), the steadily increasing *taille* (based simply on the estimate of what each taxpayer was worth) and, from the late 1440s, the *gabelle*. In 1464 a joint meeting of the estates of Poitou and five other provinces lamented 'the heaviness of taxes in general and requested that they be diminished'.[35] Yet, at the same time, they voted 100,000 *écus* as a contribution towards King Louis XI's military ventures.

Poitou is one documented example of the way in which French kings gradually, persistently and undramatically managed and moulded provincial assemblies to do their financial bidding. It also illustrates the way in which they exploited the extended crisis of the English 'threat' in their dealings with provincial estates. The history of fifteenth-century French assemblies is a classic example of the related effect of domestic and external developments on king–parliament relations. Philip Hoffman writes that, as French kings 'yoked territories to the kingdom, they confirmed traditional liberties and even conceded new privileges in order to win over a province or a city. When the strategic port of Bordeaux returned to French rule in the last stages of the Hundred Years' War, for example, Charles VII granted the inhabitants tax exemptions and considerable local political autonomy.'[36] It certainly did not amount to a policy of centralisation.

Notes

1   See above, p. 25; H.G. Koenigsberger, 'Beginnings of the States General of the Netherlands' *PER* 8, 2 (Dec. 1988) pp. 105–6.

2   See below, pp. 100–3; K. Gorski, 'The origins of the Polish Sejm' *Slavonic and East European Review* 44 (1966), pp. 125–9.

3   H.G. Koenigsberger, 'Parliaments and estates', in R.W. Davis, ed., *The Origins of Modern Freedom in the West* (Stanford, CA, 1995), pp. 174–5; see below, p. 65.

4   D.H. Sacks, 'The paradox of taxation: fiscal crises. Parliament and liberty in

England, 1450–1640', in P. T. Hoffman and K. Norberg, eds, *Fiscal Crises, Liberty and Representative Government, 1450–1789* (Stanford, CA, 1994), pp. 9–13.

5   M. Rady, *France, 1494–1610. Renaissance, Religion and Recovery* (London, 1991), p. 8; W.R. Ormrod, 'The West European monarchies in the later middle ages', in R. Bonney, ed., *Economic Systems and State Finance* (Oxford, 1995), p. 124; J. Russell Major, *From Renaissance Monarchy to Absolute Monarchy. French Kings, Nobles and Estates* (London, 1994), pp. 17–22.

6   This applies only to those assemblies to which representatives came with *plena potestas*. Where members were delegates, as in the Castilian Cortes and the states of the Low Countries, their duty to consult with their cities about royal tax requests naturally prolonged negotiations.

7   P. Blickle, 'Peasant political representation in Sweden and Switzerland – a comparison', in N. Stjernquist, ed., *The Swedish Riksdag in an International Perspective* (Stockholm, 1989), pp. 24–30.

8   See below, pp. 133, 148–9.

9   For Castile and France, see above, pp. 54–60.

10 Koenigsberger, 'Parliaments and estates', p. 166.

11 Effected by the parliamentary statutes of 1536 (27 Henry VIII c.24 and 26) and 1543 (34/35 Henry VIII, c.26), A. Luders, T.E. Tomlins, J. Raithby et al., eds, *Statutes of the Realm*, 11 vols (London, 1810–28), vol. III, pp. 555–8, 563–9, 926–37.

12 H.G. Koenigsberger, 'Composite states, representative institutions and the American Revolution' *BIHR* 62 (1989), p. 135; ibid., 'Parliaments and estates', p. 167.

13 This was to occur, for example, in the Low Countries during Philip II's reign and in Catalonia during the 1640s.

14 P.T. Hoffman, 'Early modern France, 1450–1700', in Hoffman and Norberg, eds, *Fiscal Crises*, pp. 227–30; Major, *Renaissance Monarchy to Absolute Monarchy*, pp. 21–2, 35–7.

15 A direct tax, but its application varied: it could be levied on property or simply on each taxpayer's estimated capacity to pay.

16 See Poitou, pp. 57–8.

17 N. Davies, *God's Playground. A History of Poland*, 2 vols (Oxford, 1981), vol.1, pp. 115–18.

18 J. Mallek, 'From the rebellion of the Prussian League to the autonomy of royal Prussia: the estates of Prussia and Poland in the years 1454–1526' *PER* 14, 1 (June 1994), pp. 19–29.

19 Koenigsberger, 'Parliaments and estates', pp. 170–1; E. Isenmann, 'Medieval and Renaissance theories of state finance', in Bonney, ed., *Economic Systems and State Finance*, pp. 34–5.

20 See also above, pp. 23–4.

21 E.g. the duchy of Aquitaine, when the future Henry II married Eleanor, heiress of the duke, in 1152.

22 E.g. Normandy, Maine, Anjou and Touraine.

23 H.G. Richardson and G.O. Sayles, *The Irish Parliament in the Middle Ages* (Philadelphia, PA, 1952), pp. 57–70 and 332–65.

24 S.G. Ellis, 'Parliament and community in Yorkist and Tudor Ireland', in A. Cosgrove and J.I. McGuire, eds, *Parliament and Community*, Historical Studies XIV (Belfast, 1983), pp. 43–51; S.G. Ellis, *Reform and Revival. English Government in Ireland, 1470–1534* (Woodbridge, Suffolk, 1986), pp. 143–8; Richardson and Sayles, *Irish Parliament*, pp. 215–20.

25 This may explain the apparent lack of enthusiasm for a Welsh assembly at the end of the twentieth century.

26 A useful introductory discussion of such change is to be found in R. Mackenney, *Sixteenth Century Europe. Expansion and Conflict* (London, 1993), ch.3.

27 R. Bonney, *The Limits of Absolutism in Ancien Régime France* (Aldershot, 1995), pp. ix, I, 94; D. Potter, *A History of France, 1460–1560. The Emergence of a Nation State* (London, 1995), pp. 149–53; Rady, *France, 1494–1610*, pp. 34–9.

28 See above, pp. 18–19, 30.

29 G. Donaldson, *Scotland. James V to James VII* (Edinburgh, 1965), pp. 8–9.

30 César Olivera Serrano, 'The parliamentary reforms of the Castilian Cortes in 1469: a victory for the nobility?' *PER* 10, 2 (Dec. 1990), pp. 127–31; C. Jago, 'Review essay. Crown and Cortes in early-modern Spain' *PER* 12, 2 (Dec. 1992), pp. 189–90.

31 J.H. Elliott, *Imperial Spain 1469–1716* (London, 1969), pp. 75–6, 78–81, 83–4; S. Haliczer, *The Comuneros of Castile. The Forging of a Revolution, 1475–1521* (London, 1981), pp. 34–5.

32 I.A.A. Thompson, 'Castile: polity, fiscality, and fiscal crisis', in Hoffman and Norberg, eds, *Fiscal Crises*, pp. 146–7, 153–4.

33 Jago, 'Crown and Cortes', p. 190; Elliott, *Imperial Spain*, pp. 80–1.

34 P.S. Lewis, 'The failure of the French medieval estates' *P&P* 23 (Nov. 1962), pp. 9–10; J. Russell Major, *The Monarchy, the Estates and the Aristocracy in Renaissance France* (London, 1988), VIII, pp. 248–9, 250–1; J.B. Henneman, *Royal Taxation in Fourteenth Century France. The Development of War Financing, 1322–1356* (Princeton, NJ, 1971), pp. 326–7; Koenigsberger, 'Parliaments and estates', pp. 169–70.

35 J.M. Tyrrell, *A History of the Estates of Poitou* (The Hague, 1968), Appendix A, pp. 134–46.

36 Hoffman, 'Early modern France, 1450–1700', in Hoffman and Norberg, eds, *Fiscal Crises*, p. 227.

3

Religious Reformation and Political Change, War and Rebellion: Their Impact on Parliaments in the Sixteenth Century: I

> These kingdoms beg His Majesty to see fit to return to these kingdoms immediately, and once here to remain here and to rule and govern in person . . . For it is not the custom of Castile to be left without a king, nor can it be ruled or governed thus with the peace and tranquillity that his royal service requires

> May His Highness be pleased upon his return . . . [not] to bring with him . . . Flemings, Frenchmen or men of any other nation to hold any office in the royal household. And may he appoint to such posts natives of these kingdoms only . . .

THESE WERE TWO of the demands made to their foreign king, Charles I, by the *Comuneros* during the Castilian rebellion of 1520–21. Charles had inherited Spain in 1516 and arrived there in 1518. Two years later, after raising a *servicio* (tax) and appointing the alien Adrian of Utrecht as regent, he departed for Germany, where he had been elected Holy Roman Emperor. From the moment of his arrival in Spain the new king, who could not speak a word of Castilian, exemplified many of the problems inherent in composite monarchs. He had had a Flemish upbringing and so, naturally, he brought with him a retinue of friends, confidants, his tutor Adrian and other compatriots from Flanders. They quickly acquired a reputation for rapacity – justified or exaggerated it is difficult to say – amongst Castilians who resented this foreign 'invasion'. There can be little doubt that Charles's own inexperience, shortsightedness and insensitivity contributed to the revolt of 1520. He was, however, trapped in a political dilemma from which it was difficult to escape. In Koenigsberger's words,

The ruler of a composite monarchy, by virtue of his very position, was bound to pursue political aims which could not be harmonised with the interests of his subjects in each one of the constituent parts of his monarchy as conveniently as they could be when he was the ruler over only one country with only one representative assembly to bother about.

The last point is significant because the constitutional purpose of the rebels was the preservation and, in some respects, recovery of the rights of the Castilian Cortes. Indeed, the rebels' *junta* declared itself to be a committee of the Cortes.[1]

The *junta*'s demands, as set forth in its petition, projected not a revolutionary but a conservative position. Charles had not respected what it conceived to be the traditional privileges of a representative assembly in one of his dominions. So it 'begged': that each city should return three, not two, deputies; that they should be paid by the cities; that *procuradores* (urban deputies) should not receive gifts from the crown; and that the choice of *procuradores* and their powers should be determined by the cities, not the monarchs. These were not a commentary on innovations of King Charles. The reduction of each city's deputies from three to two, for example, went back to 1429. On the other hand, Charles did demand that they come armed with *plena potestas* and he dispensed favours in order to secure a compliant assembly.[2] So incensed were the *Comuneros* by this practice that the *junta* demanded the death penalty for those deputies who accepted royal favours. Although the petition included one novel request for triennial Cortes, it was essentially a conservative document. Charles's conduct seems to have triggered the formulation of a set of demands which would restore some lost rights and protect others which his conduct threatened. It all came to naught, however, when the movement became socially radicalised and the nobles crushed it in 1521.[3]

Charles I's early Castilian 'experience' is a commentary on the problems which composite monarchies posed for both rulers and ruled. When Charles left Spain in 1520 he promised that he would be back within three years. During that time a regent would have to govern. The dominions of a composite monarchy could expect to experience visits from time to time by a peripatetic monarch.[4] But for most of the time they had to put up with a foreign administrator deputising for their (often foreign) ruler. Sicily, for example, was from the early fifteenth century governed by viceroys from Aragon. This change was not to the detriment of its governing elite. Its dominance was reflected in the structure of the *Parlamento*: three estates (or *bracci*) of clergy, nobility, and cities and towns. At the assembly's triennial meetings taxes were granted, petitions presented and the priorities of both parties to the process were by and large respected: for the viceroy internal order, stability and effective defence and for the *bracci* the social and financial benefits of sworn allegiance.

Under the Habsburgs Spanish grandees were regularly chosen to be viceroys in Sicily. In contrast English kings, between the 1480s and 1530s, frequently employed members of the Anglo-Irish (or Old English) community, especially the Geraldine earls of Kildare, in the offices of chief or deputy governor of Ireland. This made political sense, for a number of reasons. Effective English authority was restricted to the relatively small area, the Pale, on the east coast of Ireland. Beyond that power was wielded by Anglo-Irish and Gaelic leaders. Anglo-Irish families had been there for over three centuries. They had intermarried with the Irish and were part of the country's political and social landscape – above all 'the Fitzgeralds of Kildare [who] had emerged as the greatest dynastic family of the medieval colony, connected by marriage and political alliances with the leading families of both the Anglo-Irish and the Gaelic worlds, controlling the royal administration at Dublin, and invested by the English crown with a shadowy, but not insignificant, authority over all Ireland'.[5] Whilst, however, the early Tudors employed the Fitzgeralds, they did not trust them. Poynings' Law, enacted in 1494, was not designed to subordinate the Irish Parliament to Westminster, but to prevent the chief governor from manipulating it to further his own interests. The Kildares were trapped in the perpetual dilemma of conflicting priorities: service to a king in England and maintenance of their own independent lordship. The unsuccessful rebellion of 'Silken Thomas', tenth earl, in 1534–35 and his execution, together with his five uncles, in 1537 terminated English dependence on the Fitzgeralds.[6] Thenceforth the governor or lord deputy of Ireland was to be an Englishman. The consequence of this policy was already being felt before the Fitzgeralds' executions, when, in 1536, the English Lord Deputy Grey summoned an Irish Parliament from which the Gaelic Irish were excluded. It proceeded to enact revolutionary changes in the Irish Church.[7]

Not only royal viceroys but monarchs themselves could become remote, alien and even threatening figures, who rarely manifested themselves. An absentee ruler brought no obvious benefits to a dominion. As the *Comuneros* complained in 1520, Castile could not be governed effectively without a resident monarch. Aragonese assemblies too complained of royal absence. So far as governance was concerned, absence certainly did not make the heart grow fonder.[8] This is, perhaps, most dramatically evident in the case of Ireland. In 1541 the new lord deputy, Sir Anthony St Leger, summoned a Parliament which enacted that Henry VIII and his successors were to be taken and accepted not as lords but kings of Ireland. It was emphasised that this was only a change in name, not substance, because even as lord he had exercised 'kingly jurisdiction'. Nevertheless no English king was formally crowned king of Ireland or took a coronation oath to respect Irish liberties. Indeed the first royal rulers of Ireland to visit their kingdom were the deposed James II and his replacement, William III, in 1689–90 – and then their purpose was to wage war.

Of course one has to acknowledge the logistical and financial problems which inhibited the movement of monarchs around their dominions. Royal Courts from the Renaissance onwards were large, elaborate, political mechanisms and elaborate settings for royal image projection. Moving them was a complex and expensive exercise which also imposed considerable burdens on the localities through which they lumbered. The reluctance of French kings to hold general assemblies in Languedoc (southern France) was partly due to the disruption, tedium and costs of Courts on the move. Furthermore, some rulers of composite monarchies became increasingly isolated as they ceased to be migratory and instead opted for the sedentary: for example Philip II at the Escorial and Louis XIV at Versailles. Even in geographically small kingdoms a peripatetic monarch such as Elizabeth I of England was a visible queen on royal progresses only in the midlands and southern counties. She remained a stranger in the north, the far west and the principality of Wales. Only at the opening and closing ceremonies in Westminster Parliaments did men from those parts observe their monarch, perhaps even meet her at Court, and duly report back to their neighbours and constituents on their return. It was one of the important ways in which Parliaments served as a point of contact.

The public perception of the absentee monarch was markedly different from that of the ruler who was resident and therefore, presumably, working to advance the interests of the community, preserve its liberties, maintain order and defend it from external threats. A perceptible caution, even defensiveness, tended to characterise the relations between representative assemblies and rulers who were obliged to keep on the move or who, for political or personal reasons, chose to live elsewhere. The Low Countries had long experience of this kind of situation. When, by a piecemeal process in the fourteenth and fifteenth centuries, the dukes of Burgundy gained possession of the Low Countries, they had to deal with a wide range of 'provincial' assemblies, each of which was primarily concerned with local privilege and economic well-being. In some the clergy and nobility were important, but in others the cities and towns tended to call the tune, especially in Flanders and Holland. Co-operation between the towns of different provinces on economic matters was not unknown and so it was a natural extension of this practice for Duke Philip the Good to call provincial assemblies together for similar reasons during the 1420s and 1430s. Then in 1434 Philip resolved to unify the Low Countries' coinage, a matter of vital commercial concern to all of the provinces. To this end he called together the towns and estates of all the provinces in what proved to be the first States-general or general assembly of the Low Countries. Thereafter it was called frequently, not for taxes but to deal with economic matters.

That, however, changed in the 1460s and 1470s, as Philip's heir, Charles the Bold, who succeeded him in 1467, embarked on a risky and aggressive foreign policy. Increasing financial demands became the purpose and focus of meetings of both the provincial assemblies and the States-general. As Charles almost doubled ducal expenditure, between 1467 and his death a decade later, parliamentary resistance to the demands of their roaming warrior-duke likewise increased.[9] Charles's death in battle against the Swiss gave the assemblies the opportunity to strike back. His heiress, Mary, was compelled to concede the *grand privilège* to all the Netherlands' provinces. The States-general had to be consulted about taxation and its consent was required before war was launched. Furthermore, it was to meet whenever it chose and not simply at the duke's behest. It did so frequently – indeed more than once annually – during the next hundred years. Mary also had to respond to the reaction against her father, after his death, by decentralising the system. She was obliged to restore provincial autonomy and the right of each provincial parliament not to be bound by the decisions of the States-general or other provinces.

This might be regarded as a major victory for representative assemblies over authoritarian rule. In the course of time, however, Duke Charles's death simply moved the Low Countries from the now defunct Burgundian composite state to the much larger conglomerate of Charles Habsburg. He duly inherited them by descent from his grandmother Mary, who was Charles the Bold's heiress. They were just one of the many dominions in a composite monarchy which extended to the New World and reached out to the Pacific. Charles's time was increasingly consumed in the preservation of his *dominium* against foreign predators, dynastic competitors and economic interlopers. His prime needs were money and men, both of which he sought from his richest possessions, the kingdom of Castile and the composite state of the Netherlands. Inevitably, however, Charles was a ruler on the move and in the Low Countries he left the processes of negotiation and applied pressure to a succession of woman regents: his aunt, Margaret of Austria (until 1530) and then his widowed sister, Mary of Hungary (1531–55). The history of their relations with both the States-general and provincial states was characterised by the application of coercive tactics: such were proposals to revoke towns' privileges, to levy taxes without parliamentary consent, to grant supply before redress was given, and even to arrest and bring to trial members of obdurate municipal governments. The parliamentary responses ranged from strict application of the delegate principle (whereby they returned to consult their provincial estates or cities for instructions about the tax demands) to downright refusal. In 1534 Charles's proposal for a defensive union, in which all the provinces regularly contributed to the financing of a standing army, was likewise turned down. Resistance, however, could go too far. When, in 1539, the city of Ghent backed its rejection of yet more taxes by rising in rebellion, the normally absent ruler personally led the army which ended it.

Thereafter taxation continued to rise, not in order to benefit the Netherlands but to fund Charles's military operations elsewhere. The financial generosity of the assemblies could not satisfy the growing imperial demands. Already in 1542 the government's debts were so large that a special meeting of the States-general was held to approve yet more taxes. By the time Charles abdicated, in 1555, the burden of debt of the Brussels government was far worse and resentment was both widespread and growing. In this way he 'mortgaged the future for his son', who would need to proceed with political tact and a priority of financial retrenchment and recovery.[10] Unfortunately the son was Philip II.

He was a firm believer that the king of Spain should dwell in Castile and that government should be centralised and should operate from a permanent and fixed location. At the end of his life he had not changed his mind on this point. So he advised his heir that 'Travelling about one's kingdoms is neither useful nor decent.' It was not sound advice for the future ruler of a geographically scattered composite monarchy. As Elliott points out, the choice of Madrid as a permanent capital 'contradicted one of the fundamental assumptions on which the Spanish Monarchy rested. If the many territories that together constituted the Monarchy were regarded as independent units of equal rank, then they were all entitled to an equal degree of consideration.' But that was not Philip's way. This contributed to a rapid deterioration in his relations with the Netherlands. He inherited a legacy of resentment from the financial demands of his father's later years. In the 1560s the repressive policies of a remote foreign king, permanently located in far-off Madrid, led to rebellion, in which the representative assemblies played such a central role.[11]

The Netherlands' experience also illustrates another problem inherent in composite monarchies. The complexities, pressures and expense of managing such a diverse conglomerate influenced, even dictated, the ruler's priorities. However, those priorities could, and often did, penalise the economic well-being and political privileges of the component parts of that conglomerate, and also subordinate, coerce or even set aside the parliaments which represented them. We should not accuse early modern rulers of cold and calculating political cynicism. There is no reason to dismiss the coronation oaths of monarchs, when they swore to respect the rights and liberties of subjects, as words carelessly or cynically uttered, without any intention to honour them. In secular and ecclesiastical government and the law oaths were treated with the highest regard and certainly not taken lightly. At the same time rulers could claim to serve a higher cause. They were divinely appointed and also recognised as God's anointed. In the ceremony of installation, as emperor, king, duke or whatever, both his right to rule and his obligation to rule well were publicly proclaimed. This was no sixteenth-century innovation. What were novel, if only in degree, were the growing political pressures, challenges and threats to rulers. Although those who lorded it over composite monarchies were especially vulnerable, these problems were common to all princes.

As touched on at the end of the last chapter, there were three specific ongoing, often dramatically escalating pressure points for European princes. And their responses often impacted on representative assemblies. The pressure points are easy to identify because they concern three points of contact which no prince could avoid:

1   The secular-international contact with other European princes.
2   The internal or 'domestic' (i.e. regional and local) concerns within the prince's dominion(s).
3   The Church and religion. This concerned matters both spiritual and secular, internal and international. It involved heresy, morals, relations with the papacy and, in the century of religious upheaval, the enforcement of the principle *cuius regio eius religio* whereby the prince determined the religion.

Whilst, for convenience's sake, these will be examined separately, it is important to remember that, in practical terms, they are inseparable. Furthermore, representative assemblies were concerned, involved and sometimes embroiled with their princely masters in all three areas of state activity, stress and even crisis.

Secular-international politics

At the heart of European politics during the sixteenth century and beyond was the dynastic conflict between French kings and Habsburgs. The Franco-Spanish wars in Italy from the 1490s were the curtain-raiser on two centuries of diplomatic rivalry and military conflict. It was for the most part a secular contest. Both the French Valois and (after Henry IV's conversion) the Bourbon dynasties and the Habsburgs remained loyal to the catholic faith during and after the religious Reformation of the sixteenth century (although French princes were willing to ally with English, Dutch and Swedish protestants in order to promote their political fortunes).

This prolonged conflict was pursued in various theatres and ways, but especially on the battlefield, until the antagonists took a 'breather' with the treaty of Cateau-Cambrésis in 1559. Dynastic politics at this time were affected by the significant developments in military technology and the growth in both the size of armies and the scale of warfare. Such politics were also complicated by the European Reformation and consequent religious wars. This is not the time or place, nor is there the necessary space, to provide a detailed study of the long-lasting dynastic struggle.[12] It began, as already noted, with a French invasion of Italy in 1494 in support of an old Angevin claim to Naples. Over the years the fortunes of the two sides swayed back and forth as the French scored military victories at Fornovo (1495), Agnadello (1509), Ravenna (1512) and Marignano (1515) but the Habsburgs achieved success at Cerignola and Garigliano (1503), Bicocca (1522) and Pavia (1525). Campaigns were also conducted within the borders of France, Germany and the Netherlands, especially in the later decades of the Valois–Habsburg struggle. After Philip II's victories at St Quentin (1557) and Gravelines (1559) the French were prepared to make peace. At the end, what had they achieved? French dreams of an empire in Italy had gone, whilst the Habsburgs had lost Metz, Toul and Verdun. The one certain legacy was, as we shall see, financial.

The sorry story of military commitments and consequent financial burdens does not end there. Emperor Charles V had to contend both with the Islamic onslaught of the Ottoman Turkish sultan, Suleiman I, on Hungary in the 1520s and, in the following twenty-five years, with the combined forces of particularist princes and militant protestantism in Germany. Furthermore, during the prolonged Habsburg–Valois 'contest' other, lesser powers became involved, willingly or otherwise. England's King Henry VIII was certainly no reluctant participant. He sought to be the embodiment of chivalry and personification of English greatness when he revived the claim to the crown of France. His early wars in 1512–14, conducted in alliance with Ferdinand of Spain and then the Habsburg Emperor Maximilian, rewarded him with those 'ungracious dogholes', Thérouanne and Tournai. Between 1522 and 1525 and again in 1543–46 Henry resumed war with France and in 1544 acquired Boulogne. The fortification of what turned out to be tem-porary gains simply added to the king's costs. Furthermore, any such conflict reactivated the 'auld alliance' of France and Scotland. The Scottish invading army was destroyed at Flodden in 1513 and another was defeated at Solway Moss in 1542. In the process the Scots lost many men – reputedly 10,000 at Flodden – two kings (one slain and the other allegedly dying of shame) and treasure which the monarchy could ill afford.

In contrast to a politically egotistical, but militarily incompetent, monarch like Henry VIII or precipitate interventionist Scottish kings, all of whom opted for war, there was no way in which Italian states could stand aloof from the Valois–Habsburg conflict. To a greater or lesser degree the papacy, the Sforzas of Milan, the Aragonese Alfonso in Naples, the Medici in Florence, and the corporate governors of Venice were pawns or victims of that struggle. Naples and Piedmont apart, parliaments were not a feature of Italian political structures unless one includes the islands of Sicily and Sardinia.[13] In most of Europe, however, it was to representative assemblies that rulers were obliged to turn. War, especially the escalating costs of larger armies and new technology, could not be funded out of hereditary revenues. These had to be augmented by taxation which, in accordance with the *quod omnes tangit* principle, required parliamentary assent. This brings us to the second pressure point for European princes.

Internal (or domestic) concerns within the ruler's dominions: the impact of war, 1490–1559

During the time of the dynastic wars, between the 1490s and 1559, the burdens of war generally constituted the most serious, intensifying and widespread grievance held against royal governments. And it was the financial cost which had the greatest impact on crown–parliament relations (although, as we shall see, from the 1530s on religion was overtaking taxation as the most controversial issue in some assemblies). The parliamentary responses to royal expectations, demands and pressures, however, inevitably varied from country to country, and were greatly influenced by their institutional strength or lack thereof. The variety is evident in the range of Case Studies of Habsburg, Valois and Tudor assemblies on pages 72–82.

The Church and religion

Although, in 1559, the treaty of Cateau-Cambrésis ended the dynastic wars, it did not bring peace to Europe, which had been thrown into turmoil by the Reformation. Even as Charles of Spain was crowned Holy Roman Emperor in 1519, Martin Luther's challenge to the papal office and Church was impacting on Germany. During the next forty years military conflicts were the consequence not only of secular state rivalries but also of religious issues. The emergence and spread of

Lutheranism in Germany and northern Europe and of Calvinism in Geneva, the Netherlands, France and eventually England and Scotland presented challenges to catholic princes. They also laid the foundations for conflict in the century after Cateau-Cambrésis. Well before then, however, Germany became the first battleground of the Reformation. Charles V, a staunch catholic, waged war with the elector of Saxony, the landgrave of Hesse and other princes of the protestant Schmalkaldic League during the 1540s and 1550s. The Peace of Augsburg, which in 1555 brought peace to Germany, was based on the principle that each ruler determined the religion in his territory. In practice other European states adopted the same principle when the ruler or his parliament unilaterally adopted protestantism or confirmed allegiance to the papacy and catholicism. So Denmark (1526) and Sweden (1527) opted for Lutheranism. English and Irish parliaments rejected papal authority in the 1530s and eventually established a protestant Church in both countries. Meanwhile Calvinism spread into Swiss and Rhenish cities, the Low Countries and France. Religious division fuelled the fires of conflict. And, at the same time, the revival of Turkish Islamic power posed a threat to Christian Europe and, in particular, to the Habsburgs. There were Turkish advances in the Mediterranean in the 1530s, and Sultan Suleiman I conquered much of Hungary in 1526, though a parliament in the remaining territory elected Charles V's brother, Ferdinand, king of Hungary.

Whether the wars were the consequence of secular rivalries or confessional conflict, they imposed financial burdens on states and so, inevitably, growing pressures and obligations on parliaments. So far as the religious schism was concerned, however, its full impact on European politics and representative institutions was not felt until after the 1550s. If the Peace of Augsburg brought peace to the Empire for over sixty years, it also set in motion a chain of events which helped to set the stage for later sixteenth-century conflicts. Augsburg signalled Charles's failure in Germany. In 1555–56 he abdicated and his son Philip became ruler of the Netherlands and Spain; on Charles's death in 1558 his brother Ferdinand inherited the German Habsburg lands and was elected Holy Roman Emperor. Philip II was a devout unswerving Roman catholic who epitomised the aggressive uncompromising spirit of the Counter-Reformation. At the same time his wife, Mary Tudor, died (1558) and under her successor, Elizabeth I, a protestant Church was established in England (1559). In France the death of Henry II (1559) resulted in a regency and the succession of boy-kings: Francis II (1559–60) and Charles IX (1560–74). And, whilst Mary Queen of Scots resided in France, as wife then widow of Francis II, a presbyterian Church was established in Scotland. Together these events provided the scenario for four decades of conflict in western Europe: in the Low Countries, with the growth of both Calvinism and resistance to the persecuting catholicism of an absentee, foreign king; in France the polarisation of the kingdom as a dynamic, organised Calvinist (Huguenot) movement and the powerful catholic network of the Guise dukes faced up to each other; in Scotland which had, from 1560, a 'Reformed' Church and a catholic monarch; and in Ireland, where consensus gave way to increasingly bloody ethnic and religious conflict between the crown's subjects and its alien administration. It would be simplistic to consider these conflicts just in religious terms. The point to remember is that in the major, often interrelated, political *and* religious changes of the sixteenth century, before and after 1559, representative institutions were liable to be involved. Sometimes they had an important, even crucial, role to play and they could find themselves in a very exposed position.

CASE STUDIES

I Castile

The Castilian Cortes, for example, had strengthened its privileges during a period of royal weakness in the fifteenth century. But with the return of strong government under Ferdinand and Isabella the two monarchs took steps to secure a compliant assembly. As *procuradores* were not elected, but selected by city councils, the choice was subject to royal influence and even direct intervention. The crown insisted that the *procuradores* came with *plena potestas* and it exploited their venality to its advantage. According to a long-standing interpretation of Castilian parliamentary history, the Cortes' record under the Habsburgs was that of 'a corrupted and decadent parliamentary institution . . . incapable of opposing royal absolutism, and useful only as the instrument for legitimizing an ever-increasing burden of taxation on Castile'. The failure of the rising of the *Comuneros* in 1520–21 and, from 1538, the exclusion of clergy and nobles from the Cortes ensured its subjection to the monarchy and compliance with its growing tax demands. The thesis of a declining parliament, however, is no longer acceptable. 'This picture of an emasculated Cortes thoroughly dominated and exploited by the Crown is now giving way to a picture of a vigorous and vital parliament, well aware of its powers and willing to confront the monarchy as circumstances required.' Charles Jago illustrates this by citing Charles I's concessions to the Cortes well after the suppression of the *Comuneros* rising: in 1536 he and the cities of Castile negotiated the conversion of the sales tax (*alcabala*) and ecclesiastical tithes (*tercias reales*) into a composition (or fixed annual sum) known as the *encabezamiento general*; the establishment, in 1525, of a permanent parliamentary committee, the *Diputación*; and administration of both the *encabezamiento* and the Cortes' regular triennial tax grant (the *servicio*) by the parliament and the cities. These concessions should not, however, be seen as the simple outcome of confrontational politics in which a vigorous assembly won certain advantages at the crown's expense. Thompson describes it rather as 'a sort of fiscal entente reached between 1495 and 1536'. It was beneficial to the crown, which was guaranteed a known annual income from several lucrative sources but was not burdened with the administration of them.

Then, in 1538, Charles sought but failed to get the Cortes' approval for a *sisa*, a wide-ranging indirect tax on foodstuffs. This session had a significant impact on the future of the Castilian Cortes. Not only were the tax-exempt clergy and nobility removed, reducing the parliament to thirty-six *procuradores* from eighteen cities. As compensation for the failed *sisa*, the Cortes granted a *servicio extraordinario* in addition to the ordinary *servicio*. In return, the *encabezamiento* was frozen at its 1536 level. In the next twenty years Charles's military commitments and expenditure increased. At the same time the proportion of his income provided by parliamentary grants, as well as their real value, significantly diminished.[14] According to Thompson, the Cortes was marginalised: '[W]ithout the lords they were irrelevant to the politics of the Court, and their financial contribution was of declining importance.' However, if that was the situation, it was to change during Philip II's reign.[15] Furthermore, as Thompson points out elsewhere, the 1538 Cortes was less significant for the nobles' final curtain-call than for their presence. More often than not nobles and clergy had been absent during the fifteenth century and they were only summoned once between 1510 and 1538.

II The kingdoms of Aragon

Charles's other Iberian kingdoms contributed little to the royal coffers. They had smaller populations. Between the later fourteenth century and 1500, for example, Catalonia's had dropped by one-third and was under 300,000, less than one-twentieth that of Castile. The Cortes of Aragon, Valencia and Catalonia met infrequently, especially as Spain's over-committed monarchs had to be personally present. So the Aragonese parliament met only seven times under Ferdinand (1479–1516) and on the same number of occasions during the 40-year reign of Charles I. The Aragonese kingdoms and Castile continued as separate legal, administrative and parliamentary entities. Consequently the Cortes of the eastern kingdoms remained powerfully privileged assemblies and, when they did meet, they voted only very modest grants. Nor could Charles expect substantial aid from his Mediterranean island possessions. The Sardinian assembly made only a minor contribution and the *donativi*, which the Sicilian *Parlamento* voted, were needed for the island's defence against the increasing Turkish threat in the sixteenth century.

III The Holy Roman Empire

Germany, which gave Charles his most prestigious title, also afflicted him with the greatest political headaches, but without the financial means to cure them. As emperor he wielded little power in a steadily fragmenting political structure which was dominated by particularist princes who resisted his attempts to create an efficient imperial government and defence force. He could raise money from his south-eastern hereditary lands in and around Austria, but they were under serious threat from the Ottoman Turks. Within the rest of the Empire he could levy no tax without the consent of the imperial diet or *Reichstag*, where he had to treat with unco-operative and particularist princes, nobles and cities. That lack of co-operation was intensified by the Reformation, which split the Empire and the *Reichstag* between protestants and catholics. Charles was committed to the defeat of protestantism and so he shouldered yet another financial burden.

IV The Netherlands

In order to fund his various military commitments, however, Charles had to look in particular to his non-German possessions: to Castile, as we have already seen, and also to the Netherlands. Especially in the later years of his reign (from 1542 onwards) the States-general and provincial estates had to cope with a wider range of tax-raising novelties proposed by the Habsburg government in Brussels: such were export duties, taxes on estates, income from property and trade and on wine and beer. As early as 1515, the Holland states (the strongest provincial assembly of one of the wealthiest provinces of the Netherlands) had accepted responsibility for *renten* or loans, which were secured against future tax yields. Thereafter the Habsburgs looked increasingly to the sale of *renten* by the provincial estates as a source of revenue. From 1542 they were secured against the wide range of new taxes. If would-be investors were to be persuaded to purchase such interest-bearing annuities, this system required the organisation and collection of taxes to be administered by the provincial estates, not by the notoriously financially voracious Habsburg government. Then, in 1553, the interest rates were significantly increased. Long-term loans bearing an annual return of one-sixth the capital value were an attractive investment. So, by the time of Charles V's abdication, the provincial assemblies were operating a cheap, effective financial system which, in the short term, benefited Habsburg government but which left them in control of an operation which enhanced their credit. In the longer term it was a system that could be equally beneficial to the government and financial stability of an independent Netherlands.

Whilst the successful operation of the system of *renten* secured on taxes required a good deal of co-operation between central government and provincial assemblies, there was a darker side to the story. In the 1550s Charles's debts spiralled, seemingly out of control. Co-operation over the *renten* did nothing to diminish the harmful effects and widespread resentment caused by continuous and excessive Habsburg demands to fund policies which had no meaningful purpose or obvious advantage for the Netherlands.[16]

V France

If representative institutions in the dominions of the Habsburg monarchy had to cope with ongoing and increasing financial demands, at least those general assemblies under most pressure – in Castile and the Netherlands – were better equipped to do so than their counterpart in the kingdom of the Habsburgs' constant foe. The French Estates-general were neither popular with princes or community nor held in high esteem by them. Furthermore, they had no real role in the taxation process. Often their function was no more than a public acknowledgement that taxation was necessary. Even if they voted a composite national amount, the crown still had to negotiate with the provinces for their individual contributions towards that sum. Consequently, there was little point in calling the Estates-general, which did not meet as a full assembly between 1484 and 1560. In contrast, the provincial estates had an active existence in sixteen provinces in sixteenth-century France. Although, in 1484, the French monarchy resisted a move by the Estates-general to extend to all provinces the right to assemble, it did grant or confirm that right to those provinces newly incorporated in the territory directly ruled by it. It recognised their right of consent to taxation. And it also left them in control of assessment and collection of local taxes, thereby freeing the crown from an onerous and costly exercise. As Philip Hoffman points out, the early modern provincial estates' vigour was the result of a fifteenth-century revival. As we have seen, this was due 'at least in part, [to] the royal strategy of confirming local privileges in order to yoke provinces to the Crown'. Even when the supposedly autocratic Francis I, for example, conquered Navarre and Savoy, he created a new assembly in one and retained the estates in the other. He also pledged to levy no taxes in Languedoc or Brittany without parliamentary consent. They also became institutionally stronger as they emerged as legal corporations with their own syndics and bureaucracies.[17]

In the course of the sixteenth and seventeenth centuries, the dynamic of the fiscal imperative caused the French crown increasingly to regard the privileges of provinces and their estates as irksome constraints on its political authority and obstacles to increased revenue. So, in a rather piecemeal fashion, the crown sought to remove such limitations as opportunity afforded. It proceeded in a variety of ways, for example by attempts to introduce the *gabelle* (salt tax) into the previously exempt western provinces, and by the introduction of royal officials who would replace the provincial estates in tax administration. The former met with stiff resistance, often of a violent nature, as in Guyenne in the 1540s. The latter, a direct assault on the provincial estates' authority and usefulness, was finally achieved in Guyenne by Louis XIII in 1621 and, as a result, the assemblies there withered and died. Such royal success was certainly not repeated in all *pays d'états* (in Dauphiné in 1639 for example) – a commentary on the diversity of French political structures, privilege and provincial experience. In any case, in J. Russell Major's words, we have to 'abandon the liberal assumption that the kings and the estates were natural adversaries'.[18] With a small inefficient working bureaucracy it made sense to use estates in tax administration. And having only limited military strength co-operation was preferable – and safer – than confrontation. Local nobilities and assemblies were not hostile to the French state, which was increasingly a source of influence and patronage to them. Whilst taxation undoubtedly increased in the sixteenth century and French estates voted larger sums, the increases are much less significant when inflation, population and national income growth are taken into account.

VI Savoy-Piedmont

As noted above, other and lesser European states became involved in the Valois–Habsburg power struggle[19] and they too experienced the concomitant problems of such involvement, especially the military burden, external threat and internal discontent. Duke Emmanuel Philibert of Savoy-Piedmont even lost control of his duchy when, between 1536 and 1559, it was divided by opposing Habsburg and French armies. From the beginning of the wars in Italy in the 1490s the dukes had become increasingly dependent on the estates for increasing funds and those of Piedmont exploited the situation to their benefit. They were, in any case, a strong assembly which, like some of those in later medieval Germany, grew in strength during a number of minorities. Despite the wars, there was only a slight increase in the annual tax burden between 1490 and the French invasion, and in 1530 the estates insisted that the taxes which they granted should be used only for Piedmont's defence. In 1535, with the threat of French invasion growing, they refused more money. The estates' conduct during the 1530s resulted in the loss of

Savoy to France. French and Spanish armies also occupied different parts of Piedmont, though assemblies continued to meet in both parts. The exiled duke spent some time in Habsburg service, as Philip II's governor-general of the Netherlands, where he was obliged to have dealings with the States-general. Then, in accordance with the terms of the peace treaty of Cateau-Cambrésis in 1559, he was able to resume the rule of his duchy. For several reasons he was hostile to the estates: his experience of Castilian royal service in the Netherlands, which did not make him well-disposed to the limitations imposed by a strong assembly; its unco-operative attitude over tax grants which prevented effective defence of the ducal territories in the 1530s; and its collaboration with the French government in Piedmont. In June 1560 Emmanuel Philibert met the estates and, having obtained an enormous salt tax, dissolved them. They did not meet again. The duke used his army of 24,000 to ensure the collection of this tax and the imposition of further ones without reference to a parliament. As a result Piedmont's tax burden increased more than six-fold.[20]

VII England

The geographical location of Emmanuel Philibert's duchy meant that he could not avoid involvement in the Valois–Habsburg Italian wars. In contrast, England's participation was the consequence of royal choice. The priorities of the first Tudor king, Henry VII, were the firm establishment of his dynasty, financial solvency, pacification of the realm and restoration of law and order after the fifteenth-century dynastic wars. His foreign policy was non-interventionist and even isolationist. Henry VIII was a complete contrast. His father's dedicated service gave the new king a security of tenure together with a degree of internal stability and financial solvency which Henry VII had not enjoyed in 1485. The second Tudor was extrovert, self-conscious and anxious to cut a dash on the continent. He had a grossly inflated opinion of his own prowess, of his ability to influence European affairs and of the kingdom's capacity and willingness to support his continental adventures.

So, at various times, he claimed the French crown, sought to recapture lost French provinces, stood for election to the imperial office, or simply sought the reputation of a warrior-king. Henry was, however, realistic enough to understand that such expansive and expensive policies could not be financed from his hereditary revenues. As he was to do throughout his reign, so, at its very beginning, he turned to parliaments for assistance. Between 1510 and 1515 six parliamentary sessions were held for the prime purpose of funding war. Henry received the traditional grant of tunnage and poundage (additional customs duties) for life in 1510; fifteenths and tenths (a moveable property tax of 10 per cent on crown lands and urban property and one-fifteenth elsewhere); a graduated poll tax (1513); and the subsidy, a tax on income from land and wages, in 1513–15. Henry VII had already experimented with an income tax on the laity in 1489, 1497 and 1504. Under Henry VIII and thereafter it became the chief parliamentary tax on both laity and clergy. However, the regular parliamentary taxes, the subsidy and the fifteenth and tenth, had serious limitations. The new subsidy failed to realise its anticipated return. In 1334 the yield of the fifteenth and tenth had become a fixed amount, apportioned amongst localities, and it had long since ceased to bear any relationship to actual property values. To offset this several fifteenths and tenths might be granted, but even this practice did not produce a realistic yield.

The development of the parliamentary subsidy in Henry VIII's reign was initially the work of Thomas Wolsey. He became archbishop of York in 1514, cardinal and lord chancellor in 1515 and for fourteen years thereafter the king's chief minister. In 1518 he negotiated the treaty of London, a peace treaty between the warring powers of Europe. The peace did not last long and by 1522 England was persuaded back into war as Charles V's ally against France. Costs soared as English expeditionary forces campaigned in France in 1523–24. Wolsey attempted to foot the bill with a loan which in 1522–23 produced over a quarter of a million pounds. Therefore it is hardly surprising that parliament was in less than generous mood when King Henry summoned it in 1523 and Wolsey requested a subsidy, assessed at the unprecedented rate of four shillings in the pound. 'After long reasoning [in the commons], there was certain [men] appointed to declare the impossibility of this [latest] demand to the cardinal, which according to their commission declared to him substantially the poverty and scarceness of the realm.' They besought him 'to move the king's highness to be content with a more easier sum . . . [H]e answered that he would rather have his tongue plucked out of his head with a pair of pinsons, than to move the king to take any less sum'. After an unusually prolonged parliament, lasting almost four months, Wolsey had to settle for a subsidy rate of two shillings in the pound, payable over two years. Anxious for speedy payment he offered easier terms for those who were willing to pay sooner than the time designated by parliament.

The capture of the French king, Francis I, by Charles Habsburg's army at the battle of Pavia in 1525 was an opportune moment for Henry VIII to reactivate his claim to the French crown or at least to regain some lost provinces. Of course it required more money. King and minister proposed to raise it by the euphemistically (albeit unrealistically) styled 'Amicable Grant'. The word 'grant' is crucial. As G.W. Bernard explains, what they 'demanded in 1525 was always a grant, a non-refundable contribution, never, as is sometimes supposed, a loan that would be one day repaid, for example as a charge on future parliamentary taxation'. It amounted to a levy of non-parliamentary taxation at the rate of one-third of clerical and one-sixth lay income. Widespread opposition and, in some places, open resistance and refusal to pay caused the king to abandon the scheme.[21]

In the years which followed Henry became increasingly involved in another matter, the annulment of his first marriage, and by 1529, when Wolsey fell, the king ceased to be directly involved in the dynastic politics of the continent. That did not change during the 1530s. It was a circumstance which naturally eased the crown's financial problems, especially as, in 1529, Parliament had cancelled Henry's obligation to repay forced loans. Between 1529 and 1540 parliamentary taxation was requested on only four occasions although eleven sessions were held during that time. It was, however, customary for the king to fund government from his ordinary (hereditary) income and to apply to Parliament for extraordinary revenue (taxation) only in emergencies, the commonest of which was war. During the 1530s England was not at war. Therefore it is not surprising that, in 1532, commons' opposition to a proposed fifteenth and tenth caused Henry's government to give up the attempt, or that another tax request in 1539 also failed. During Thomas Cromwell's time as chief minister and parliamentary manager, however, he did succeed twice in obtaining peacetime tax grants. These were important precedents for the future.[22]

In 1540 Cromwell lost not only his pre-eminent place in the king's counsels, but also his offices, liberty and eventually his life. During the early 1540s Henry turned back to war against the 'auld alliance': campaigns against the Scots and an invasion of France which gained him the dubious prize of Boulogne. By the time the treaty of Ardres brought peace with the French in 1546, these wars had cost the English state two–three million pounds. Parliaments contributed over £650,000, an unprecedented amount in such a short period. The rest was raised by land sales (mainly expropriated Church property), loans and debasement of the coinage: all means which mortgaged the state's financial future, harmed the economy and brought nearer royal financial dependence on Parliament.

Henry VIII died in January 1547, but war did not die with him. The duke of Somerset, the young King Edward VI's uncle, guardian and the Protector of the Realm, pursued his obsessive desire to conquer Scotland, marry Edward to the infant Scottish queen, Mary, and achieve a union of the two crowns. His invasion of Scotland in 1547 was followed by the establishment of a network of garrisons. This expensive exercise, together with Henry VIII's war debts, could not be funded from the crown's hereditary resources. Somerset turned to Parliament, which dissolved the chantries (religious foundations endowed to say masses for the souls of their benefactors) and granted their assets to the crown, as well as a tax on sheep, wool and cloth in 1548/49. The failure of Somerset's Scottish policy contributed to his downfall in 1549. He left behind him a virtually bankrupted state. Many of its assets had been liquidated and it was burdened with debt. Although coinage debasement, loans and land sales contributed far more than parliamentary taxes to the war budget, Parliament would be expected not only to come to the rescue of a debt-burdened state, but, in the long term, to make a considerable and regular contribution to its ordinary operating costs.[23]

England remained at peace for the remainder of Edward's reign and for much of Mary's. In 1557, however, Queen Mary was persuaded into war against France by her Spanish consort Philip. The English were involved in the defeat of the French at the siege of Saint-Quentin, but in January 1558 France recovered Calais, England's sole remaining French possession. The house of commons' favourable response to financial requests, even in wartime, could never be guaranteed. When Parliament met in January 1558, shortly after the loss of Calais, it resisted a privy council demand for a subsidy set at four times the normal rate. The country was suffering from a succession of bad harvests, high mortality, debased coinage, the impact of a forced loan yielding more than £100,000 in 1557 and, according to a privy council memorandum, 'the smarte of the last warres'. There was also more concern about national defence than attempts to recover Calais. Nevertheless, the tax finally voted by Parliament produced as much as Mary's father had ever received in a single grant. The assembly of 1558 exemplifies the impact of the necessities of war on crown–Parliament relations in England: it imposed strains and stresses on the relationship; it occasioned the airing of grievances and cries of distress; but in the end the government obtained a substantial proportion of what it had sought from an essentially loyal Parliament.[24]

Notes

1 J.H. Elliott, *Imperial Spain, 1469–1716* (London, 1969), pp. 135–42; H.G. Koenigsberger, 'Parliaments and estates', in R.W. Davis, ed., *The Origins of Modern Freedom in the West* (Stanford, CA, 1995), p. 168.

2 This too was no novelty. Isabella had been lavish with such payments to *procuradores*. H.G. Koenigsberger, 'Parliaments in the sixteenth century and beyond', in Davis, ed., *Origins of Modern Freedom*, pp. 274–5.

3 Ibid., p. 275.

4 This was not, however, true of Charles's son Philip II (1556–98) who after 1559 did not budge from his Spanish kingdom for most of his reign.

5 T.W. Moody, F.X. Martin, F.J. Byrne, eds, *A New History of Ireland, 1534–1691*, 10 vols (Oxford, 1978), vol. 3, pp. xxxix–xl.

6 Ibid., pp. 40–3; S.G. Ellis, *Tudor Ireland. Crown, Community and the Conflict of Cultures, 1470–1603* (London, 1985), pp. 124–31.

7 Moody et al. (eds), *New History of Ireland*, vol. 3, pp. 55–8.

8 Charles I's treatment of Scotland exemplifies this. See below, pp. 145–60.

9 H.G. Koenigsberger, 'Beginnings of the States General of the Netherlands' *PER* 8, 2 (Dec. 1988), pp. 109–14.

10 A.J. Veenendaal, 'Fiscal crises and constitutional freedom in the Netherlands, 1450–1795', in P.T. Hoffman and K. Norberg, eds, *Fiscal Crises, Liberty and Representative Government, 1450–1789* (Stanford, CA, 1994), pp. 100–2; D. Maland, *Europe in the Sixteenth Century* (2nd edn, London, 1987), pp. 211–12; J.D. Tracy, *A Financial Revolution in the Habsburg Netherlands* (Berkeley, CA, 1985), pp. 34–5.

11 G. Parker, *Philip II* (London, 1979), pp. 24–5; Elliott, *Imperial Spain*, pp. 246–8.

12 A lucid, compact study of Habsburg–Valois relations between 1494 and 1559 is to be found in R. Mackenney, *Sixteenth Century Europe. Expansion and Conflict* (London, 1993), pp. 219–42.

13 H.G. Koenigsberger, *Estates and Revolutions* (Ithaca, NY, 1971), pp. 19–21. Koenigsberger dismissed the Neapolitan assembly as irregular and unable to place limits on its ruler's power.

14 C. Jago, 'Review Essay. Crown and Cortes in early-modern Spain' *PER* 12, 2 (Dec. 1992), pp. 177–81, 189–90; I.A.A. Thompson, 'Castile: polity, fiscality, and fiscal

crisis', in Hoffman and Norberg, eds, *Fiscal Crises*, pp. 155–7, 165–7; I.A.A. Thompson, 'Castile: absolutism, constitutionalism and liberty', also in Hoffman and Norberg, eds, *Fiscal Crises*, pp. 182–4.

15   Thompson, 'Castile: absolutism, constitutionalism and liberty', p. 184; see below, pp. 92–3; I.A.A. Thompson, *Crown and Cortes* (Aldershot, 1993), IX, p. 74.

16   Veenendaal, 'Fiscal crises', pp. 100–2; Tracy, *A Financial Revolution*, chs 2–3; Koenigsberger, 'Parliaments in the sixteenth century and beyond', pp. 291–3; J.D. Tracy, *Holland under Habsburg Rule, 1506–1566. The Formation of a Body Politic* (Oxford, 1990), pp. 211–12.

17   See above, p. 57; P.T. Hoffman, 'Early modern France, 1450–1700', in Hoffman and Norberg, eds, *Fiscal Crises*, pp. 240–1; J. Russell Major, *From Renaissance Monarchy to Absolute Monarchy. French Kings, Nobles and Estates* (London, 1994), pp. 35–7.

18   E.g. J. Powis, 'Guyenne 1548: the crown, the province and social order' *European Studies Review* 12, 1 (Jan. 1982), pp. 1–15; D. Hickey, *The Coming of French Absolutism: The Struggle for Tax Reform in the Province of Dauphine, 1540–1640* (Toronto, 1986), pp. 34–7, 74–6, 171–3; J. Russell Major, 'Henry IV and Guyenne. A study concerning the origins of royal absolutism' *French Historical Studies* 4, 4 (1966), pp. 363–83; D. Potter, *A History of France, 1460–1560. The Emergence of a Nation State* (London, 1995), pp. 284–7; Major, *Renaissance Monarchy to Absolute Monarchy*, pp. 43, 49–50.

19   See above, pp. 69–70.

20   Koenigsberger, *Estates and Revolutions*, pp. 19–23, 63–79; ibid., 'Parliaments in the sixteenth century and beyond', pp. 272–3; A. Marongiu, *Medieval Parliaments. A Comparative Study* (London, 1968), pp. 204–5.

21   M.A.R. Graves, *The Tudor Parliaments. Crown, Lords and Commons, 1485–1603* (London, 1985), pp. 41–4, 61–2; M.A.R. Graves, *Early Tudor Parliaments, 1485–1558* (London, 1990), pp. 16–17, 39–41, 105; G.W. Bernard, *War, Taxation and Rebellion in Early Tudor England. Henry VIII, Wolsey and the Amicable Grant of 1525* (Brighton, 1986), p. 55.

22   See below, p. 105.

23   Bernard, *War, Taxation and Rebellion*, p. 53; J. Guy, *Tudor England* (Oxford, 1988), pp. 190–2; M.L. Bush, *The Government Policy of Protector Somerset* (London, 1975), pp. 9–39.

24   C.S.L. Davies, 'England and the French War, 1557–9', in J. Loach and R. Tittler, eds, *The Mid-Tudor Polity c.1540–1560* (London, 1980), pp. 161–2, 165–6, 179–80; J. Loach, *Parliament and the Crown in the Reign of Mary Tudor* (Oxford, 1986), pp. 159–61.

4

Religious Reformation and Political Change, War and Rebellion: Their Impact on Parliaments in the Sixteenth Century: II

The increasing commitments and burdens of monarchies

THE INCIDENCE and scale of dynastic and politico-religious conflict were the most obvious, indeed dramatic, examples of the broadening range of sustained pressures on strictly limited princely resources. They must be seen, however, in the context of the changing nature of monarchy in early modern Europe. From the later fifteenth century, so-called Renaissance monarchy focused on royal image projection – an extravagant Court, as a point of contact with the great men of the community, and the seductive purveyor of patronage as a means of control over them. It made government much more expensive and that is true even of monarchs who did not aspire to achieve absolutism.

Some sought to regulate their subjects' affairs and to exercise more direct control of their domains, whether they were scattered or contiguous. They did not, however, as was once believed, seek to replace the old, autonomous governing elites of nobles and upper clergy by career-orientated, ambitious and obedient, largely landless but professionally skilled bureaucracies. The old elites had provided voluntary and largely unpaid service, as indeed they continued to do, for example, in England. Where bureaucracies were developed, as in early modern France and Spain,[1] they grew up alongside and complementary to the old elites. This involved a dramatic cost-growth and increased social burden. Bureaucrats were salaried and they grew rapidly in number, partly because early modern states increased their functions and powers, but particularly because offices were created and sold as a revenue-raising device. Many were duplicated offices or sinecures. So alongside useful civil services there developed parasitic bureaucracies and somehow they both had to be funded.

The early modern European power-system was, as we have seen, characterised by a growth in the scale, incidence and duration of wars. These were not only secular, dynastic and territorial in nature but increasingly, especially after 1559, politico-religious. There were major changes in military technology and tactics. Firepower replaced the lance and bow. Small medieval armies, dominated by aristocratic cavalry, were superseded by massed pike formations and musketeers. Naval warfare also changed. Mediterranean man-powered galleys were unsuitable for oceanic sailing. Therefore, as colonial empires grew, fleets of sophisticated and much more costly galleons, equipped with cannon, were developed. Siege warfare and complex fortifications became features of the new military technology and capacity. But it all cost money, much of which parliaments were expected to grant on behalf of their communities.[2]

The aspirations of princes, who were bred in the political climate of the Renaissance or later influenced by Bodinian sovereignty theories, provided the potential for divergence and conflict between rulers and their assemblies. So too did the growing financial burdens of their Courts, governments and diplomatic corps. The tensions, disagreements and parliamentary resistance which resulted, especially over the inexorable financial demands of war, would drive some rulers to pressurise, coerce or even bypass their assemblies. The potential for conflict, however, did not end there. The European Reformation also had its parliamentary repercussions: for example, in the English Parliaments of 1529–59, the States-general of the Low Countries during the 1560s and beyond, and the Parliaments of Elizabethan Ireland as the crown pursued policies of plantation and the persecution of Gaelic and Anglo-Irish catholics. As European princes, before and after 1559, firmly adhered to the principle *cuius regio eius religio*,[3] parliamentary criticism or resistance to their religious positions amounted to disobedience to them.

All of these early modern developments had an impact on local and regional privileges, priorities, prosperity, political and religious affiliations and loyalties. When rulers sought *auxilium*, representative assemblies were the natural places to air these concerns and vent grievances. The years 1555–60 marked a period of transition when the German wars ended, and a new generation of rulers assumed control in much of Europe.[4] With a new scenario of resurgent Counter-Reformation catholicism and a new cast of princely politicians, confessional politics and conflict became more important in Europe and its assemblies. They did not, however, displace dynastic rivalries. Princes in pursuit of religious and dynastic triumphs looked to parliaments *or* beyond for the necessary political and financial support.

The European experience

As the case studies in the following pages will show, everywhere crown–parliament relations during the sixteenth century were affected, even determined, by a basic albeit varying combination of circumstances and developments:

1   The burdensome consequences, especially financial, of inflated royal aspirations, bureaucratic growth (especially in France and Castile), increased government functions, diplomatic activity and above all, in France, England, German principalities and the lands of the Habsburg composite monarchy, military involvement.

2   The stresses within social structures, especially when they affected nobles who were prominent or powerful in parliament.

3   Official efforts to manage or pressurise parliaments to productive ends, or even to bypass them in order to increase tax yields. The responses, as in the cities of Castile and the Netherlands and in the French provinces, were frequently those of parliamentary resistance and opposition by regional, local or social interests.[5]

4   Ethnic and national hostilities, especially in the Castilian *Comuneros*, the anti-Philippic Dutch revolt and the later sixteenth-century Irish parliaments.

5   The significance of religion (for example in the Swedish and British parliaments and many estates of the German principalities and Habsburg lands) or the avoidance of pressing religious issues, as in the French Estates-general of 1560–61.

6   Dynastic problems, caused by royal minorities[6] and regencies, male attitudes to female regents, childless or unmarried queens,[7] the threatened or actual end of dynasties,[8] elected monarchs,[9] disputed successions and the prospects of partition,[10] could have serious parliamentary repercussions.

7   As Koenigsberger has pointed out, 'unique political decisions' and 'intervention of outside powers in the struggles between kings and their parliaments' also played a part, though these were more important in the seventeenth century.[11]

European assemblies experienced mixed fortunes in the sixteenth century. In the elective monarchies of Poland and the Empire the central parliaments were already powerful in 1500 and grew more so in the next hundred years. The newcomer, Sweden's *Riksdåg*, quickly learned to perform one important parliamentary function, that of *consilium*. By 1600 it was on the way to superseding the role of the provincial assemblies, the *landsting*, as the provider of *auxilium*. In England the Tudor parliamentary houses of lords and commons were capable of persisting with grievances, criticising royal policies and practices and even rejecting bills favoured or promoted by the monarch. Such occurrences, however, were within a firm framework of loyalty to the ruler. Furthermore, as a consequence of events in the 1530s, the parliamentary trinity of monarch, lords and commons had together become the sovereign and unlimited legislative authority in the kingdom. Elsewhere in Europe, however, many representative institutions were being coerced, bought off, sidelined, or simply no longer called by ambitious, hard-pressed or autocratically inclined rulers. Some of those rulers found the constraint of *quod omnes tangit* unacceptable and sought *auxilium* elsewhere or by other means. Long before the seventeenth century assemblies were infrequently, even rarely, called in Aragon, Catalonia, Valencia and Ireland. In Castile the dualism of king and Cortes was tending to give way to direct royal contact with cities and a triple relationship between crown, assembly and the cities which it represented. The estates in Piedmont had already been laid to rest and they were to be followed by the French Estates-general after one final flurry in 1614–15. More corpses would be carried to the parliamentary graveyard during the next half-century.

CASE STUDIES

I France

The Estates-general, which served little financial purpose, had not been summoned since 1484. In 1560, however, the royal minority following the death of Henry II necessitated a regency. Discontented and ambitious politicians were much less reluctant to intrigue and muster opposition against a regent than an adult prince. So the regent, Catherine de Medici, was in a relatively weak position and needed public confirmation of her position. Furthermore, the crown's finances were in a critical state. Its debts amounted to more than 43 million *livres*, including 19 million of unpaid loans – yet the government continued to issue bonds and alienate estates and tax revenues as repayment. Meanwhile the threat of religious wars between a highly organised Huguenot Church in alliance with feudal magnates and the forces of the catholic Guise family made a political arrangement of some kind an urgent priority. In 1560 (at Orléans) and 1561 (at Pontoise) Catherine twice summoned the Estates-general. The assembly of 1560 was not a co-operative one. Some deputies were reluctant simply to accept the authority of the regency without the assembly's approval, whilst the membership would not discuss the crown's financial plight because its electors had not instructed it to do so. The government called fresh elections for a new assembly in 1561. This time members came with instructions to discuss the crown's finances. Whilst, however, the assembly discussed the state of government and religion, nothing was done to restore the royal treasury to financial health. The third estate advised the king how to solve his problems, but offered no practical assistance. Although the clergy made a separate grant, the Estates-general as such did nothing. Once again, in both its financial and advisory functions, it had failed the monarchy in time of crisis.[12]

In 1562 the French civil wars began and continued, intermittently but often savagely, into the 1590s. They were not only episodes in a prolonged religious conflict, but also stages in a continuous power struggle between the royal and leading noble dynasties, catholic and protestant. European powers, including Spain, England and the Dutch, also intervened on one side or the other. But it was not until 1575 that the beleaguered monarchy sought parliamentary assistance. The delay is hardly surprising. The Estates-general of 1560–61 had shown its incapacity to assist the crown. The government had lost both the parliamentary initiative and managerial control, whilst the assembly had preferred to offer criticism, rather than constructive advice and tax approval. By 1575, however, the crown was in crisis. Henry III borrowed, raised some taxes from provincial estates, sold a harvest of new and duplicated offices, and then in 1575 and 1576 called general assemblies. He sought advice and the necessary money to end internal conflict and establish religious uniformity. Neither *consilium* nor *auxilium* was forthcoming.

Future meetings of the Estates-general were called or controlled by other forces, in particular by the Huguenots, and in 1588, 1593 and 1597 by the catholic league. When Henry III summoned it in 1588, it was suborned by the Guise leaders of the league and, as in 1575 and 1576, there was no *auxilium*. For a quarter of a century the crown had no further recourse to the Estates-general for money. After the assassination of Henry III, who was the last of the Valois, it took the first Bourbon king, Henry IV, almost a decade to pacify the kingdom and assert his authority. It did not augur well for the future of the national assembly. Henry IV was a king of autocratic temper, with little time or patience for it. He preferred to raise revenue by local negotiations or, sometimes, by the establishment of *élections* (fiscal districts in which finance courts managed direct taxation) as in Guyenne in 1603, or by the attempted introduction of the *gabelle* and other taxes into previously exempt provinces.[13] In any case, the provinces, cities and other localities preferred direct tax negotiations with the monarchy without the seemingly wasted time and effort of a preparatory general assembly.[14] It was not called again until Henry IV's assassination in 1610 resulted in a royal minority and a regency government in need of public support.[15]

II Castile

Religion was never an issue in the Cortes of Roman catholic Castile. In practice its purpose and function under the Habsburg monarchy was financial. Debates, disputes and disagreements concerned taxation. Recent revisionism has reassessed the role and authority of the Castilian Cortes not only under Charles I but also in the reigns of Philip II, Philip III and Philip IV (1556–1665).[16] Its fiscal role was defined by a number of agreements, which cities negotiated with their first Habsburg king. First, the establishment of the *encabezamiento general* for the *alcabala* in 1536, the continued right of each city to negotiate its share, and the delegation of tax management to the cities and Cortes resulted in a system characterised by 'autonomy and administrative decentralisation'.[17] Secondly, the Cortes successfully resisted attempts by Charles (and his successors) to impose general ongoing regular taxation. So his attempt to impose a general *sisa* (food tax) in the Cortes of 1538–39 failed. He was granted instead an extraordinary *servicio*, in addition to the ordinary *servicio*. Thereafter the amount of the *servicios* was fixed and they were granted every three years by the 'Kingdom' in the Cortes. 'The Kingdom, therefore, rejected all attempts to establish any kind of general and permanent taxation in favour of the periodic concession of temporary subsidies for specific purposes, and in return for redress through the particular conditions of the grant.' In this way the Cortes was now better equipped to secure royal consideration of its grievances and indeed in the following reigns it was in practice able to extract concessions before the voting of supply.[18]

A fiscal system in which the range of taxes was strictly limited and subject to regular re-grant, the yield was largely fixed, and management was chiefly in the control of Cortes and cities, was clearly unsatisfactory and disadvantageous from the crown's point of view. Philip II's accession in 1556 marked a significant change in royal attitude and conduct. The formidable public debt which he had inherited resulted in 'bankruptcies' in 1557 and 1560 whilst, in the 1560s and 1570s, his military commitments grew. He had no choice but to increase royal revenue and one way to do so was to introduce new regular taxes. Gone was Charles's rather conciliatory policy towards Cortes and cities.[19]

Any discussion of the early modern Castilian Cortes under Habsburg kings needs to be circumspect and qualified. This is because in the last twenty years there has appeared in print a thoroughgoing revision of the traditional picture of a powerful Habsburg monarchy exerting effective control over a weak susceptible assembly. As elsewhere (e.g. parliaments in England) revision tends to produce diversity if not disagreement, rather than one unified new interpretation. Furthermore, the process of revisionism continues to change perspectives. So it has brought to the forefront the Castilian cities. They no longer figure as the obedient, complaisant tax targets of hungry Habsburgs, but as powerful and, as occasion demanded, politically combative corporate bodies. The Cortes was their instrument, through which they protected their interests. Early modern Castilian parliamentary history needs to be considered in terms of a triple relationship between crown, Cortes and cities. It was a relationship of growing significance in the reigns of the Philips.[20]

Philip II sought new and permanent taxes for which more subjects were eligible and which did not require parliamentary consent: such were the levies on wool and salt and the proposed tax on grain. Naturally these were resisted by the Cortes. In March 1567

The *procuradores* . . . all together said that for some years certain new and uncustomary taxes have been created, increased and collected in the kingdom, and the price of salt has gone up generally . . . and all this has been done without summoning the kingdom together in Cortes and without the agreement of its *procuradores* as is stipulated in the laws of these kingdoms and as has always been their custom . . . [T]he kingdom . . . does not consent, implicitly or explicitly, to any new or increased tax or due . . . created now or in the future outside of the Cortes and without the consent of the *procuradores* of the kingdom.

Although, in the Cortes commencing in 1573, *procuradores* were prepared to consider a grain tax, it failed because most cities were opposed to it. Philip II retaliated in 1575 with a new, unilaterally imposed *encabezamiento general*, which was worth three times the previous one. The Cortes, however, secured its reduction by 40 per cent and, as usual, limited the time-span of its operation, insisted on its regular renewal, administered it and required an end to all non-parliamentary taxes. Royal attempts to manage the assembly, by influencing the choice of *procuradores* and greasing the palms of those chosen, were on the increase. On the other hand, the cities were becoming more emphatic about the delegate role of *procuradores*, in contrast to the crown's insistence that they came to the Cortes with *plena potestas*. Furthermore, according to Fortea Pérez, many cities refused to accept the apportioned amounts they were supposed to pay in accordance with the new *encabezamiento general*.[21]

The tensions which such practices and positions suggest were hardly surprising. As Philip II's needs grew, so did both his efforts to increase his revenue and his subjects' consequent financial burdens. The crown's real income in the 1580s was four times that of the 1520s. On the other hand, Philip had not succeeded in restructuring the financial system, in which the cities of the Cortes were so important. Then the failed Armada against England in 1588 triggered a major debt crisis which obliged him to turn to the assembly for additional help. He did not seek a new tax or expansion of the *alcabala* but a subsidy: the *millones* in 1590 and the 500 *cuentos* six years later. This suited the Cortes' preference for temporary grants of fixed term. It also enabled the assembly to bargain for redress of grievances. Before the *millones* agreement was signed Philip had to accept the Cortes cities' right to determine the *arbitrios* — how the money was to be raised — as well as specific conditions imposed by some of them. Those conditions became standardised features of future *millones* contracts. A second *millones*, called the 500 *cuentos*, was sought in 1596. Negotiations ran into difficulties over the conditions imposed by the Cortes, especially its full administrative control of the tax. Although agreement was finally reached, largely on its terms, the Cortes insisted that the *voto decisivo* lay with the cities. Their response was highly unfavourable and, although wide-ranging concessions secured the vote of a majority of municipal councils, its unpopularity and its diminished value caused the new king, Philip III, to withdraw it in 1598. In 1601, however, the *millones* was re-introduced and thereafter regularly renegotiated.[22]

There is no general agreement about the political consequences of the *millones* for crown, Cortes and cities. Certainly it has caused historians to give more attention to the Cortes cities, whose importance has previously been neglected or unrecognised: in particular, their continued exercise of the *voto decisivo* in Philip III's reign emphasises that, in Fortea Pérez's words, 'As an assembly of the communities of the kingdom the Cortes of Castile could not act independently of the governing bodies of those cities which were summoned by the king to attend him in Cortes'. Beyond this, however, conclusions differ. Some revisionist historians argue that the *millones* extended the constitutional authority of Cortes and cities. It did so by giving them extensive administrative control of the tax system and limiting the king's authority and manoeuvrability by contractual agreements containing restrictive conditions. In contrast, it has been argued that political reality was very different from the terms of those contracts. According to Jago, Philip II's successor sought to protect the crown's fiscal and jurisdictional autonomy, the Cortes to control tax administration and influence royal policies, and the cities to preserve their local interests and autonomy from both monarchy and parliament. And he concludes that, in Philip II and Philip III's reigns, there were 'no clear winners'.[23]

III The kingdoms of Aragon

The sixteenth-century history of the Cortes of the eastern kingdoms of Aragon, Valencia and Catalonia was a significant contrast to that of the Castilian assembly. When Spain was under Habsburg rule, royal visits to the Aragonese kingdoms became progressively more infrequent. As the king's presence was necessary for a meeting of the Cortes, they too were convened only rarely. In Aragon, for example, they met only three times under Philip II and not even once under Philip III. The common European preference for a resident ruler, as expressed by the Castilian *Comuneros* in 1520, was also frustrated here and the prolonged absences of alien Castilianised kings promoted a sense of remoteness and neglect. As kings usually called assemblies for financial aid, the eastern parliaments were spared the frequent demands made on the Castilian Cortes. However, their smaller populations and weaker economies made them less attractive targets to Philip II's financially straitened government. Amounts voted were small, usually fixed and had little favourable impact on the royal treasury. Furthermore, he also had to work with the Aragonese Cortes in a contractual relationship, put up with the principle of unanimous voting and, in all three assemblies, the presentation of grievances before supply. Nevertheless, only once in the sixteenth century did a significant crown–Cortes crisis occur in eastern Spain. Violent anti-Castilian riots in Aragon led to Philip's invasion and subjugation of the kingdom and the imposition of constitutional changes at a Cortes in 1592. The alterations to Aragonese *fueros* (liberties) were modest and reveal the king's profound respect for legality and privilege, but they did affect the Cortes: the unanimity principle was replaced by a majority vote, except for the approval of taxes; the power of the *Diputación* (the permanent committee of the Cortes) to spend money was restricted but it continued to collect and hold tax revenue. Although the *Justicia*, custodian of Aragonese *fueros*, was no longer appointed for life but during royal pleasure, the *fueros* of kingdom and Cortes remained largely intact.[24]

If the Cortes of the Aragonese kingdoms, with their constitutional safeguards and powerful noble components, escaped with only modest contributions to the Habsburg war-chest, the 'colonial' parliaments were less fortunate. This is not simply because they were all weak parliaments. In Sardinia, Naples and Sicily assemblies exercised the taxing power and were prepared to assert themselves against the king's representative. Nevertheless royal needs intensified financial pressure on them during the sixteenth century. This was particularly true of Naples, where Charles V's viceroy, Pedro de Toledo, extracted escalating sums in the 1540s and 1550s.[25] Altogether the Neapolitan Cortes was called about forty times for tax purposes during the century. It was a weak assembly with little capacity for resistance or effective bargaining. Its *capitoli* (petitions) could be and frequently were rejected and the viceroy effectively controlled its permanent watchdog committee, the *Deputazione delle grazie*. As for Sicily, it became the Christian and Habsburg imperial stronghold and outpost against the waves of Ottoman Turkish revival and expansion. A constant supply of money was needed for the Spanish garrison and Sicilian naval defences, especially at the height of the Turkish threat, when the *Parlamento* met thirty-three times in forty-five years (1532–77). Thereafter Philip needed to divert resources to his military commitments in western Europe. The figures tell the story. In the fifteenth century the basic parliamentary grant was 50,000 *scudi*. Even allowing for inflation this was a modest figure compared to the peak of 278,000 *scudi* in 1594. Between 1549–59 and 1590–99 parliamentary taxation doubled. Yet the three *bracci* of prelates, nobles and townsmen, who comprised the *Parlamento*, normally co-operated and voted the necessary *auxilium*.[26] Venality and their ability to pass on tax liability to others probably account for such compliance, although they do not explain why, in 1591, the only (and unsuccessful) parliamentary tax revolt of the century occurred in the noble house. Prolonged and rising taxation in the next century would eventually cause violent and far more serious disruption.

IV Portugal

Although the Cortes of early modern Portugal was not a strong representative institution, it had a symbolic importance, which was given expression in its elaborate rituals and ceremonies. It also met quite often in long sessions. However, it had no legislative or judicial authority. Members were expected to exercise a *voto decisivo* on important matters without reference back to their constituents, but their decisions did not have to be accepted by the king. So far as he was concerned the Cortes was a purely consultative body. Its one vital function and power was consent to taxation and this seems to have determined the rhythm of its meetings. It also appears that, under the ruling Portuguese dynasty, the Cortes had limited capacity to resist the royal will. Then, in 1580, Philip II, backed by an hereditary claim and an army, acquired Portugal. At the Cortes in April 1581 he swore to respect Portuguese laws and liberties, a set of articles preserving the kingdom's autonomy, and the right of the Cortes to convene only in Portugal. Philip II generally respected the arrangement and, in response to Portuguese desire for a resident monarch, he stayed in Lisbon until 1583 and then left his nephew, the Cardinal Archduke Albert, as viceroy. Philip's successors, however, were less sensitive to Portuguese anti-Castilian sentiments and primarily concerned to increase the tax yield.[27]

V The Low Countries

Unlike Castile and the kingdoms and colonies of Aragon, crown–parliament relations were not dominated by the one issue of finance. Undoubtedly the cost of Habsburg wars and the resultant indebtedness were causes of acute discontent when Philip inherited the Netherlands. In 1557–58, at a time of poor harvests, high bread prices and wide-spread urban unemployment, the States-general gave the king less than he demanded and it hedged in the grant with conditions, including parliamentary control over its collection and disbursement. But finance was not the only or the prime concern. The presence of Spanish troops was seen as a threat to liberties. Philip's controversial plan to create fourteen bishoprics and the Inquisition's activity against Calvinist heresy, which had spread into the Netherlands from France in the 1550s, created another and, in this case, potentially explosive issue. All of these were matters of relevance, indeed importance, to members of both the provincial estates and States-general. During the 1560s relations between an alien absentee king and the Netherlands deteriorated with the spread and increased persecution of Calvinism. After widespread iconoclastic riots in 1566, Philip II appointed the duke of Alba with an army. His tasks were to stamp out heresy and political opposition and to impose a range of new taxes which the States-general was instructed to approve. It was Alba's brutal regime which led to the revolt of Holland and Zealand and eventually to a political revolution in the north. Holland and Zealand set up a government headed by William prince of Orange but resting on the authority of the provincial estates. Eventually they, together with five other northern provinces, formed the independent state of the United Provinces. In 1581 allegiance to Philip II was formally ended. Although William of Orange exercised executive powers and commanded the army, he served a republican state in which the sovereignty resided in the provincial estates and those whom they chose to serve in the States-general.[28] Nevertheless, within this structure the prince of Orange assumed a quasi-monarchical role.

Although he stated that he recognised the States-general as the superior authority, he conducted himself like the monarchs of contemporary Europe. So he tended to hold Court and use courtly skills to manage the parliamentary members. 'He always entertained some five or six of the most credit; the needy ones with pensions, the rest with presents, and all with calling them to his table and society. Through these he wrought upon the rest and there was nothing handled in their assemblies but he knew of it beforehand.' Parliamentary skills were needed to overcome divisions of opinion, reluctance to act and unwillingness to pay, but the princes of Orange applied them in much the same way as the Tudor Henry VIII or the Habsburg Charles I in Castile. Such quasi-regality did not threaten the alliance of princes and estates in wartime but, once peace with Spain came (between 1609 and 1621 and again in 1648) 'the estates and their substitute monarchy found themselves engaged in struggles for power – just like any legitimate monarchy and its parliaments'.[29]

VI The German principalities

Emperor Charles V, the catholic champion, failed to achieve religious unity in Germany, either by military victory over the protestants or by a *rapprochement* between the two religions. However, the *Reichstag*, the imperial parliament (in which those princes who elected him were supreme) and the only imperial institution which might have helped him achieve one or other of his goals, proved instead to be an obstacle. It was particularist and, from the 1520s onwards, divided by religion. Although Charles had an extensive power-base in the hereditary Habsburg lands of Austria, Styria, Carinthia and, from 1526, Bohemia and west Hungary, as elected emperor he enjoyed great prestige but wielded little power outside these territories. Repeatedly his efforts to strengthen the machinery and funding of the state, its defensive capability, and the catholic faith were killed by the opposition of the princes in the *Reichstag*, even after his victory over the Lutheran Schmalkaldic League. By the end of his reign it was accepted in the treaty of Augsburg (1555) that each prince should determine the religion of his subjects.

Those princes too had to manage assemblies (*Landtage*) in their own principalities. Despite the political diversity within the medieval and early modern German political system,[30] it is possible to generalise about the history of princes' estates in that period. It was during the fifteenth and sixteenth centuries that estates, both in the German principalities and in hereditary Habsburg lands, reached the height of their influence, effectiveness and local control. As governments expanded their armies and developed their administrations they became more dependent on the taxing powers of representative assemblies to fund such activities. In many cases the nobles, who often enjoyed a prominent, even predominant place in those assemblies, used them as a lever to extract concessions from the ruler and to preserve their privileges and local autonomy. Furthermore, where princes remained catholics but many of their subjects, including those who sat in the estates, converted to Lutheranism, the protestants employed the estates to defend their right to freedom of conscience. Of course, estates' relations with individual princes were liable to differ, if only because of variables such as princely personalities, internal and external circumstances and accidents of fate.

In 1514, for example, the *Württemberg* Diet extracted from its duke the treaty of Tübingen, which became the basis of the duchy's privileges. By its terms the estates voted and administered taxes, whilst their consent was required for war. In the following twenty years the Diet met regularly and during that time improved its organisation, especially in 1521 with the introduction of permanent committees. During the long, arbitrary and turbulent rule of Duke Ulrich the estates certainly had a chequered history, but after his death in 1550 their importance was re-established and consolidated. In 1553 they assumed responsibility for ducal debts and henceforth controlled the levy, collection and spending of taxes. Fortunes again fluctuated under Frederick (1593–1608), but when he died the estates re-asserted their financial control and they even influenced policy decisions. So they required the new duke to justify his membership of the union of protestant princes.[31]

The *Saxon* estates were a success story. They enjoyed a harmonious relationship with Duke George and during his reign (1500–39) asserted the sole right to tax and to effect changes in the law. Throughout the sixteenth century an 'equilibrium between the prince and the Estates, and within them between the nobility and the towns, was preserved'.[32] The assembly willingly granted increasing sums of money to the ruler. At the same time their privileges, structure and organisation were clearly defined and they came to influence religious and foreign policy.

The story of success was not repeated everywhere. By the sixteenth century the *Bavarian* estates 'had acquired very far-reaching privileges, which entitled them to participate in the government and administration of the duchy, and had become a well-organized corporation'.[33] During the reigns of William IV and Albert V (1508–79), however, the power of the estates significantly declined. This was partly a consequence of a deliberate policy pursued by Duke William and his chancellor, Dr Eck. Prince–parliament relations in Albert's reign were dominated by religious conflict. Catholic Albert defeated the estates' support for Lutheran concessions. He also wore down their resistance to increasing taxation. By the early seventeenth century they had become ineffective and submissive to ducal direction.[34]

The Bavarian experience was exceptional. More typical of estates in sixteenth-century principalities were those in *Brandenburg*, where the nobility came to predominate. Successive margraves, desperate for cash, made significant concessions to them in return for tax grants: to make no alliance without their consent; to cede administrative management of taxation to them; to surrender control over the raising, training and funding of the state's military forces. And in *Prussia* the strength of the nobility ensured that the 'power of the Estates was . . . secured more firmly than in any other German principality'.[35]

VII The Habsburg hereditary lands

There are a number of common denominators between estates in these territories and in the German principalities. The Reformation raised problems in ruler–assembly relations. The presence of a powerful nobility, who used the estates to their own advantage against the ruler, could also complicate the relationship. Both Habsburgs and German princes incurred increasing expenses from the growth of the Court, the administration and the military establishment, and this in turn made them dependent on estates, most of which held the purse-strings. Princes engaged in petty wars over territory or succession disputes and many were drawn into the religious conflicts of Emperor Charles V's reign. All such military excursions were costly, but nothing compared to the Habsburgs' enormous financial outlay on defensive wars against the Turks, who were a sustained threat to their hereditary lands. This external threat and the internal upheaval caused by the Reformation often required a rapid response. The Habsburg government on its hereditary lands, however, was not a centralised monarchy and it required the assent of a dozen parliaments to equip it for military action. The process was slow and success was not guaranteed and so the Court was tempted to circumvent or ignore this requirement.[36] The resultant problems for assemblies in the Habsburg hereditary lands during the sixteenth century can be illustrated by a brief survey of three of the most important of them.

Austria: The administrative reorganisation of Habsburg hereditary lands by Emperor Maximilian I (1493–1519) was regarded as threatening to the estates' role in policy matters and so, at the Austrian Diet of 1518, they presented a list of grievances. The result was an agreement whereby the emperor received a sizeable tax, on condition that the grievances were dealt with and in return for which the estates would be involved in defence and 'common affairs' of the state. Although Maximilian died in the following year, grievances and supply were effectively linked under Ferdinand, the younger brother of Emperor Charles V who ceded the Austrian territories to him. The dominant parliamentary concerns during Ferdinand's rule (1519–64) were the enormous costs of defence against the Turks and the estates' desire for Lutheran religious concessions, such as communion in both kinds and clerical marriage. Indeed, they sometimes exploited Ferdinand's financial need and dependence by linking aid and religion. Changes of ruler made little difference. Ferdinand's successors, Maximilian II (1564–76) and Rudolf II (1576–1612), still had to contend with Turkish attacks and with demands for religious reform by the assembly which supplied the funding for defence.[37]

Hungary: Here the Turkish threat became a disastrous fact when much of the country was overrun in 1526. The Diet of the surviving Habsburg kingdom of Hungary had legislative and taxing power as well as administrative control of the taxes. Nevertheless grievances abounded, because an absentee monarchy excluded Hungarians from management of the kingdom's affairs. Under Maximilian II and Rudolf II the estates' demands for autonomy were frustrated but, at the same time, they would not vote taxes to desperately needy rulers for more than two years at a time. Then the Diet had to be summoned again. So it displayed the same preference as the Castilian Cortes for temporary grants rather than permanent taxes. Neither side could score a victory and so they maintained a kind of balance which included a good deal of co-operation. It was religion which repeatedly soured relations between ruler and assembly: when Ferdinand demanded action against protestant heresy and the estates refused (for example, in 1543, 1553 and 1556). As protestantism spread and penetrated the estates and as Calvinism displaced Lutheranism, Emperor Rudolf often clashed with them. Finally, in 1604, the Hungarian protestants under their leader Stephen Bocskai, leader of the estates, went to war with Rudolf.[38]

Bohemia: The three estates of the central parliament or *Sněm* had evolved to become the key Bohemian institution by the beginning of the sixteenth century. They controlled taxation, defence and even the choice of the king. After his election as monarch in 1526, however, Ferdinand asserted his authority over the estates to the point where they rebelled in 1547. The ongoing issues between king and parliament were the usual ones, common to all the Habsburg estates: religion, their political rights, and the financial needs of war against the Turks. During the rest of the sixteenth and the early decades of the seventeenth century the religious question came to dominate relations between sovereign and estates, between catholic Habsburgs and an assembly in which non-catholic nobility were prominent and active. Unfortunately for the Bohemian estates, whilst their meetings were 'a focus for resistance to the demands of the crown' they also 'proved to be an equal focus for the disunity of the opposition'.[39]

Whilst each of the Habsburg estates had its own story, they shared a number of common circumstances, developments and sources of tension: increasingly autocratic rulers; the assertion of parliamentary liberties; the escalating costs of government and war; the external Islamic threat to Christian states; and the internal conflict between catholics and protestants within those states. Some of the parliaments in the Habsburg lands and German principalities would become victims of such developments in the next century.

VIII Poland-Lithuania[40]

The German and Polish monarchies were afflicted with common problems. From 1386 the kings of Poland, like the Holy Roman Emperors, had been elected and the electoral process usually involved concessions, *douceurs*, and promises by those seeking election. Indeed, from 1454 the *Sejm*, the Polish central parliament, decided what the elected king's concessions were to be. Furthermore, their monarchies were neither strong nor centralised. By the sixteenth century power within Poland resided in a very numerous nobility, who owned most of the land and dominated, indeed monopolised, the provincial parliaments, the *sejmiki*, and the national assembly, the *Sejm*.[41] Through this two-tier system of parliaments, which was an expression not only of the feudal obligations of *consilium et auxilium* but also of *quod omnes tangit*, the nobility strengthened its place in the state.[42] The monarchs' vulnerability to noble pressure was enhanced by the fact that, like the Habsburgs, the Jagellons were forever in need of subsidies and soldiers to fight aggressive neighbours, in this case Muscovy and the Turks.

It would be wrong, however, to dismiss the kings of the Jagellon dynasty as mere figureheads or puppets. Casimir IV (1447–92) was an autocrat by temperament and an astute politician. He developed a power-base in the Church and used loyal noble magnates to manage the one-chamber *Sejm* in which his council sat. In the years between 1492 and 1506, immediately following his death, magnates and lesser nobles, the *szlachta*, carried through significant constitutional changes beneficial to them. Casimir left five sons and the *Sejm* elected not the eldest, but younger brothers, first John Albert (1492–1501) and then Alexander (1501–6). Siblings were potential if not actual rivals and this encouraged those chosen to make concessions in order to secure support. So the *Sejm* became bicameral: a senate of magnates (including the royal councillors) and a chamber of *szlachta* from the *sejmiki*. Between 1496 and 1520 the *Sejm* ensured a noble monopoly of land and of higher ecclesiastical offices and it also reduced the peasantry to a state of serfdom. In 1505 John Albert's successor, Alexander, accepted the constitution of *Nihil Novi* which ruled that 'nothing new' – that is, no new laws – could be introduced without the approval of both houses of the *Sejm*. It was the embodiment of the principle *quod omnes tangit*.

Nevertheless, according to James Miller, under Sigismund I (1506–48) 'the Polish Renaissance monarchy was at its height', whilst Czaplinski describes the last Jagellon, Sigismund Augustus (1548–72), as a ruler 'who knew how to impose his will on both the Senate and the [*szlachta*]'. The two Sigismunds displayed skill and patience and they pursued consensus, conciliation and compromise as they sought productive parliaments. They both had to deal, however, with a growing *szlachta* movement which was hostile to both magnates and the crown. The *szlachta* demanded a law against *incompatibilitas* – magnates holding more than one office. They also campaigned for a more efficient operation of the judicial system. By the 1560s, however, this 'execution of the laws' movement was running out of steam. Then, in 1572, the last of the Jagellonian kings died.[43]

From then on the *Sejm* elected foreign princes to rule Poland. This was to prove both a major blow to the power of the monarchy and a significant boost to that of the *Sejm*. When foreign candidates sought election they were primarily concerned to advance the interests of their own homelands or, at least, their own position there. They had little or no interest in the long-term future of the Polish monarchy and so they were willing to make any concessions which would ensure election. After a brief interregnum (1572–74) Henry Valois was elected by the *Sejm*. He was hoping to secure a coalition of Poles and Turks against the Habsburgs and so willingly swore the coronation oath and approved the *pacta conventa*, acknowledging his personal, military and financial contributions. Furthermore, in the Henrician articles he agreed to biennial *Sejms*, a permanent committee of senators to 'assist' him between sessions, and the *Sejm*'s sole right of consent to taxes and troop levies. Shortly afterwards, however, Henry returned to France as Charles IX's successor. The *Sejm* proceeded to elect Stefan Bathory, prince of Transylvania (1576–86), and after him Sigismund Vasa (1587–1632). One of Stefan's chief concerns was Transylvanian security, whilst Sigismund's priority was always Sweden. Catholic Sigismund succeeded John III as king of Lutheran Sweden in 1593, but six years later he was deposed. For the rest of his reign the king of Poland maintained his claim to the throne of Sweden and the two countries repeatedly went to war.

The rise of the noble *Sejm* brought with it liabilities and burdens. As it controlled the Polish military machine and war-chest, so it was responsible for finding the manpower and money to wage the many wars against Poland's neighbours. After the extinction of the Jagellon line, it also had to find the resources for the military adventures and priorities of its foreign kings. Furthermore, it was not a united assembly. Apart from the factional divisions, feuds and vendettas which marked the Polish nobility, there was the *szlachta* hostility towards the magnates and widespread noble suspicion of the king and his supporters in the Church and on the royal council in the senate. The Reformation and Lutheran penetration in northern Poland was another cause of division. The one circumstance which could guarantee noble unity was defence of noble privilege. In the *Sejm* this defence rested on the principles of unity and unanimity which embodied the principle of consent by all to proposed legislation.[44]

IX Sweden

The Swedish *Riksdag* was the youngest of Europe's representative assemblies. Although an assembly of sorts was called at times during the fifteenth century, it did not become a recognisable and recognised national parliament until Sweden broke away from the Scandinavian Union of Kalmar with Denmark and Norway in the early 1520s. Gustav Vasa was confirmed as the king of Sweden by the *Riksdag* in 1523. In a classic piece of theatre at another meeting, four years later, he declared his intention to abdicate because of poverty and charges of Lutheran heresy against him. The parliamentary response was to transfer much of the Church's wealth to the crown. It also appealed to Gustav that, as right was on the Lutherans' side, 'God's Word may be purely preached everywhere in the realm'. The *Riksdag*, however, was still a rather primitive constitutional organ, without clearly defined rights, privileges or even functions. The *landsting*, the older provincial assemblies, exercised the right to legislate and vote taxes. Nevertheless Gustav Vasa's willingness to defer to the *Riksdag* on significant national matters meant that it rapidly came to exercise one of the important functions of parliaments, that of advice. It also registered approval of actual or proposed changes: so in 1544 it confirmed the protestant Reformation and recognised the crown as hereditary within the Vasa family. Furthermore, in 1544 and 1560, the king even sought the *Riksdag*'s initial approval of new taxes before they were submitted to the *landsting*.

Gustav Vasa died in 1560. During the remainder of the sixteenth century the national parliament was, on occasions, involved in political decisions of the highest importance, because of the dynastic disputes between his heirs and successors. In 1569 the estates declared King Erik XIV deposed and his brother John succeeded him 'upon a title which had undeniably more of an electoral than a hereditary flavour'. At his coronation King John III promised not to make war without approval by 'the leading Estates'. In 1587 John's Roman catholic son, Sigismund, was elected king of Poland. When, after John III's death, Sigismund returned for his coronation in 1594, he was obliged to accept the *Riksdag*'s demands, in particular an unqualified acceptance of the Swedish Church and his subjects' religious freedom. Eventually, in 1599, Sigismund, resident in Poland, was deposed by the *Riksdag*, which also excluded his heirs and offered the crown to Karl, his uncle. Karl declined and it was not until 1604 that he indicated his willingness to accept. By deposing and electing kings the national parliament had acquired considerable political importance, because it had come to speak for the political nation. Unlike most other European assemblies in the sixteenth century, however, it had not become burdened with the task of supplying money for defensive or aggressive war. As yet the power of taxation continued to reside in the provincial assemblies.[45]

X England

In contrast to the Swedish *Riksdag* the English Parliaments were amongst the older European assemblies. It had long since been established that laws and taxes required their assent.[46] They also enjoyed the right to present grievances, though they did not claim the right to redress before supply. These powers enabled them to fulfil their undoubted obligation to provide the king with *auxilium* and *consilium*.[47] There were, however, clear limits to the authority of Parliament (or, to be precise, of 'king-in-parliament' for, by the sixteenth century, the monarch was recognised as an integral part of the assembly). Statute could not deal with matters spiritual, nor did it encroach on property rights in any general way. That all changed during Henry VIII's reign. The pope's refusal to annul the first marriage of the king, so that he could marry a younger woman who might provide him with a male heir, caused Henry and his chief adviser, Thomas Cromwell, to resort to a parliamentary solution. In 1532–34 the spiritual and temporal powers of the papacy were transferred to the crown and Henry VIII was recognised as 'the only supreme head in earth of the Church of England'.[48] When, in 1536, Parliament dissolved the lesser monasteries, suppressed the franchises (bodies and areas with special liberties and immunities) and enacted the statute of uses (which invalidated bequests of property by will), it effected a statutory property revolution. The 1530s established the supremacy of king-in-parliament and the omnicompetence of Parliament. This was not immediately apparent to contemporaries. However, the acts of 1534, 1536 and 1544 (which ordered the royal succession), the act of six articles (which in 1539 lay down a body of orthodox catholic doctrine), the protestant Reformation and prayer books (enacted in the Edwardian parliamentary sessions of 1547, 1548/49 and 1552), the restoration of Roman catholicism (in the Marian assemblies of 1553–55) and, in 1559, the re-establishment of a protestant Church under Elizabeth as supreme governor had a cumulative effect: it became clear that Parliament was sovereign. It could make new laws and repeal or annul existing law on anything and everything.

In such circumstances it might be assumed that, in her long reign, Elizabeth would burden this powerful institution with many tasks, responsibilities and commitments, especially as she was increasingly beset with internal and external problems and threats. Quite the contrary. The queen prohibited debate and proposed new laws on a variety of subjects which were of major concern to members of the two houses of commons and lords: Elizabeth's marriage, the succession, Mary Queen of Scots' claim to the English crown, and any matter which touched the royal prerogative. In particular, she would not allow either further reformation of the Church after 1559 or parliamentary consideration of the matter. Frustration contributed to the emergence, in 1572, of the presbyterian movement, which rejected the office of bishop. During the 1580s, its adherents repeatedly, albeit unsuccessfully, promoted religious legislation in the commons. Nevertheless the queen's resolve was unshaken. In her reign, therefore, the range of activities of a sovereign parliament, wielding omnicompetent statute, did not expand but instead contracted. Apart from 1559 and two occasions (1572 and 1586/87) when, under pressure, she called meetings to consider the threat of Mary Stuart, her sole reason for summoning the assembly was money. Six times between her accession and 1584 she successfully requested peacetime subsidies from parliaments. They built on the Cromwellian precedents,[49] as official spokesmen and statute preambles justified them on the grounds of the benefits of government, especially in religion, the preservation of peace and, at the same time, the need to be prepared for possible attack.[50] Elizabeth and her councillors transformed parliamentary taxation into a largely unquestioned, frequent source of peacetime revenue: between 1559 and 1584 six subsidies and eleven fifteenths and tenths.[51]

War against Spain, of course, was accompanied by the demand for more supply, in both frequency and amount: between 1584 and 1603 fourteen subsidies and twenty-eight fifteenths and tenths.[52] Multi-subsidies were introduced: two in 1588, three in 1593 and 1597 and a quadruple subsidy in 1601. Inflation, under-assessment and tax evasion all helped to reduce the yield. Sir Walter Raleigh, complaining about false declarations of income, told the commons in 1601 that 'our estates are £30 or £40 in the Queen's books – not the hundredth part of our wealth'. Nevertheless, like most of the later sixteenth-century continental assemblies, funding government especially in war was the Elizabethan Parliaments' chief service. They also enacted a number of important laws for poor relief and against recusants, Jesuits and seminaries, but generally she sought *auxilium* and not *consilium*.

XI Ireland

Henry VIII's preference for dealing with Irish matters in a constitutional manner was demonstrated by his use of the Irish Parliaments, in 1536–37 and 1541–43, to extend the breach with Rome to Ireland and declare himself its king. Steve Ellis argues that the king appreciated the value of the Irish assembly in the government of Ireland and especially 'to promote unity and co-operation from the magnates'. His execution of policy tended to be gradual and cautious and, in particular, he avoided coercion of the Anglo-Irish. By the end of the reign, however, the king and his privy council were undergoing a change of attitude. They were dissatisfied with the size of Irish parliamentary tax grants. They had also come to recognise that the problems of managing the Pale were largely due to 'the survival of an independent Gaelic polity beyond, which had hitherto been largely ignored'. That Gaelic polity had to be reduced to a state of submission and dependence. So, beginning late in Henry VIII's reign and developing over the following decades, was the gradual replacement of consensus politics by a coercive policy of 'plantation' – land confiscation and colonisation – and conquest. It was not, however, a straightforward process because, as late as the governor-ships of Sir Henry Sidney and Sir John Perrott, between the 1560s and 1580s, there were also moves to pursue a policy of assimilation by cultural reforms and an internal restructuring based on English law and government. It failed, partly because it was successfully resisted by the Anglo-Irish of the Pale, particularly in the Parliament of 1585–86.

As English government became less concerned to communicate with the localities, placate the Anglo-Irish and maintain good terms with powerful magnates, Parliaments became less significant. At the same time the government increasingly funded its activities by non-parliamentary means, such as the *cess* (for provisioning soldiers), unpaid military service, billeting of soldiers, free labour for building defences and carts to transport provisions. Parliaments became few and far between; after 1543 only four were summoned during the next seventy years, in 1557, 1560, 1569 and 1585. The 1560 Parliament established Elizabeth's succession and her Anglican Church in Ireland. Thereafter it was chiefly used to promote the policy of confiscation, conquest and exploitation. Unlike some of its European contemporaries the scope of its business and the frequency of its meetings dramatically diminished from the mid-sixteenth century onwards.[53]

XII Scotland

In the feudal kingdom of Scotland Parliament was 'the head court of the king and his vassals'. Traditionally the assemblies met frequently because the dispensing of justice was their chief concern. Legislation was not an important function and, as we have seen, taxes could also be granted by the alternative conventions of nobles or estates whilst the task of devising the terms of required taxes and laws was delegated to a committee of lords of the articles. Parliaments were not of major importance, even during the frequent minorities and absences of monarchs, when they might have performed an important stabilising role. This was also the case after the accession of James V's infant daughter Mary in 1542. The treaties of Greenwich, which in 1543 established an Anglo-Scottish peace and agreed on a future marriage between Mary and England's Prince Edward, were rejected by the Scottish Parliament. Until 1551 Scotland suffered invasions by armies of Henry VIII and Edward VI. By then Mary Stuart was in France and, in her absence, the kingdom was governed by her mother Mary of Guise. As regent she attempted, unsuccessfully, to use Parliament to pursue the somewhat contradictory policies of political reconciliation and increased taxation. In the Reformation crisis of 1559–60 (during which Mary of Guise died) a parliament abolished the mass and rejected papal authority. It also accepted a protestant confession of faith but without requiring subscription to it. It was the general assembly which, in the following years, effectively established a presbyterian Kirk. Even so, the 1560 Parliament had breached Mary Stuart's instruction not to deal in religious matters. Both in 1560 and 1563 she would not ratify its religious legislation, but she changed her position in 1567, when she was in desperate political crisis.[54]

Between Mary Stuart's enforced abdication in 1567 and James VI's assumption of personal control in the mid-1580s, rival Parliaments were sometimes held by parties for and against the ex-queen: six in a mere ten months in 1571–72. These apart, thirteen Parliaments and twenty-two conventions were summoned during the eighteen years between 1567 and 1584. During the nineteen years between 1585 and 1603, when James VI was personal ruler and resident in Scotland, he called only seven Parliaments but fifty conventions. Frequency, however, was no yardstick of importance. Whilst both had the power to tax and legislate, conventions were increasingly called simply to provide financial assistance. And finance was a major problem, due partly to government growth but also inflation, exacerbated by currency debasement in the 1570s. In the process of reviving royal authority James VI made extensive use of Parliaments to reconcile opposing interests. At the same time it became an important legislative body. In 1579, for the first time, it enacted more than fifty laws; in 1581 over a hundred; and the scope of its legislation spread, for example into social welfare.

In one respect James was fortunate. The earl of Arran's regime (1583–85) secured the 'Black Acts' in 1584. These subordinated the Kirk to the crown, forbade any assembly without royal licence, and condemned anything which impugned or attempted to reduce the authority of Parliament. When Arran fell in 1585, the Black Acts remained. So the general assembly met by royal consent and the 'golden act' of 1592, which confirmed the Kirk's privileges, required the king or his commissioner at each meeting to designate the venue and time of its next meeting. In the years following Arran's fall James displayed a desire to broaden political consensus and harmony. In 1587 he promised Parliament that he would not 'prejuge the libertie of frie voting and ressoning of the saidis estaitis'.[55] That consensus-building, however, did not last. Financial necessity made Parliaments and conventions into tax targets. Even allowing for inflation, the size of tax grants underwent a significant increase. In 1566 a convention had voted £12,000 for James's baptism; for that of his son Henry in 1594 another convention provided £100,000. According to Julian Goodare, 'There was a large increase in first the frequency and then the level of taxation, beginning in the 1580s, which was important in establishing the principle that the government was entitled to tax and that taxation was granted by Parliament or convention of estates'. However, whilst the yield was much less than it might have been, because of the continued application of antiquated methods of assessment, the growth of the tax burden, especially in the 1590s, led to opposition. It was sometimes successful, especially in 1599–1600 when conventions of estates prevented revision of the tax assessment machinery.[56] Nevertheless, by the time James VI became James I of England too, he was presiding over a government which was more Court-focused, which had more authority over Church and society and an expanding role, and which cost much more. Parliaments occupied an important place in this process. Indeed, it has been persuasively argued that from the 1580s the Parliament of Scotland became 'almost a different assembly'.

The transformation of the 'lords' or 'committee' of the articles was crucial to such development and change. In 1424 it was formally empowered not only to draft articles for new laws and taxes but also to consider articles submitted by the king. The general body of members met only twice: to elect the committee and later, in one sitting, to ratify the articles. The lords of the articles were not therefore a managerial instrument created by the crown, but a device enabling most members to escape the tedium, expense and other burdens of parliamentary service. James VI, however, did transform the lords of the articles into a managerial tool. By the early seventeenth century it consisted of an equal number – eight – of clergy, nobles, barons, burgesses and royal councillors. Its loyal, reliable membership and the king's frequent presence at its meetings ensured effective royal control of parliamentary business.[57]

Notes

1 Despite bureaucratic growth nobles remained important and powerful in regional and local government. They were also sensitive about their privileges, especially (where it applied) tax-exemption, e.g. Castile (after 1538), France and, in practice, Sicily. H.M. Scott, *The European Nobilities in the Seventeenth and Eighteenth Centuries* 2 vols (London, 1995), Vol. 1, *Western Europe*, pp. 35–43. Parliaments were a natural arena for the defence of such privileges, as in Castile in 1538 (see above, p. 73) and France in 1614–15 (see below, pp. 132–3).

2 L.J. Reeve, 'The politics of war finance in an age of confessional strife: a comparative Anglo-European view' *Parergon*, New Ser., 14, 1 (1996), pp. 85–8.

3 The ruler determined the religion in his domains.

4   E.g. in Spain and the Low Countries, Sicily and Naples, the Holy Roman Empire, France, England and Sweden.

5   See above, pp. 73, 75–6.

6   E.g. in England, Scotland and France.

7   E.g. the Tudor dynasty.

8   E.g. France and England.

9   In Poland and the Empire.

10   E.g. German principalities.

11   H.G. Koenigsberger, 'Dominium regale or dominium politicum et regale: monarchies and parliaments in early modern Europe', in *Politicians and Virtuosi* (London, 1986), p. 23.

12   J. Russell Major, *The Estates General of 1560* (Princeton, NJ, 1951), pp. 101–2, 105, 110–14, 119–20; J. Russell Major, 'The third estate in the Estates General of Pontoise, 1561' *Speculum* 29 (1954), pp. 461–3, 469–73, 474–6.

13   It was a profitable practice for kings to create *élections* or introduce *élus* (royal tax officers) in *pays d'états* and then remove them in return for compensation. J. Russell Major, *From Renaissance Monarchy to Absolute Monarchy. French Kings, Nobles and Estates* (London, 1994), pp. 41, 190–3; J. Russell Major, *The Monarchy, the Estates and the Aristocracy in Renaissance France* (London, 1988), V, pp. 702–6, 709–13; VIII, pp. 253–5, 259; e.g. Poitou and Guyenne.

14   The provinces, however, needed to be watchful and on their guard with the new king. In Guyenne, for example, Henry IV attempted to establish *élections*, in which his officials would replace those of the provincial estates in the apportioning and collection of taxes. J. Russell Major, 'Henry IV and Guyenne. A study concerning the origins of royal absolutism' *French Historical Studies* 4, 4 (1966), pp. 369–81.

15   See below, p. 116.

16   See above, pp. 90–2.

17   José I. Fortea Pérez, 'The Cortes of Castile and Philip II's fiscal policy' *PER* 11, 2 (Dec. 1991), p. 119.

18   Ibid., p. 120.

19   I.A.A. Thompson, 'Castile: polity, fiscality, and fiscal crisis', in P.T. Hoffman and K. Norberg, eds, *Fiscal Crises, Liberty, and Representative Government, 1450–1789* (Stanford, CA, 1994), pp. 168–9.

20   Particular use has been made of the following revisionist works in this study of the Castilian Cortes: C. Jago, 'Habsburg absolutism and the Cortes of Castile' *AHR* 86, 2 (1981), pp. 307–26; C. Jago, 'Philip II and the Cortes of Castile: the case of the Cortes of 1576' *P&P* 109 (Nov. 1985), pp. 24–43; I.A.A. Thompson, 'Crown and Cortes in Castile, 1590–1665' *PER* 2, 1 (June 1982), pp. 29–45; Fortea Pérez, 'Cortes of Castile', pp. 117–38; C. Jago, 'Review Essay. Crown and Cortes in early-modern Spain' *PER* 12, 2 (Dec. 1992), pp. 177–92; C. Jago, 'Parliament, subsidies and constitutional change in Castile, 1601–1621' *PER* 13, 2 (Dec. 1993), pp. 123–37; Thompson, 'Polity, fiscality, and fiscal crisis', pp. 140–80; I.A.A. Thompson, 'Castile: absolutism, constitutionalism and liberty', in Hoffman and Norberg, eds, *Fiscal Crises*, pp. 181–225.

21 G. Griffiths, *Representative Government in Western Europe in the Sixteenth Century* (Oxford, 1968), p. 60; Fortea Pérez, 'Cortes of Castile', pp. 122–8; Jago, 'Crown and Cortes', pp. 182–3; Thompson, 'Polity, fiscality, and fiscal crisis', pp. 168–9; ibid., 'Absolutism, constitutionalism and liberty', pp. 184–5.

22 Ibid., pp. 186–7; Fortea Pérez, 'Cortes of Castile', pp. 128–30, 134–5.

23 Ibid., p. 134; Jago, 'Change in Castile, 1601–1621', pp. 123–4, 136–7.

24 X. Gil, 'Crown and Cortes in early modern Aragon: reassessing revisionisms' *PER* 13, 2 (Dec. 1993), pp. 112, 114–16, 118–22.

25 E.g. 150,000 ducats in 1543 and 500,000 ducats in 1552. D. Maland, *Europe in the Sixteenth Century* (2nd edn, London, 1987), p. 221; A.R. Myers, *Parliaments and Estates of Europe to 1789* (London, 1975), p. 94.

26 H.G. Koenigsberger, 'The Italian Parliaments from their origins to the end of the 18th century', in *Politicians and Virtuosi* (London, 1986), pp. 40–6; H.G. Koenigsberger, *The Government of Sicily under Philip II of Spain* (Kettering, 1951), pp. 124–5, 128–9, 132–5, 142.

27 P. Cardim, 'Ceremonial and ritual in the Cortes of Portugal (1581–1698)' *PER* 12, 1 (June 1992), pp. 4–6, 9–11; P. Cardim, 'Politics and power relations in Portugal (sixteenth–eighteenth centuries)' *PER* 13, 2 (Dec. 1993), pp. 95–6, 105–7; A.H. de Oliveira Marques, *History of Portugal* 2 vols (New York, 1972), vol. I, pp. 298, 314–15; J.H. Elliott, 'The Spanish monarchy and the kingdom of Portugal, 1580–1640', in M. Greengrass, ed., *Conquest and Coalescence* (London, 1991), pp. 53–4, 57–63.

28 H.G. Koenigsberger, 'Parliaments in the sixteenth century and beyond', in R.W. Davis, ed., *Origins of Freedom in the West* (Stanford, CA, 1995), pp. 293–7; H.G. Koenigsberger, 'Why did the States General of the Netherlands become revolutionary in the sixteenth century?' *PER* 2, 2 (Dec. 1982), pp. 104–6; ibid., 'Dominium regale', pp. 16–19; A.J. Veenendaal, 'Fiscal crises and constitutional freedom in the Netherlands, 1450–1795', in Hoffman and Norberg, eds, *Fiscal Crises*, pp. 102–6; H.G. Koenigsberger, 'Riksdag, Parliament and States General in the sixteenth and seventeenth centuries', in N. Stjernquist, ed., *The Swedish Riksdag in an International Perspective* (Stockholm, 1989), pp. 63–6, 71–2.

29 S.C. Lomas and A.B. Hinds, eds, *Calendar of State Papers Foreign Series* (London, 1929), vol. 21, pt 3 (1587), p. 164; Koenigsberger, 'Riksdag, Parliament and States General', p. 66; ibid., 'Dominium regale', pp. 18–19.

30 See above, pp. 22–4.

31 F.L. Carsten, *Princes and Parliaments in Germany* (Oxford, 1959), pp. 9, 11–49; V. Press, 'The system of estates in the Austrian hereditary lands and . . . Empire. A comparison', in R.J.W. Evans and T.V. Thomas, eds, *Crown, Church and Estates. Central European Politics in the Sixteenth and Seventeenth Centuries* (London, 1991), pp. 3, 10–11; Koenigsberger, 'Parliaments in the sixteenth century and beyond', p. 283.

32 Carsten, *Princes and Parliaments*, pp. 201–28.

33 Ibid., p. 356.

34 Ibid., pp. 356–87; Koenigsberger, 'Parliaments in the sixteenth century and beyond', p. 284.

35 F.L. Carsten, *The Origins of Prussia* (Oxford, 1954), pp. 165–9.

36 Kálmán Benda, 'Habsburg absolutism and the resistance of the Hungarian estates in the sixteenth and seventeenth centuries', in Evans and Thomas, eds, *Crown, Church and Estates*, pp. 124–5.

37 A. Kohler, 'Ferdinand I and the estates, 1521–64'; G.R. Burkert, 'Protestantism and defence of liberties in the Austrian lands under Ferdinand I'; and Sergii Vilfan, 'Crown, estates and the financing of defence in Inner Austria, 1500–1630', in Evans and Thomas, eds, *Crown, Church and Estates*, pp. 48–66, 72–6.

38 László Makkai, 'The crown and the diets of Hungary and Transylvania in the sixteenth century', in Evans and Thomas, eds, *Crown, Church and Estates*, pp. 80–7; Koenigsberger, 'Parliaments in the sixteenth century and beyond', p. 284.

39 Winfried Eberhard, 'The political system and the intellectual traditions of the Bohemian Ständestaat from the thirteenth to the sixteenth century' and Jaroslav Pánek, 'The religious question and the political system of Bohemia before and after the battle of the White Mountain', both in Evans and Thomas, eds, *Crown, Church and Estates*, pp. 30–4, 132–9; R.J.W. Evans, 'The Habsburg Monarchy and Bohemia, 1526–1848', in Greengrass, ed., *Conquest and Coalescence*, p. 138.

40 The gradual merger of Poland and Lithuania was finalised in an act of union in 1569.

41 See above, p. 37.

42 H. Olszewski, 'Review of J. Bardach's Polish Parliamentary System in Contemporary Historiography' *APH* 73 (1996), p. 179.

43 W. Uruszczak, 'The implementation of domestic policy in Poland under the last two Jagellonian kings, 1506–1572' *PER* 7, 2 (Dec. 1987), pp. 135–8; J. Miller, 'The Polish nobility and the Renaissance monarchy: the execution of the laws' movement: part one' *PER* 3, 3 (Dec. 1983), pp. 74–8; ibid., 'Part two', *PER* 4, 1 (June 1984), pp. 1–10; W. Czaplinski, 'Polish Seym in the light of recent research' *APH* 22 (1970), pp. 182–3.

44 See below, p. 150.

45 M. Roberts, *The Early Vasas. A History of Sweden, 1523–1611* (Cambridge, 1968), pp. 39, 75–8, 140–2, 190–3, 242.

46 Nevertheless, as Wolsey's benevolence, the 'Amicable Grant', illustrates, the crown was still capable of trying to raise non-parliamentary taxation by forced loans or benevolences, despite the 1484 statute declaring the latter to be illegal.

47 See above, p. 40.

48 Act of Supremacy, 26 Henry VIII, c.1, *Stats Realm*, vol. III, p. 492.

49 See above, p. 80.

50 G.R. Elton, 'Taxation for war and peace in early-Tudor England', in *Studies in Tudor and Stuart Politics and Government*, 4 vols (Cambridge, 1983), vol. 3, pp. 222–8, 231.

51 J.D. Alsop, 'Parliament and taxation', in D.M. Dean and N.L. Jones, eds, *The Parliaments of Elizabethan England* (Oxford, 1990), p. 93.

52 Ibid., p. 93.

53 T.W. Moody, F.X. Martin, F.J. Byrne, eds, *A New History of Ireland, 1534–1691* (Oxford, 1978), vol. 3, pp. 61, 77–83, 92–3; S.G. Ellis, 'Parliament and community

in Yorkist and Tudor Ireland', in A. Cosgrove and J.I. McGuire, eds, *Parliament and Community*, *Historical Studies* XIV (Belfast, 1983), pp. 56–63; C. Brady, 'Comparable histories?', in S.G. Ellis and S. Barber, *Conquest and Union. Fashioning a British State, 1485–1725* (London, 1995), pp. 78–9, 81–4.

54 M. Lynch, *Scotland. A New History* (London, 1994), pp. 196–200, 205–9; J.M. Goodare, 'Parliament and society in Scotland, 1560–1603' PhD, University of Edinburgh, 1989, pp. 7–8; G. Donaldson, *The Scottish Reformation* (Cambridge, 1960), pp. 54–5, 66–8.

55 Lynch, *Scotland*, pp. 183, 231, 235–6; Goodare, 'Parliament and society', pp. 8, 10, 13–19, 491–8; Donaldson, *Scottish Reformation*, pp. 211–12, 219, 231–3.

56 J.M. Goodare, 'Parliamentary taxation in Scotland, 1560–1603' *SHR* 68, 1 (April 1989), pp. 23, 43–5, 47–52; ibid., 'Parliament and society', p. 25; see below, p. 194.

57 J. Scally, 'Constitutional revolution, party and faction in the Scottish parliaments of Charles I', in C. Jones, ed., *The Scots and Parliament* (Edinburgh, 1996), pp. 57–8.

5

Mixed Fortunes of Seventeenth-century Parliaments: Eclipse, Survival and Triumph

DURING THE YEARS which ended one century and began another, peace at last came to much of Europe. Some of the wars which now concluded had been between foreign powers, but others had been internal conflicts, in some of which treason had been synonymous with heresy. In 1598 the treaties of Nantes and Vervins ended the French religious wars and hostilities between France and Spain. Philip III acknowledged the *de facto* independence of the Dutch, when Spain and the United Provinces signed a twelve-year truce in 1609. Meanwhile, in 1603, James VI of Scotland succeeded the last Tudor, Elizabeth I, as king of England. This union of the English and Scottish crowns ended centuries-old border lawlessness, conflict and forays, and intermittent warfare, invasion and counter-invasion between the two kingdoms. When the earl of Tyrone's Ulster-based rebellion of the 1590s finally collapsed and he surrendered in 1603, the English conquest of Ireland was brought to a successful conclusion.

Although the peace imposed on Ireland was, in effect, accomplished by the time James became king of England, it certainly accorded with his ongoing, driving wish for peace, not only in the British Isles but on the European continent too. In 1604, after almost two decades of war, he secured Anglo-Spanish peace by the treaty of London. During the following years he had a hand in persuading Spain and the Dutch to sign the twelve-year truce and, in 1614, in averting a major German war over the contested succession to the duchy of Cleves-Julich. He helped to negotiate the settlement which ended a rebellion against the French regent, Marie de Medici, in 1615–16 and his diplomats in Copenhagen and Stockholm brought to an end the war of Kalmar (1611–13) between Denmark and Sweden. James wished to be recognised as *rex pacificus*, the royal peacemaker, and his efforts certainly justified such a reputation.

He was not always successful. He could not achieve a constitutional Anglo-Scottish union, which would have been a much stronger guarantee of peace between the two kingdoms than a personal union of crowns. But, at least, in 1605 peace was brought to the borderlands by an Anglo-Scottish commission. He also followed the settlement with Spain by a trade treaty with France. Furthermore, he pursued not only internal peace within European states and pacific international relations between them. He was just as consistent and persistent in his search for religious reconciliation, within England and amongst protestant Churches in Europe.[1] He even looked beyond to a general Christian unity involving the Greek orthodox and Roman catholic Churches.[2]

James's achievements as peacemaker were limited and short in duration, but his efforts harmonised with the mood of the time. The push for peace was not confined to Christian Europe. In 1581 Philip II of Spain and the Ottoman sultan, Selim, concluded a truce. A quarter of a century later the Habsburgs and Turks signed a peace treaty. Not that there was a 'universal' absence of war. The competitive politics of Scandinavia and eastern Europe ensured that. Nevertheless, between 1598 and 1609 west, central and southern Europe moved to a period of peace, albeit a very brief one.

Peace brought some relief to the beleaguered exchequers of princes. Parliaments, however, tended not to experience the pleasant consequences of war's end. Although the conclusion of hostilities with Spain initially removed a major financial strain on the English crown's finances, the inherited war debts of Elizabeth I and the greatly increased household expenditure of an extravagant married king with a family meant continued demands on parliament.[3] Other combatants in the sixteenth-century wars had to grapple with much larger accumulated debts when peace came. In Spain it was the Castilian Cortes, or rather the cities whose *procuradores* sat there, which continued to bear the burden, just as they had done in wartime. As the Cortes of the eastern kingdoms of Aragon continued to meet infrequently and make only a modest financial contribution, it was increasingly the Castilian assembly which propped up the government. In 1573 it had provided a quarter of the crown's gross revenue but by the 1650s that portion had risen to three-fifths.[4] Between 1601 and 1621, as peace came to Spain (only to end with the expiry of the truce with the Dutch), so the *millones*, the compactual tax arrangement regularly re-negotiated by the Cortes, became an inherent part of Castile's financial burden.

In one important case, a national assembly proved incapable of providing financial aid to the government. Between the 1590s and 1610 Henry IV of France and his finance minister, the duke of Sully, sought to increase royal revenues. The king preferred to avoid the Estates-general, which, during the religious wars, had sought to place limits on royal authority. In 1593 it had even tried to find a catholic alternative to Henry, who had yet to renounce the protestant faith. King and minister pursued their objectives in a variety of ways, such as the *droit annuel* or *paulette* on officeholders (who thereby acquired hereditary possession of their offices), exploitation of indirect taxes, increased demands on the provincial estates and the extension of non-parliamentary levies into previously exempt provinces.[5] In 1610, however, Henry IV was assassinated and there followed the usual problems associated with a regency, especially a greater willingness to resist a regent – in this case Marie de Medici, Henry IV's widow – than an anointed monarch. Indeed, the noble rebellion against the regency government in 1614 led to the summoning of the Estates-general once more.[6]

There is considerable debate about this final meeting of the national representative assembly,[7] especially the reasons for its failure. The basic problem was that it was not equipped to satisfy royal needs and expectations. Any tax vote was no more than a recommendation. It had no legislative power and, whilst the presentation of grievances was a regular practice, serious and productive discussion on matters placed before it was inhibited by social and geographical divisions. This was particularly so in 1614–15, when the estates clashed over the distribution of offices and nobles' pensions, the relationship between the papacy and the monarchy and the *cahiers* of grievances. Richard Bonney, however, plays down 'tension between the orders' as *the* reason for the assembly's failure. He emphasises the hostility of other French institutions, such as the Paris *parlement*, and the failure of the Estates-general to work in collaboration with the provincial estates. Whatever the cause, the crown was not encouraged to call it again, especially during the years (1624–42) when Cardinal Richelieu was Louis XIII's chief minister. Richelieu, who sat in the first estate in 1614–15, later recalled that it was incapable of remedying faults. Thenceforth the government reverted to the more rewarding process of direct negotiation with provincial assemblies on a variety of matters, including taxation.[8]

As the English, Castilian and French examples show, debt-burdened monarchies sometimes lacked the will or, in particular, the resources to pay off their creditors. They certainly lacked the time. In 1618 there began what is misleadingly known as the Thirty Years' War. It began as a political and confessional crisis in the German Habsburg hereditary lands and erupted into rebellion in Bohemia. It rapidly enlarged to involve leagues of protestant and catholic German princes, France, Spain and its possessions in the Low Countries and Mediterranean, England, the United Provinces and Sweden. It was, at one and the same time, a reassertion of the German Habsburgs' authority in their hereditary lands, a confessional conflict, a renewal of the French–Habsburg dynastic wars, the Dutch defence of their *de facto* independence and the launch of Sweden's imperial career. It was both offensive and defensive, involving quests for territorial expansion and frontier security. The chief theatre of war was Germany, but campaigns were also waged in many of the participating countries and at sea in the Channel and the Mediterranean. Furthermore, military and naval operations extended into colonies, commercial bases and markets in the Americas, Caribbean and Asia.[9] The Thirty Years' War was not one conflict but a series of concurrent wars, some though not all of which were interrelated. Some of the combatants were engaged on a number of fronts and with several enemies at the same time. Spain was the classic example of the over-stretched monarchy. Philip III (1598–1621) and Philip IV (1621–65), propped up by the Castilian Cortes, waged war with the United Provinces (1621–48), France (1627–29 and 1635–59) and England (1624–30), as well as contending with rebellions in Portugal (1640–68) and Catalonia (1640–52). But Spain was not the only over-committed state. Sweden, for example, took on the German Habsburgs (1630–48), Poland (1632–35) and Denmark (1643–45). Furthermore, although the Peace of Westphalia (1648) brought some of the wars to an end, that between France and Spain and a general conflagration through northern and eastern Europe – especially Sweden, Denmark, Muscovy and Poland – continued for more than another decade.

Over forty years of European conflict on a grand scale tested the capacity of states to conduct long wars on more than one front. There were the constant and growing demands: recruitment, training, up-to-date and sufficient weaponry, an adequate, effectively operating commissariat and, above all, the money to pay for it all. In a political climate which was favourably disposed to the growth of more autocratic monarchy, practical necessity – the needs of war – provided additional impetus in that direction. After all, in many European countries the development of the 'fiscal-military' state was based on larger armies, more centralised and stronger royal government and increasing taxation. Parliaments and their response were central to this whole process, because it was there that concerns, grievances and resistance to growing financial burdens could be expressed. A dramatic example of this is to be found in Denmark, which Sweden invaded in 1658 and 1659 and on which it imposed the humiliating peace of Oliva in 1660. Blame was placed on the noble-dominated council (*Rigsraad*) and parliament (*Rigsdag*) for their resistance to the war. King Frederick III became an hereditary absolute monarch and the *Rigsdag* was consigned to oblivion until 1835.[10]

In the tiered system of multiple parliaments which operated in France the picture was a more diverse and less clear-cut one. The 'disappearance' of the Estates-general made little practical difference because it was normal practice for agents of the French kings to bargain with the provincial assemblies in the *pays d'états* for their tax quotas. Their importance, however, was diminishing. By 1600, six of the sixteen provincial estates had ceased to meet. During the seventeenth century others followed them, whilst the estates of Normandy were suppressed by the crown. Even before then, however, the estates of Normandy in 1629 complained 'of the great and excessive *tailles* demanded of us . . . [together with] surtaxes as excessive and onerous, or more so, than the *taille* itself, [all] in the name of a worthless group of officers . . . which, like caterpillars . . . gnaw on and ruin your people'. Some, such as Languedoc, Brittany, Burgundy and Provence, remained significant and their management required some political skill. Nevertheless, for several reasons, even they were becoming less and less important. First, the overall costs of war, in men, equipment and money, escalated. French military manpower trebled from 50,000 to more than 150,000, between the sixteenth century and the 1630s. As Philip Hoffman explains, although the bewilderingly diverse and often secretive nature of the French fiscal system makes it impossible to provide accurate tax figures, the estimates of total gross tax revenue reveal a dramatic upward trend: from 31.6 million *livres* in 1581 to 33.7 in 1620 and 77.8 in 1640. The urgent needs of war could not brook delay from reluctant taxpayers or obstructive local assemblies. As royal commissioners, the *intendants*, began to operate regularly in most parts of France in the 1630s and 1640s, they supervised local institutions and they were able to channel royal favours to those who co-operated, including members of provincial estates. They also negotiated with local elites, thereby assuming an old function of those estates. In these ways the estates were sometimes suborned, sidelined and rendered less effective as the tax burden rapidly became heavier. That burden suddenly increased in 1630–34, when the *pays d'états* were obligated to pay heavily for the revocation of *élections* which had been introduced in 1628 and which, in the process, had undermined the estates' financial control. Some showed spirited resistance when, for example, in 1633–34 the Languedoc assembly twice refused Louis XIII's demands. The crown, however, usually got its way with flattery, *douceurs*, or, as in 1657–59, threats to quarter troops and establish *élections* in Languedoc. In any case, in Brittany and elsewhere estates were inclined to reward themselves lavishly too when they voted taxes.[11]

Unlike the French Estates-general, the central assembly of the Castilian kingdom continued to be very active because it was respons-ible for voting and, especially since the introduction of the *millones*, administering an increasing portion of the state's revenue. According to Fortea Pérez, Charles I's negotiated financial arrangement or 'pact' with the Cortes and cities in 1536–38 determined the basis of the state's financial system for over a century. Initiated in 1590, the *millones* agree-ments were regularly re-negotiated contracts which bound Philip III and Philip IV to honour a variety of obligations, in return for conditional and limited-term grants of subsidies. This was hard bargaining but it does not denote an unwillingness to make financial provision for the king. One should not think of conflict as characteristic of crown–Cortes relations. Castilians were noted for their loyalty and willingness to obey the king and, as the Cortes' chief function was consent to taxation, that was one way in which cities and *procuradores* could express their devotion. Furthermore, fiscal crises, adverse economic conditions and the enormous expense of prolonged wars on a number of fronts made the crown ever more dependent on the assembly. It was this which led to the successive grants of subsidies, the *millones*, from the 1590s. Despite some years of peace with France, England and the Dutch, the decades between 1600 and 1620 brought no financial relief. Castile's economic decline, its eroding tax base and the state's debts (which, in 1623, were ten times greater than its annual revenue) made sure of that. This increased the financial role of the Cortes and also its political importance, especially because of the restraints placed on the king by his signature on a formal *millones* contract from 1600 on. The Cortes' power rested in administration of the *millones* tax arrangement, through a special commission in each city (the *comisión de millones*) and in the appropriation of the revenue.[12]

Of course the *millones*, constituting yet another burden, were never popular. The negotiations for successive grants in 1601, 1603, 1610, 1619 and beyond were always protracted. They met stiff resistance in some cities and consent was never unanimous. Furthermore, the government frequently intervened in the cities' administration of the *millones*. It attempted to control the *Diputación*, which was the Cortes' watchdog when it was not in session, and, after 1610, the *comisión*, to which the Cortes gave complete administrative control. It also diverted appropriated revenue to other purposes. There was not only a public perception of the Cortes' status and importance but also a royal concern to control it. The distribution of royal patronage amongst difficult *procuradores* became more important, widespread and lavish and so the crown spent progressively more for holding the Cortes. The monthly cost of holding the parliament in the 1650s was seven times greater than in the 1590s. City councillors and others involved in the urban administration of the *millones* were also reputedly creaming off handsome profits.[13]

There were undoubtedly shortcomings in the *millones* system. And there were grounds for royal dissatisfaction, disapproval, even rejection of the tripartite structure, in which the other two parties, the cities and Cortes, controlled the levying, collection and audit of very sizeable revenues. The *millones* illustrate Thompson's point that '[t]he constitutional history of Castile in the early-modern period is in effect the history of a struggle between Crown and cities for control of the Cortes'.[14] So long as the *procuradores* were issued with strict instructions by their cities, from which they had to obtain a decision to any request by the crown, they remained servants and delegates of those cities. Times were changing, however, especially in the *millones* era. The crown wanted the *procuradores* to come with full, independent decision-making power to a parliament which acted for the whole kingdom. At the same time there was a divergence of interests between the Cortes and the cities. *Procuradores* were *increasingly* anxious to promote and protect the assembly's authority as the intermediary between the cities of Castile and the king. At the same time longer Cortes' sessions isolated them from their cities, and they became more susceptible to royal pressure and financial benefits. So there occurred a physical separation and a divergence of interests between cities and Cortes.[15]

When Philip III died in 1621, votes by the Cortes were still based on decisions reached in at least a majority of the cities who sent *procuradores* there. Philip IV's objective was to reassert royal control over finances and, to this end, he sought to end the Cortes' subordination as the mouthpiece of the cities. In 1632 he won, when the cities capitulated under pressure and sent their members with *plena potestas*. The *procuradores* were now, and in the future, free to vote on anything put before them without reference back to the cities. By then Philip IV was also reasserting control over the *millones* administration and by 1658 the process was complete when the *comisión de millones* was absorbed into the royal council of finance. The key change, however, occurred in 1632. A decade before then Philip IV had attempted to negotiate directly with the cities, without calling the Cortes. Then he had been unsuccessful precisely because he tried to bypass the parliament. When he did so in 1643 the cities responded positively and he obtained what he sought. Philip had ended the Cortes' dependence on the cities and the result was a division of functions: the Cortes made financial decisions without reference back to the cities, which simply carried out those decisions. The 'victory', however, belonged rather to the cities. The Cortes wielded no political power and it lost its administrative role, which was assumed by the cities. The last decades of Philip IV's reign were a time of economic collapse, perpetual fiscal crisis, to which an unfettered Cortes contributed with new taxes, and military disaster. During the last years of the reign, 1660–64, the Cortes were in session. They did not meet again and thereafter the king dealt directly with the cities, in a decentralised financial structure characterised by particularism.[16]

The Cortes of the eastern Spanish kingdoms were, to some extent, the financial beneficiaries of the king's continuing and growing reliance on the Castilian tax base. Even the modifications imposed by Philip II on the Aragonese assembly during the constitutional crisis of 1592[17] did not have a significant adverse impact on its authority. It was called only twice during the reigns of Philip III and Philip IV (1598–1665) and the Cortes of Valencia and Catalonia also met infrequently. As their assent for taxation was necessary, few parliaments meant few taxes, and the amounts which they did grant were very modest. There was, however, increasing pressure for more money, especially from the 1620s under Philip IV's chief minister, the Conde Duque de Olivares. In 1626 he extracted sizeable grants from Aragon and Valencia, but he obtained nothing from Catalonia. In any case the Aragonese Cortes retained a good deal of their strength. When they met, they continued to deal with money-matters, legislation and political concerns and they retained their taxing authority.[18] They excluded courtier-nobles, royal ministers and officers and so, unlike the Castilian Cortes, they prevented the infiltration of a royal managerial network. Furthermore, the strong standing committee of the Aragonese Cortes, the *diputación permanente* (and likewise the Catalan *diputació*), provided institutional continuity and so it mattered much less that the full assembly met only rarely.[19]

Nevertheless the Cortes of the eastern kingdoms were under increasing pressure in the first half of the seventeenth century. They had, in fact, a long-standing grievance, that the king resided far away in Madrid and seldom visited them or held Cortes, which required his personal presence and where he could commune with his subjects, grant favours, consider grievances and, of course, negotiate taxes. *Auxilium* was, after all, a recognised obligation and expression of devotion by loving subjects. Although he was annually in Zaragosa between 1642 and 1646, royal visits were usually rare, whilst the pressure for military supplies of both money and men intensified. The government was ready to create and exploit opportunities. So an absent king nonetheless made extensive use of royal patronage in Aragon and he worked through smaller bodies, such as *juntas* (committees) in Valencia and *brazos* (estates) in Aragon, in an effort to obtain financial help. Although the *brazos* could not vote *general* taxes and thereby act as a substitute for the full Cortes, Philip IV's government in the 1640s and 1650s raised money and recruited men for service abroad, without prior parliamentary consultation. Its justification was that, whilst Philip IV was king of a multi-national state, he had specific obligations to each component part. In this case he was making provision for the Aragonese kingdom's defence, especially during the Catalonian war of 1640–52. Indeed, the future prospects of Spanish parliaments were bleak. The autocratic Philip IV, speaking with specific reference to the States-general of the Spanish Netherlands, dismissed assemblies as 'pernicious at all times and in all monarchies'. After 1645–46 the Cortes of Aragon did not meet for thirty-one years, whilst those of Valencia were not called again.[20]

Some European states were more fortunately placed than the major powers, Spain and France. Such were the United Provinces, England and Sweden. The Dutch had heavy and prolonged military commitments and they, like Spain, enjoyed a respite only during the twelve years' truce (1609–21). However, the federal structure of the new Dutch breakaway state, in which the sovereign provincial estates, composed largely of merchants and industrialists, exercised the taxing power, guaranteed both an adequate war-chest and financial stability. In dramatic contrast to the sequence of Spanish Habsburg bankruptcies, the independent Dutch republic did not experience one serious fiscal crisis in the seventeenth century. It 'presented a picture of almost un-believable financial stability'. Certainly the new state had problems, which were not confined to matters of defence against Spanish armies. There were deep religious divisions until the victory of orthodox Calvinism over Arminianism in 1619. The prince and other members of the house of Nassau-Orange, who provided the military leadership of the new state and were regularly appointed stadholders, the highest provincial officials and military commanders, constituted a surrogate monarchy. Sometimes a conjunction of autocratic temper and pressing military circumstances caused them to behave in an inappropriate regal manner, which in turn gave rise to political tensions. Powerful prov-incialism was a guarantee against the growth of a strong central government, but it also prevented urgent decisions. Problems there undoubtedly were, but they were resolved without damage to the structure and stability of the new state. Meanwhile, with its maritime and economic resources, the most advanced credit structure in Europe, a successful policy of empire-building (partly at Spain's expense), taxation of the rich rather than the poor, and a focus on profitable colonial and commercial war, the Dutch state, a non-absolutist fiscal-military state, finally won its independence in 1648 without losing its prosperity. Throughout the struggle for independence the States-general was the assembly which considered matters of common interest, especially the war. But it could not impose its will or taxes on the provincial estates, whom its deputies had to consult frequently for their positions on any given matter.[21]

England and the United Provinces had much in common. They were both maritime powers, Calvinist in religion, and friends and allies since Elizabeth's reign. They were also states in which representative institutions controlled the taxing power and which tended to tax the more prosperous. Unlike the Dutch, however, the English were not involved in foreign wars over an extended period. Between the Anglo-Spanish peace of 1604 and 1638–42, when the British Isles were overtaken by civil conflict, England was at war for only five years

(1625–30). Nevertheless, during that relatively brief period Charles I displayed a masterly and characteristic capacity for breathtaking folly when he engaged in simultaneous wars with both of Europe's major powers, Spain and France. As an island nation and maritime power England did not need a standing army (as the Dutch did against Spain). Its logical strategy was naval and commercial war combined with national defence, assistance to the Dutch and quick strikes against key installations such as Cadiz. Such a strategy was cheaper and much more likely to succeed than commitment to extended and extensive land warfare. This had been practised in Elizabeth's reign and there was still widespread – and vocal – support for it in the 1620s.[22] On five occasions – in 1625 (twice), 1626, 1628 and 1629 – Charles called Parliaments to fund his wars, but only twice did he obtain subsidies. Unlike the Dutch, the English were not fighting for their independence and so there was less enthusiasm for war, especially for the French war which seemed to have little to do with the national interest. Furthermore, Charles was already committed by his late father to the wasteful and useless subsidising of a German mercenary, Count Mansfeld, and to support the defence of Denmark, the kingdom of his uncle Christian IV. The diplomatic ineptitude of Charles's favourite, the duke of Buckingham, in embroiling England in two wars at once, together with his military incompetence, which led to the disastrous expeditions to Cadiz (1625) and La Rochelle (1627), stiffened parliamentary reluctance to waste money on war. Charles's dependence on Buckingham, his devotion to him and the exclusion of many both from the perquisites of favour and office and especially from royal counsels focused parliamentary hostility on him.

Meanwhile, non-parliamentary levies such as the forced loan of 1626, the arbitrary imprisonment of some who refused to pay and Charles's Arminian position in religion all added fuel to the fires of discontent. In 1626 the king forestalled Parliament's attempt to impeach his favourite by dissolving it. Two years later Buckingham's assassination and Charles's apparent acceptance of the parliamentary petition of right, which affirmed the illegality of non-parliamentary taxes, imprisonment without cause given and other recent authoritarian actions, provided the prerequisites for an improved political climate. When, however, Parliament was recalled for money in 1629, the priority of many commons' members was pursuit of grievances in both state and Church. Charles ended the Parliament and blamed its failure on 'turbulent and ill-affected spirits', who had pursued 'their wicked intentions, dangerous to the State'.[23] He did not call another for eleven years. In the process of breakdown between 1625 and 1629, Charles's authoritarian instinct played a greater part than either the strains of warfare on a financially ill-equipped state or the sinister designs of ill-affected spirits.

Sweden was, like England and the United Provinces, a territorially small protestant state and largely dependent on naval power for its economic well-being and national security. It faced an array of foes across the Baltic waters: Denmark had been a traditional enemy since the break-up of the Union of Kalmar; the Habsburgs another, since the Lutheran Reformation; and Poland, since Sigismund's deposition from the Swedish throne. When Karl IX died (1611) he left a seventeen-year-old son, Gustav Adolf, who, according to the succession pact of 1604, could not succeed until he was eighteen or take full control of government until he was twenty-four. It was a critical state of affairs at a time of pending Danish and Polish military threats, but the crisis was resolved by a *Riksdag* at Nyköping. It presented the young king with an accession charter which embodied a number of royal concessions to prevent a recurrence of the abuses committed in the previous reign. Gustav's immediate accession was conditional upon his acceptance of these.

The resultant charter of 1611 recognised the constitutional place of the *Riksdag* in Swedish government, but the king was free to consult individual estates and also provincial assemblies. The charter was also less than precise about what we might regard as the key powers and functions of an effective representative assembly. So it specified that laws would not be made, amended or repealed, wars would not be waged nor treaties concluded without the consent of 'the Council of the Realm and all the Estates'. It did not, however, state that such functions should be carried out by the estates at a meeting of the *Riksdag*. The estates were not even mentioned in relation to taxation: only that appropriations of revenue would not occur without the 'knowledge and advice of the *råd* [council] and without the consent of those who are concerned'. There is an air of uncertainty as to whether, at this stage, *landsting* or *Riksdag* embodied the taxing power. Perhaps the ambiguities of wording mattered less than the practice. There followed an effective working relationship between the warrior-king Gustav Adolf, his chancellor and ally, the noble Axel Oxenstierna, and the estates of the

Riksdag. The charter was originally a safeguard against royal abuses, but in practice it was flexibly applied under an able, popular royal ruler, who worked with the *Riksdag* in the interests of Sweden's imperial career. Gustav II's military achievements, which included defeats of Denmark, the acquisition of Ingria and Kexholm from Russia, Poland's concession of Livonia and his intervention in Germany from 1630, were funded by French and Dutch subsidies and especially by the territories which he occupied. It was, however, imperative to maintain internal political stability, especially as the king was abroad for such lengthy periods. This was achieved by continual collaboration between king, nobility, *råd* and *Riksdag*, the managerial skills of Oxenstierna, the king's ability as a popular speaker and the more effective organisation of the parliament in the *Riksdag* ordinance (1617) and the ordinance for the noble estate in 1626.

In November 1632 Gustav Adolf's death at the battle of Lutzen challenged Oxenstierna's maintenance of that stability. His legacy included his heir, Christina, a long minority (1632–44) and a Lutheran country committed to wars against catholicism and its old national enemies and also in pursuit and defence of its imperial career.[24] It was a legacy and an experience which already, in 1635, was causing financial stress, and makeshift measures by a nervous, even distracted government. So Count Per Brahe advised the *råd* that, if it could not reach peace terms with the emperor, 'we go on fighting. If we win a victory, we must exploit it; if we are beaten, then that disposes of the soldiers' [wage] arrears, and we can defend the strong places on the coast with the survivors.' Unrelenting war, financial burdens and consequent social stress would contribute to a *Riksdag*-focused crisis in mid-century.[25]

It is clear that prolonged international conflicts and the demands which they imposed upon princes, communities and their elected members in representative assemblies, by creating the necessity and therefore dynamic for the growth of the fiscal state, played an important part in parliamentary history. They contributed to the demise of some assemblies and, as we shall see, they helped to trigger a spate of mid-seventeenth-century crises, in some of which parliaments had a central role. The cause–effect relationship, however, was not a uniform one. Wars could also activate and enhance the importance of parliaments, because of the fiscal-military needs of monarchs. There is a natural temptation to seek out common causality or to construct theories, models or general principles which will accommodate the experience of most, if not all, representative institutions. It would be simplistic, indeed wrong, however, to attribute early modern parliamentary developments chiefly to the financial consequences of extended war.[26] The history of assemblies could also be significantly affected by their structure and composition, inter-cameral relations and the extent to which members were liable to, or exempt from, direct taxation.[27] Royal war-driven needs were, in any case, just one, albeit a very important one, of a wide and varying combination of financial and economic, political, religious and social problems which impacted on the fortunes and fate of parliaments in the early and mid-seventeenth century.[28]

The autocratic tendencies of early modern hereditary rulers

The institutional diversity, decentralisation and even independent jurisdictions of late medieval territories encouraged the growth of autocratic tendencies which were necessary to achieve more effective royal control. In pursuit of this end some rulers appealed to absolutist ideology. War could give a sense of urgency to the process, as it could no longer be sustained from the old royal hereditary revenues. This could enhance the bargaining position and political authority of parliaments but equally it could encourage rulers to seek alternatives. Even then, as in France when monarchs no longer called the Estates-general after 1614–15, all was not what it seems in retrospect. It was not an obstacle to royal authority which was laid to rest, but an unrewarding, time-consuming institution which was rendered ineffective for a variety of reasons: geographical, social and cameral divisions, lack of legislative or financial powers, the absence of any working link with the more frequent provincial estates, and the hostility of other institutions, such as the Paris *parlement*, towards it.

The Holy Roman Empire provides more convincing evidence of estates as victims of autocratic princes. Yet even here the picture is one of contrasts. The seventeenth-century imperial diet remained an unreformed assembly which increasingly resembled a gathering of diplomats representing effectively independent principalities and cities. It met infrequently (in 1613, 1640–41, 1653–54) until 1663, when a permanent diet was established at Regensburg. This made little difference, because it was divided by religion, minority rights were protected, and it lacked the power to raise funds for effective imperial defence and administration. In any case it was the assembly of a decentralised empire in which, as a consequence of the Thirty Years' War (1618–48), the princes were recognised as territorial sovereigns. As such they could ignore or reject any of the diet's actions which impinged on that sovereignty. Weak though the diet was, neither its authority nor its existence were under threat from a powerful ruler, because the emperor's role after the Thirty Years' War was little more than that of a figurehead.

Among the estates of the German principalities, those of Württemberg flourished after the war, in which the duchy had become a battleground. This was due, however, not to some kind of parliamentary triumph over the dynastic ambition and autocratic aspirations of the ruling prince. It was the consequence of the prince, Eberhard III (1633–74), whose traditional approach to government was based upon a co-operative relationship with the *Landtag* and a respect for its rights. This ducal policy was reinforced by the government's financial dependence on the assembly. The war, which had involved heavy taxation, Habsburg military occupation, looting and the destruction of property by marauding soldiers, left a ruined economy, an empty treasury and debt which obliged Eberhard to look to the estates for assistance. So, for a variety of reasons, his reign was marked by the activity of a revitalised *Landtag*.[29]

Saxony, like Württemberg, was ravaged by the Thirty Years' War. It was spared the direct impact of military operations until 1630. Thereafter it became the victim of Swedish and imperial armies, which waged war on each other on Saxon territory. During and after the war, however, the estates strengthened their position, partly because of the personal weakness of Elector John George I (1611–56). He was financially dependent and also repeatedly deferred to them for advice on policy matters. Nevertheless he did not call an assembly after 1640. Then, when he died, the estates firmly and successfully opposed the partition of the principality amongst his sons. Under his heir, the new Elector John George II, they secured guarantees of their right to advise and to tax. So 'the equilibrium between the prince and the Estates remained, to the advantage of the country'.[30]

Württemberg and Saxony were the exceptions rather than the rule. In most of the important principalities autocratic tempers, the imperious needs of war, or the two in combination put estates under siege.

Even before the Thirty Years' War the Bavarian Elector Maximilian (1597–1651) legislated, controlled foreign policy, and made war and peace without reference to the *Landtag*. He exercised wide-ranging financial powers and regarded the estates' grant of taxes as an electoral right. He summoned the estates only twice – in 1605 and 1612 – during his long reign and thereafter he looked to the permanent parliamentary committee of sixteen to extend and repeat previous tax levies. Conflict between a cash-needy prince in time of war and an overburdened society resulted in a victory for Maximilian, who decreed new taxes, imposed his control on the committee and extracted large parliamentary grants without resistance. After Maximilian's death the estates met only once more, in 1669.[31] In other principalities, relations between rulers and estates were similarly affected by a divergence of interests during pro-longed war. Hesse was also afflicted by the common curses of partition and religious conflict.[32] Such divisions weakened the regime of Maurice of Hesse-Cassel (1592–1627) and made him dependent on the estates for military alliances and defences and the necessary funding of them. His weakness defeated his attempts to establish a permanent parliamentary committee to act on the estates' behalf. Whilst they favoured neutrality, he sought to enter the Thirty Years' War on the protestant side. Finally, in 1627, under pressure from the estates, he abdicated in favour of his son William V (1627–37), in order to placate the invading imperial forces. The strength of the estates, however, was in the long term undermined by division between the nobility and the towns. This eventually enabled William VI to weaken significantly their authority. By an agreement of 1655, he could impose taxes unilaterally in emergencies and, when convenient, obtain the estates' retrospective approval.[33]

Similarly, the seventeenth-century history of the estates in Brandenburg and Prussia has some of the characteristics common to the German principalities. The electors of Brandenburg, George William (to 1640) and then Frederick William (1640–88), were typically faced with military crises, widespread devastation, defensive needs, invasions, contributions levied by occupying powers and a desperate need of money. These priorities clashed with the estates' resistance to excessive taxation and the nobles' hostile response to the harmful effects on their economic bases. Frederick William's eventual answer to such opposition was to manage without them. The Brandenburg assembly did not meet again after 1652–53. In his new acquisition of Prussia, acknowledged by foreign powers in 1660, defensive needs, especially the maintenance of a powerful army, took priority over the estates' rights. Their claim to inalienable rights, which limited the elector's authority, led to a parliamentary crisis over his assumption of sovereignty (1661–63) and a confrontation over tax demands. Thereafter the elector proceeded to levy an excise, land and poll taxes without calling the estates, or dictating his requirements when they met. As so often happened in Germany, including the hereditary Habsburg dominions, the exercise of absolute authority in Brandenburg-Prussia was the end-result of conflicting priorities, practical necessity, reinforced autocratic impulses and divided estates. In addition, Frederick William consistently worked to establish a mutually advantageous relationship with the nobility, thereby preventing any possibility of parliamentary unity amongst the estates.[34]

Unlike many of the German princes, the power of the Spanish Habsburgs was in decline. As their territories came under increasing threat from the French, Dutch, English and Turks, and as they became involved in geographically scattered theatres of war, they became more impatient and inclined to resort to autocratic responses when confronted with parliamentary resistance. In the previous century the Sardinian parliament had met approximately once every decade, but in sessions stretching over several years. Crown–parliament relations had generally been stable: taxes were voted on request and privileges were respected. But, as so often, the political climate significantly changed there in the seventeenth century. Major confrontations occurred between Spanish viceroys and parliamentary opponents, over royal tax demands and threats to privilege, especially in 1624–25, 1654–55 and 1665–68. The opposition consisted variously of nobility, clergy and cities. The conflicts encompassed a broadening range of issues, including appointments to Sardinian offices, noble privileges and the crown's right to plead necessity and override privilege. They also became progressively more serious until, in the 1660s, the viceroy was murdered and his opponents were executed. Only three more sessions were held under Spanish rule: in 1677, 1688–89 and 1697–99.

On the Italian mainland, Habsburg patience ran out much earlier. After two difficult sessions over growing taxation, in 1639 and 1642, the Spanish viceroy advised the government in Madrid that the Neapolitan parliament was a threat both to the crown's needs and to public order in Naples. It did not meet again.[35] In the Low Countries, growing Habsburg impatience with obstreperous assemblies had been reinforced by the great rebellion of Philip II's reign. After the reconquest of the southern provinces, the States-general of these Spanish Netherlands had a short life. They met on only four occasions and no more after 1632. Although provincial estates continued to meet, they were weak and taxation continuously increased, with or without consent.[36] Once again, as in other Habsburg dominions, military necessity encouraged the Spanish monarch to exert increasing control over assemblies or to leave them in abeyance. It became evident, however, that such royal conduct or inaction was also the product of an autocratic temper which manifested itself in social, ethnic and religious policies too.

In two instances when monarchs 'broke' with their assemblies, in England and Denmark, it cannot be argued that they did so because they were driven on by the exigencies of war. In 1629 the blinkered Stuart, Charles I, dissolved Parliament and in a proclamation he intimated, in obscure terms, that it would not be summoned again for the time being. This was the consequence of deteriorating relations between the government and an increasing number in both lords and commons. Some issues were directly war-related, but others concerned religion, an over-weening favourite and authoritarian royal conduct. Charles did not, however, dispense with difficult parliaments in order to pursue his wars and fund them with arbitrary non-parliamentary levies. Indeed he made peace with France and Spain in 1629–30.

Whereas Charles just suspended relations with his parliament, the same cannot be said of Frederick III of Denmark. Furthermore, the Danish king did not make his move until after the signing of a peace treaty ending three years of war between his kingdom and Sweden in 1660. It had been a humiliating and devastating experience for Denmark and the immediate legacies were cession of territory, formidable debts and an impatient, unpaid army. The *Rigsdag*, representing nobles, clergy and towns, was called to deal with the pressing financial problems. When the nobility asserted their traditional right to tax-exemption they were isolated by a hostile parliamentary coalition of clergy and citizens. Aristocratic intransigence led the coalition to seek a restructuring of the political system in order to break noble power. That power was entrenched in the *Rigsraad* or state council, which shared with the elected king the exercise of sovereignty, and in the *Rigsdag*. The key proposal of the coalition – to change from an elective monarchy, which had given the nobles great influence, to an hereditary one – received widespread support. An isolated nobility capitulated and, in October 1660, the estates offered Frederick III hereditary status for himself and his heirs.

His acceptance effectively ended more than a century of noble ascendancy. He was then empowered to make constitutional changes appropriate to his new status. The unsurprising outcome was the establishment of absolute monarchy, which was formalised with a written declaration in 1661 and the *Lex Regia* four years later.

The events of 1660–65 in Denmark, however, should not be seen merely as the working-out of a postwar political crisis. They constituted both a reaction against a lengthy noble ascendancy and the modernisation of an outmoded political structure.[37] That kind of archaic system was repeated elsewhere in Europe: an early modern state encumbered with medieval administrative structures and practices and a domanial-based financial structure, in all of which a privileged noble elite exercised considerable, sometimes disproportionate, influence. In a few drama-packed weeks in 1660 the estates facilitated the shift towards a fiscal-military state appropriate to the financial demands of the seventeenth century. It was, however, also a situation skilfully exploited by a king who had autocratic aspirations, but who ostensibly attributed the change to God's will. At each stage of the process he appeared simply to respond to public demand. He did, however, apply military pressure to overcome noble resistance, whilst the estates' amenable conduct was partly responsive to discreet royal persuasion and encouragement.

Stresses within the social structure

Social stress could have significant parliamentary repercussions, because it usually involved the nobility. It was and remained usually the most influential political order. Along with the crown and Church it was collectively the greatest domanial proprietor. And apart from some provincial estates (especially in the Low Countries but also in some French *pays d'états*) and, after 1538, the Cortes of Castile, the nobility was usually present and a prominent, powerful, even pre-eminent parliamentary order. Furthermore, in one of those exceptions, the Castilian Cortes, great nobles showed a renewed interest in the seventeenth century and, for a variety of reasons, secured election as *procuradores*. Where the nobility was present in strength, threats to their privilege and position and the threat which they in turn posed to other orders were likely to surface in the parliament-time, as in Denmark.[38]

In France the nobility was sometimes at loggerheads with the other social orders during the parliament-time. As in Denmark and elsewhere, the privileges and royal favours enjoyed by the *noblesse* were often the target of representatives of the tax-burdened third estate. The last meeting of the Estates-general, in 1614, also exposed serious social differences. They were to some extent, however, blurred by other considerations such as religion. Furthermore, the representatives of the third estate consisted largely of royal officials, parlementarians and other lawyers, provincial and urban officials, but very few merchants and no peasants. In other words, it was composed rather of members of administrative and legal elites than of a social order. Nevertheless the issues which divided the three estates certainly reflected distinct and predictable social attitudes. When the estates would not resolve their differences over venality, privilege, royal patronage and other matters, they appealed to the king to arbitrate, thereby publicly acknowledging his absolute authority. The nobility in particular, under pressure from the third estate, was supportive of the monarchy.[39]

This episode can, however, convey a misleading picture. Research in recent years has resuscitated European nobilities. They remained powerful, prominent, even pre-eminent in society and in regional and local politics. In France the *noblesse de robe* reinforced the place of nobility. They did not pose some kind of rival force – a number were even in origin *noblesse de race*. Away from the Estates-general and back in the provinces nobles and *sieurs* were connected elites in control of military and civil administration respectively.

Some nobilities in contemporary Europe actually grew in strength. The Swedish Queen Christina's practice of alienating by grant or sale to noblemen the right to crown lands, rents or taxes from freehold peasants caused widespread and escalating discontent during the 1640s. Freehold peasantry were liable to be burdened with increased taxes and they were threatened with social degradation to the status of nobles' peasants, overburdened and without rights. A nobility, rapidly swollen in numbers, wealth and social control, was to become the target of the other estates' hostility when the *Riksdag* met in 1650 and 1655. At least the Swedish freehold peasantry had recognised constitutional rights and a place in the national assembly to express their discontent and protest against injustices.[40] But not in Germany, where the imperial diet was dominated by the electoral and imperial princes and where, in Brandenburg, Prussia and other principalities, the rise of autocratic rulers rested on aristocratic co-operation and the dismantling of assemblies. In the Habsburg hereditary lands of Bohemia, Hungary and Austria powerful independent-tempered nobilities dominated their societies and assemblies.

Nowhere, however, could elites match the success of the Polish nobility. In the late fifteenth and early sixteenth centuries they effectively monopolised the *Sejm*, which from 1493 onwards was bicameral. The peasants were reduced to a state of serfdom. The clergy dealt separately with the king through their synods, and under Sigismund I (1507–48) the towns were excluded, with the exception of Cracow, whose members had observer status only. Burgesses were prevented by law from acquiring landed estates and peasants were reduced to a state of serfdom. The contemporary description of Poland as 'the noble nation' was indeed an apt one. Nonetheless social stress was present in the *Sejm* in the form of hostility between the magnates, who sat in the senate, and the *szlachta* (lesser nobility) in the chamber of deputies. This was expressed especially in the 'execution of the laws' movement, which was at its height in the first half of the sixteenth century. The *szlachta* were loud in complaint about the chronic crime rate, delays in legal process and the king's failure to enforce the laws. These, they believed, were partly the consequence of inefficient and corrupt royal law courts. It was their right to appeal directly and personally to the king as the highest judge in the kingdom. He performed this time-consuming duty during sessions of the *Sejm*, but time invariably ran out, leaving many appeals unheard and many *szlachta* frustrated. So through the *Sejm* the *szlachta* sought a simplification and codification of the laws and procedures and other reforms. Thus far they were canvassing the king to carry out his duties of interpreting the law and ensuring its due process. At the same time, however, they believed that magnates in favour at Court and recipients of offices and other patronage were obstructing the 'execution of the laws' movement'. During the 1540s and 1550s it became increasingly directed against the magnates, sessions of the *Sejm* were turbulent and other issues were left unresolved. Although by 1570 the movement had ended, it illustrated how tensions within one social order could preoccupy and dominate political life and especially parliamentary meetings over a long period. Mutual magnate–*szlachta* suspicion and distrust continued into the seventeenth century.[41]

Ethnic and national hostilities

In the composite monarchies of early modern Europe such hostilities could focus on an 'alien' ruler and his foreign advisers, favourites, courtiers, military commanders and bureaucrats. Such hostilities were easily exacerbated if the monarch ignored or abused custom and traditional liberties and privileges or simply if he was an absentee ruler. The Castilian revolt of the *Comuneros* in 1520–21 was a dramatic example of this. Later, absentee and Castilianised Habsburg kings caused widespread alienation and even rebellion, for example in the Low Countries under Philip II and in Catalonia in 1640–52, during Philip IV's reign.[42] Representative assemblies were prominent in all of these violent statements of national resistance to alien rule.

This was not, however, always the case in early modern Europe. Parliaments were not the focus and driving force of the Scottish and Irish rebellions, which began in 1638–39 and 1641 respectively, in response to the policies of English royal government. Unlike the Spanish assemblies, the Parliaments of the Gaelic kingdoms did not provide leadership. When they were in session their membership, procedures and business were under effective royal control. This had enabled successive monarchs from Mary I to Charles I to authorise and legitimise the plantation of Irish lands; it had also facilitated James VI's imposition of important liturgical reforms, the Five Articles of Perth, on the Scottish presbyterian Kirk in 1621, overcoming parliamentary opposition in the process. Admittedly, despite Charles I's presence, there were protests and anti-government votes in 1633 during the coronation Parliament, which was designed to display royal pomp and power. Nevertheless, Charles used the occasion to tighten up further royal legislative control, developed by his father through the lords of the articles, which had to approve all proposed new laws.[43] Opposition had no possibility of promoting an alternative programme. In any case the Gaelic Parliaments were not in practice appropriate places for concerted and persistent criticism of royal policies. In Ireland they met infrequently: only six times between 1558 and the rebellion in 1641. Whilst Scottish Parliaments met more often (until Charles I's reign) they were still not regular, their sessions were very brief and, in the convention, there was an alternative source of laws and taxes. Above all, the British Parliaments lacked permanent committees which looked after the assembly's interests between sessions and, as in Spain, could provide leadership in rebellions against royal misrule.

This is not to say, however, that British Parliaments never provided opportunities for voicing ethnic or national hostility. When, for example, the Irish Parliament of 1569 began, the English administration was immediately challenged by an organised Anglo-Irish coalition of land-owners. Under the leadership of Sir Edmund Butler and Sir Christopher Barnewall, they accused the government of electoral malpractice and set the tone for a tense and obstructive session.[44]

Ethnic and national hostilities could go even further and overthrow cherished royal schemes, no more so than in the British multiple monarchy. In 1604 James VI and I presented to the English Parliament, in vague, undefined terms, his objective of an Anglo-Scottish union. Gradually, over the next three years, he outlined his goals more precisely: 'one body of both kingdoms', which would provide 'a general union of laws', naturalisation of Scots born before and after James's accession to the English throne and 'community of commerce'. It was the central issue in the sessions of 1604 and 1606–7, but in the end it foundered on the mutual hostility of both English and Scots, as voiced in their respective Parliaments. In England the parliamentary voice spoke for the common dislike, distrust and even contempt for the 'barbarous Scots'. They were likened to a herd of cattle seeking to feed in rich English pastures. James's Scottish courtiers, descending on Whitehall in 1603, were perceived as ravenous and power hungry. Sir Anthony Weldon, an English courtier who went north with James in 1617, witnessed Scottish nobles on their homesoil. He described their wives as their slaves, their horses as their masters and their swords as their judges. He summed up the Scottish capital, Edinburgh, as 'stinking' and Scotland as 'lousy'. Parliament was certainly in tune with public opinion. As for the Scots, they were no better disposed to union because they feared subordination and control in politics, government and law by their stronger, aggressive southern neighbour.[45] It would take a common enemy, Charles I, to bring about a degree of voluntary cross-border collaboration during the 1640s.

Religion

The inevitable and often major impact of the sixteenth-century Reformation on relations between rulers and their parliaments has already been considered. Because it was a fundamental of people's existence, a fundamental for which many were prepared to kill and were willing to die, religion could supersede or at least impact upon other loyalties, issues and priorities. It cannot, therefore, be considered apart from those other concerns, such as the political aims and needs of governments, elites and assemblies. For example, Sergij Vilfan has demonstrated, with reference to sixteenth- and early seventeenth-century Inner Austria, the clear 'links between defence, finances, Reformation and the struggle between estates and absolute monarchs'.[46] This was particularly true within the Empire because of the legacy of division left by the Reformation. The *Reichstag* included opposing catholic and protestant princes and free cities who nonetheless had to confer constructively together about defence against the Turkish menace. It met only six times between 1555 and 1603. Because religious differences often made compromise solutions impossible, after 1608 it met only once more, in 1613, before a 27-year gap ensued. The treaty of Augsburg which, in 1555, signalled the end of the German religious wars, adopted the principle *cuius regio eius religio*, whereby princes could opt for catholicism or Lutheranism for their territories. Calvinism was not included, but some princes chose it nonetheless, for example former Lutherans such as the elector palatine in 1559–60 and the count of Nassau in 1578. In 1613 the elector of Brandenburg became a Calvinist, ruling over a largely Lutheran principality. In 1605 Maurice of Hesse-Cassel switched to Calvinism, but his estates and his cousin Louis of Hesse-Darmstadt remained Lutheran. In the spirit of the Counter-Reformation Albert of Bavaria (1550–79) used a mixture of firmness, concessions, patronage and re-staffing of the state to restore catholicism.[47] The German Habsburgs, however, had to contend with powerful and independent protestant nobilities. Into the seventeenth century these nobilities continued to dominate the communities and estates of the Habsburg domains, which needed defence against Turkish military power. Everywhere there was religious division.

In the Habsburg domains, however, there was also religious change in the seventeenth century. These territories, which constituted a composite state in south-eastern Germany, stretched from the Tyrol ('Further Austria'), Carinthia, Carniola and Styria ('Inner Austria'), north-westwards through the duchies of 'Upper' and 'Lower' Austria to the newest additions – Bohemia and, to the east, the northern and western parts of Hungary. In 1526–27 the estates of the kingdoms of Bohemia and of what remained of Hungary, after the Turks' crushing victory of Mohacz in 1526,[48] elected Ferdinand I as their king. The nobility was powerful and to a large extent firmly protestant in all the Habsburg territories. In the older parliamentary estates of Bohemia, Hungary and, after 1564, the newly created assemblies in all the Austrian lands, the protestant nobles occupied a dominant position. Any province or assembly which experienced Habsburg intimidation or oppression could expect support from the others. Furthermore, the Habsburgs' regular need for money and men to combat the ongoing Turkish menace enabled the estates to strike bargains, including religious concessions, with their catholic rulers. Indeed the estates became important as a protestant frontline of defence against the Counter-Reformation spirit of the later sixteenth century. In 'Further', 'Inner' and 'Lower' Austria anti-protestant measures were introduced by Habsburgs from the 1570s onwards. Although Bohemia and Hungary were protected by old constitutional rights against the exercise of absolute authority, this did not prevent Emperor Rudolf II from taking action against 'heresy' in both kingdoms. In 1604 Hungarian protestants, backed by the estates, rebelled against his Counter-Reformation policies, which had included a ban on parliamentary discussions about religion. Austrian, Bohemian and Moravian co-religionists gave their support. The protestant-dominated estates of the Habsburg domains also benefited from family in-fighting between Rudolf and his younger brother Matthias, who sought to unseat him. Both made concessions on religion to them in order to gain their support: untrammelled religious freedom to their Hungarian (1606) and Bohemian (1609) protestants.

Tension between catholic rulers and protestant estates continued, however, and in 1618 conflict renewed. In the following year the Bohemian estates summoned a general assembly, including representatives from the Austrian and Hungarian estates. It deposed their new king, Ferdinand II, and chose Frederick V, elector palatine, instead. The nobility weakened their cause because they remained exclusive and did not recruit the active support of towns or peasantry. In any case Ferdinand was able to enlist greater military help, and the rebellion was decisively put down in 1619–20. The result was that the participating estates lost most of their powers. After 1620 the general Bohemian Diet was not called again for 228 years. Provincial assemblies, however, continued to meet and in them the noble estate retained its influence. In accordance with the 'renewed' or revised constitution of 1627 the Bohemian monarchy became hereditary and, on paper, it became absolute. In practice, however, much autonomy survived in the hands of a small powerful landed elite, which provided the government's officials and used the diets to represent their interests to the king. Only the Hungarian parliament retained its formidable strength, because the crown continued to need its assistance in maintaining defences against the Turks. Later in the century, Emperor Leopold I (1658–1705) did not call the estates for twenty years (1662–81) and conducted repressive policies against protestants. Hungarian resistance, however, was such that in 1681 he negotiated a settlement, which granted religious freedom to the estates. As noted at the beginning of this section, religion was often a major issue and the cause of conflict between rulers and estates. Yet, as the German-imperial experience illustrates, it was more often than not inseparable from geographical and social loyalties, defence concerns and conflicting constitutional positions.[49]

Religion was important in the representative assemblies of other European states. Conflicting interpretations of the French king's religious authority occurred in the Estates-general of 1614–15, when the third estate clashed with the others over the demarcation of royal and papal power in the French Church.[50] Amongst the diverse issues which divided Charles I of England and his Parliaments in 1625–29, religion loomed progressively larger during the five parliamentary sessions of those few short years. In his proclamation justifying the dissolution of the 1628–29 Parliament, he accused difficult members of lies and malice: '[A]lthough our proceeding before the Parliament, about matters of religion, might have satisfied any moderate men of our zealous care thereof . . . yet, as bad stomachs turn the best things into their own nature for want of good digestion, so those distempered persons have done the like of our good intents by a bad and sinister interpretation'.[51] Religion also caused parliamentary problems for the early Stuart monarchy in Scotland in 1621, when James sought the statutory enactment of the Five Articles of Perth, which introduced English liturgical practices.[52] Although they passed into Scottish law, James did not attempt to enforce them because they had aroused such hostility in the Scottish Parliament. It should be added, however, that his tax demands also contributed to a heated and disturbed session. Not that, in any case, the Stuarts always used Parliaments to advance religious policies or to bring the Churches of England, Scotland and Ireland into a state of 'congruity'[53] or harmony and peace. Charles I's disastrous move in 1636–37, when he introduced new canons and a prayer book designed to effect major liturgical changes in the Scottish Church, was made without reference to the general assembly or Parliament. After the military conquest of Ireland in 1603 the English government proceeded to replace Gaelic by feudal land tenures. This was not carried out by the authority of the Irish Parliament, which was not consulted. It was achieved by a series of judicial decisions, handed down by judges who were English common lawyers.[54]

Dynastic problems and other 'wildcards'

These took a variety of forms, all of which could provoke undesirable parliamentary consequences. Moves to partition German principalities amongst co-heirs usually met with the stiff resistances of the estates. A royal minority – the absence of an adult anointed and active ruler – always weakened a monarchy, even if the succession was undisputed. This was because various interests then took the opportunity to challenge its authority.[55] So in France, during Louis XIII's minority (1610–17), a consequence of Henry IV's assassination in 1610, the princes of the blood rose in rebellion against the regency of the queen mother, Marie de Medici. She was obliged to call the Estates-general, although the young king's proclamation of his majority strengthened the government's hand when it met. Nevertheless, as we have seen, the assembled estates spent much of their time in inter-cameral bickering rather than in assisting the crown.

Choice of a royal consort was crucial for the perpetuation of the ruling dynasty. But an unpopular or impolitic choice was liable to lead to trouble in the parliament-time. When James I of England sought a marriage alliance between his heir and the Spanish king's daughter, the house of commons petitioned in 1621 that Charles should marry 'one of our own religion'. The result was rapid crisis: James told the commons to mind its own business, or at least to keep its nose out of his, namely foreign policy; the commons claimed freedom of speech; James counter-claimed that it derived from royal grace; the lower house protested that it was an ancient right and recorded the protest in the commons' journal, from which the king tore it before dissolving Parliament and imprisoning several commons' members. The Anglo-Spanish marriage did not eventuate, but its replacement, Charles's marriage to the catholic Henrietta Maria, Louis XIII's sister, had just as much explosive potential. The marriage contract, negotiated in 1624, included a secret but widely suspected promise to suspend the penal laws against English catholics. When the secret became public knowledge it caused much parliamentary anxiety, suspicion and anger. The queen's public chapel, also allowed by the contract, became a meeting place for English catholics and a constant irritant to protestant Parliaments.

Dynastic problems could also occur when a monarch changed religion in a state which did not rest on the *cuius regio* principle. In 1599 Sweden, whose Church observed the Lutheran confession and condemned any deviation, had deposed King Sigismund, both for autocratic constitutional conduct and his Roman catholicism. Fifty years later Queen Christina declared her intention not to marry. She intended to abdicate and withdraw to Rome. Therefore, in order to perpetuate the Vasa dynasty, she sought approval of her cousin Karl Gustav and his heirs as her successors. To this end she summoned the *Riksdag* in 1650. Her intention contributed to a strained, often heated session, in which a reluctant nobility was isolated and put under pressure by royal exploitation of the other estates' grievances.[56]

Some dynastic crises, triggered by inopportune deaths or other threats to the succession, might be regarded as 'wildcards' in the story of parliaments. The same term might also be applied to 'unique' political decisions in a particular context: such were Charles I's introduction of the canons and prayer book into Scotland in 1636–37 and the Spanish government's decision to shoulder a greater military burden in 1640, during the Thirty Years' War. The former resulted in Scottish resistance and rebellion, which eventually forced the king to call the Long Parliament; the latter caused a revolt under the leadership of the Catalan Cortes' permanent committee. The intervention of a French army on the Catalans' side introduces another 'wildcard', that of the 'external power'. Indeed, the combination of circumstances, events and developments in each state is so complex and diverse that the history of each European parliament might itself be described as unique. Undoubtedly there were, as already considered, a number of general trends or processes common to a number of assemblies: autocratic aspirations of princes; the move to tax-based states; social, ethnic, national and religious divisions, tensions, conflicts and so on. Common institutional characteristics concerning membership, organisation, privileges and powers are also important and await consideration.[57] Each of these contributes, usually in combination, to an explanation of parliamentary fortunes in some European states. Beyond that it is questionable how far one can go in the formulation of general processes of change. Despite the persuasiveness of some aspects of theses which have been put forward, none of those models, typologies or schema has achieved anything near comprehensiveness.[58] In particular, there is no model which provides a consistent or convincing and encompassing explanation for the demise of some representative assemblies in seventeenth-century Europe: for example, the Castilian Cortes, French Estates-general, Danish *Rigsdag*, and estates in Naples, Sardinia, Bohemia, Austria and the Spanish Netherlands.[59]

Mid-seventeenth-century crises

The same is true of the role of representative assemblies in the spate of crises which occurred in the middle decades of the seventeenth century. Those crises ranged from civil wars and rebellions in the British Isles, France, Catalonia, Portugal, Naples and Sicily to seventeenth-century constitutional crises or confrontations in Denmark, the Dutch state and Sweden. During the 1970s H.R. Trevor-Roper triggered an historical debate when he postulated a thesis of 'general crisis', based on an attempt to prove common causes. Fortunately it serves no useful purpose to rehearse the debate here, but it is important to note one common denominator: that the crises were all precipitated by the actions or policies of monarchs or, in the Dutch case, of the princes of Orange, who represented the monarchical principle. Beyond that, however, the picture is one of great diversity, especially as far as the parliaments are concerned. In several cases they played no part at all. In Naples the parliament had been put to sleep five years before rebellion broke out in 1647. The Sicilian revolt, which began in the same summer, was a popular uprising, the leaders of whom would not have dreamt of appealing to the elitist *Parlamento*. In a similar position was the Irish Parliament. Since the mid-sixteenth century it had been one of the instruments employed by the English government to oppress the Gaelic catholic population and increasingly penalise the Anglo-Irish. It could play no part in the bloody rebellion of both Irish and Anglo-Irish in 1641.[60]

On the European continent France provided yet another example. Between 1648 and 1653 there occurred the Frondes. These were a series of revolts against prolonged war and its accompaniments of tax burdens and ever more new financial expedients imposed by a government in desperate financial need. The rebels were an unnatural coalition of princes of the blood and peasants, greater and lesser nobles, the normally royalist *parlement* of Paris and hostile provincialism. During the uprising, proposals for an Estates-general were aired. In 1649 and 1651 elections were held and *cahiers* were drawn, but each time the meeting was cancelled, although in February–March 1651 lesser nobles held a special protest assembly of their own in Paris. The rebellion failed and a national parliament ceased to be an option, even though further assemblies of lesser nobles were still demanding the recall of the Estates-general as late as 1657–59.

In contrast, there were the Spanish, British, Dutch and Swedish crises, in all of which parliaments figured at some point. In most they were active, prominent or even the very focus and dynamic of change or of resistance to change. The Catalan and Portuguese rebellions and proclaimed revolutions illustrate the problems inherent in the diverse and loose structure of a composite monarchy. The crown's financial demands on the individual territorial components of a decentralised system had to be modest if they were to be satisfied. The resumption of hostilities with the Dutch in the 1620s and the Thirty Years' War (1618–48) compelled the Spanish monarchy to increase those demands and, moreover, to spread the load. The Union of Arms was the immediate answer of Philip IV's chief minister, the Conde Duque de Olivares. It was a project to establish a common imperial defence force, towards which all territories would provide, equip and maintain a fixed quota of soldiers: Castile 44,000, Aragon 10,000 and so on. The proposed contributions of Catalonia and Portugal were 16,000 each. When Philip IV sought this, in addition to the traditional taxes, the result was a disaster in public relations between the crown and the Catalan Corts. The assembly's rejection of royal demands in 1626 was followed by a lengthy suspension and a final session ending in impasse. The failure of the Corts of 1626–32, 'a farce with irreparable consequences', was followed by mutual recriminations: on the one hand, excessive royal demands, on the other, a conspiracy by privileged groups (notably the municipal government of Barcelona, and the *diputació* or permanent committee of the Catalan Corts) to control Catalonia and sideline the crown.[61]

In 1640 a desperate Olivares billeted an army in Catalonia as a means of exerting pressure on the Corts, which he intended to call in order to revise the constitution. In doing so he triggered riots, revolt and, under the leadership of the *diputació*, a self-proclaimed independent Catalan republic. Harsh realities caused the republican ideal quickly to wither and die. Catalonia had to enlist the military support of absolutist France and the Catalan aristocracy became the hated target of the poor, unemployed and long-oppressed majority. Divided loyalties, the Frondes which diverted French military resources back into France, plague and food-shortage led to Catalan capitulation to Philip IV in 1652. He granted a general pardon and promised to respect its liberties. The rebellion and the Corts were now things of the past.[62]

As in Catalonia so in Portugal, attempts to extract wealth and manpower for military purposes alienated the local political elite. When in 1619, after a gap of thirty-eight years, the Portuguese Cortes were summoned, chiefly to welcome Philip III on his visit to Lisbon after twenty-one years as king, they presented a list of complaints. These concerned increased taxation and the crown's failure to honour promises made to it in 1582, after Philip II's acquisition of Portugal and its empire. Olivares chose to manage the kingdom and raise revenue without calling the Cortes. Then, in 1634, the alien Margaret of Savoy, Philip IV's second cousin, was appointed viceroy in order to exploit Portuguese resources more effectively. Riots across northern Portugal were followed by southern revolt and Spanish military intervention (1637–38), and a conspiracy which in 1640, when Olivares demanded assistance against the Catalan rebels, became a military coup. The duke of Braganza, head of Portugal's greatest noble house, was declared to be the legitimate ruler and acclaimed King John IV. When the Cortes were called in 1641 they recognised him as such. They also confirmed Philip II's acknowledgement of 1581, that taxation was only by the community's consent. During the Portuguese war of independence the Cortes met in 1642, 1645, 1653 and 1668. All Spanish attempts to reverse the Portuguese 'revolution' failed and, in 1668, the independence of Portugal was formally recognised. Thereafter the Cortes met only three times: in 1673, 1679 and 1698.[63]

In contrast to the Spanish crises in the Iberian peninsula, the concurrent British crisis occurred when its monarchy was not engaged in debilitating European wars. Both, however, illustrate the complex problems inherent in the management of composite monarchy. The British Isles, governed by one monarch from 1603, constituted an ethnic, national and religious mix which was rich in potential or actual hostilities: most notably, but by no means only, between Goidelic Celt and Anglo-Saxon, Scots and English, catholics and protestants. Royal attitudes sometimes reflected English prejudices. The first two Stuart British kings, like Elizabeth before them, were not crowned monarchs of Ireland and they did not visit their Irish kingdom. Meanwhile it was subject to military conquest, persecution of catholicism, and confiscation of Irish and Anglo-Irish property, which was planted by English and Scottish protestants. Although the bloody catholic rebellion of 1641–50 was a complex affair, it was to some extent the simple consequence of long-term neglect and cruel repression.

Furthermore, when royal attitudes ran counter to English ethnic prejudices, they could founder. In 1604 and 1606–7 widespread parliamentary opposition in the commons ensured that James's dreams of an Anglo-Scottish union did just that.[64] It should be added, however, that, as Jenny Wormald has shown and as noted before, James did not define in precise terms what he meant by union and, furthermore, that this lack of definition was deliberate, because of mutual Anglo-Scottish hostility to the 'British' idea. Indeed, Wormald emphasises that 'there are grounds for doubting the extent of James's commitment to a British identity'.[65] Nevertheless, the whole episode emphasises the importance of an early modern parliament as a safeguard of national liberties and identity.

Although 'union', whatever James meant by that, failed, he maintained political stability within and between England and Scotland. He achieved a lively yet peaceful latitudinarian Church in England and, in contrast to the flanking reigns of Elizabeth I and Charles I, religion was not a subject of controversy or dispute within Parliaments. He also established harmony between the English and Scottish Churches, because he sought not conformity but 'congruency' between them. When the Five Articles of Perth (1621), his attempt to introduce more ceremonial into Scottish worship, encountered stiff resistance, James did not attempt to enforce them. Peace was his priority. Not so with Charles I. He commenced his reign in Scotland in 1625 by issuing a revocation which intended to cancel all royal or ecclesiastical land grants since 1542; despite frequent rumours of a pending visit in the later 1620s and 1631 he did not go there for his coronation and first Scottish Parliament until 1633. That Parliament, in which he sat and took notes, enacted unpopular or at least highly suspect religious legislation, and imposed fresh taxes. It amounted to intervention and exploitation by a neglectful absentee king. Then in 1637 he introduced canons and a Scottish prayer book which imposed unpalatable changes.

In a composite monarchy an absentee king could not govern without the support and co-operation of the political elite and the clergy. Charles's revocation and his religious changes alienated them both. There followed within a few years a Scottish rebellion (from 1638), an English Parliament, called to fund its suppression but in which a majority were alienated by the king's record in Church and state (1640), the Irish rebellion (1641), which caused the English Parliament to challenge the untrustworthy king's constitutional right to command an army against the rebels and, finally, civil war between English royalists and parliamentarians who were, from 1643, assisted by a Scottish army. It was a British crisis, one common cause of which was Charles's pursuit of religious conformity. This did not, however, mean conformity with the Anglican Church. The king sought changes in all his Churches, the purpose of which was conformity with *his* ideal.[66]

During the civil war and the revolution which followed there was a dramatic contrast between the roles of the English and the Gaelic Parliaments. The 'Long Parliament' (1640–53), consisting of those peers and commons' members who opposed the king, organised and funded the successful war-effort against him (1642–46). A 'rump' of members, survivors of a purge by the Army which it had created, authorised the trial and execution of the king and established a republican form of government (1648–49). Throughout the revolutionary years (1649–60) Parliament remained a more or less constant feature of attempts by the victorious coalition to arrive at an enduring constitutional arrangement. Its structure, powers and life, however, were dependent on Oliver Cromwell and other military commanders, because the Army remained the sole arbiter. So, in April 1653, Cromwell expelled the 'Rump'. It was replaced, briefly, by an assembly of nominated 'saints' (July–December 1653) and then by the Parliaments of the Protectorate (1653–59). As head of the executive Protector Cromwell, increasingly a quasi-king, quickly became acquainted with some of the problems which monarchs experienced in their relations with representative assemblies. Sessions of the Protectorate Parliaments (initially single chamber but in 1657 bicameral) were marked by clashes over religion, parliamentary liberties, the constitutional place of the Army and finance. Cromwell's death (1658) was followed by the disintegration of the republic and, in 1660, the restoration of the traditional form of government. It was, however, a weaker monarchy and a stronger Parliament of lords and commons than had existed in 1640: not just in terms of specific powers, but also because there existed the precedent of a king who had been called to account by Parliament and paid the ultimate price for his faults.

Between 1639 and 1651 the Scottish assembly continued to meet as a 'full and frie' Parliament, in accordance with a new triennial act. The Parliament which enacted it lasted from August 1639 to November 1641 and the two triennial Parliaments (June 1644–March 1647 and March 1648–June 1651) which resulted effectively governed the kingdom and organised the war-effort, first against Charles I and then in support of his son. It also established a committee of the estates to sit between Parliaments.

In contrast to the English Parliament, however, the Irish and Scottish assemblies experienced a total eclipse during the British revolution. In 1649–51 Cromwell led an army to end the Irish rebellion and to defeat Scottish military support for the executed king's son, crowned Charles II at Scone. The Celtic Parliaments were suppressed and, in the Instrument of Government which, in 1653, established the Protectorate, Scots and Irish were each given thirty seats in the 460-member unicameral British Parliament at Westminster.[67] Although separate Celtic Parliaments were restored along with the monarchy, they were firmly under royal control. A solitary catholic sat in the Irish assembly which in 1661 generally upheld the massive Cromwellian confiscation of Irish catholic lands during the 1650s. It was, however, the Irish protestants who successfully resisted legislative proposals devised in England and so caused Parliament to be called no more. When, at the Restoration, the Scottish Parliament was revived, the powers which it had assumed in the 1640s were restored to the crown. It dutifully voted Charles II an annuity of £480,000 Scots for life – and even more in the following years. Furthermore, the lords of the articles returned to control parliamentary business in the king's interest.[68]

In contrast to the British, Spanish and other crises, which were characterised by violent upheaval, those in Denmark, the United Provinces and Sweden were resolved by political action within the existing constitutional structures. Only chance, however, prevented the Dutch crisis from degenerating into violence. On the other hand, the potential for crisis had been there from the inception of the new state in the sixteenth century. It was a loose republic consisting of seven privilege-protective provinces, which controlled all important decisions including tax-grants. Central government consisted of little more than the national assembly – the States-general – and the military structure controlled by the princes of Orange through the council of state and based on the office of provincial stadholder or governor. The small governing 'regent' class of about 2,000 families, however, governed the republic's cities and towns and also nominated the members of the provincial assemblies. They provided the state with some cohesion. So too did the province of Holland, which from 1616 provided more than 58 per cent of the state's revenue. There were, nonetheless, tensions within the new state, caused in particular by jealousy of Holland's preponderance and by the political ambitions of the house of Orange-Nassau. The princes provided the military leadership which helped to secure and maintain the independence of the new state. They were also surrogate monarchs, holding Court, entertaining, distributing patronage and building up a loyal following. The Holland regents, however, were troubled by Orange aspirations and ambitions. A power struggle in 1617–19 enabled Prince Maurice to carry out a purge of opponents in many towns, but Holland remained a powerful force.[69]

Renewed war with Spain required continued collaboration but then, in 1648, the regents at last achieved peace. That robbed the house of Orange-Nassau of its chief value to the republic. In this case peace triggered a crisis. Prince William II, frustrated by his failure to continue the war, eventually attempted a military occupation of Holland's most powerful city, Amsterdam, in 1650. That too failed. Then William suddenly died of smallpox. Divine intervention or chance? No matter which, it was providential for the Dutch republic. As he left no adult male heir, the regents of Holland and most other provinces left the office of stadholder vacant and so stripped down the Orange power structure. Government was now secure in the hands of the regents, operating through municipal governments, provincial assemblies and their delegates to the 22-man States-general.

Whereas the Dutch regents conducted their sometimes difficult relations with the Orange 'party' both within and outside their parliamentary assemblies, the sole political arena of the Swedish crisis was the *Riksdag*. It was there that the divisions were exposed, grievances were aired, confrontation occurred, manoeuvrings took place and a compromise achieved a modicum of consensus. The circumstances in which the diet of 1650 met have already been discussed.[70] To a considerable extent Queen Christina was the culprit. She it was who wished to remain unmarried and, despite a reluctant nobility, to abdicate in favour of her cousin Karl Gustav. Furthermore, her reckless generosity, in enriching some nobles with lands, offices and taxes, aroused the resent-ment of burghers, clergy and other nobles, who had not benefited, and of taxpaying peasants who felt their free status threatened. At the same time, it was Christina who manipulated the situation to her advantage. She encouraged the other estates to attack the nobility, who sur-rendered to her wishes in return for her protection. By a judicious distribution of clerical privileges, royal safeguards for the peasantry and offices for burghers, she then defused the crisis. The whole episode illustrates the effectiveness of the *Riksdag* as a place for the public airing and resolution of grievances, as a mechanism for prompt solutions to political problems and as a 'point of contact' between crown and community. Cousin Karl Gustav was also to demonstrate this, when he succeeded Christina as Karl X Gustav. At a meeting of the *Riksdag* in 1655 he was willing to use the other estates in order to extract from the nobility a resumption of about 25 per cent of crown grants.[71]

Fortunes of the seventeenth-century parliaments

Although no theory or model has yet encompassed the fortunes and fates of all or even most parliaments, there were undoubtedly common forces and developments impacting upon their effectiveness, and their capacity to protect the community, serve the government and maintain their integrity, durability and institutional strength. Such were autocratic tendencies, the pressure to create fiscal-military states, re-ligious, social and ethnic conflict. They were not, however, universal. Furthermore, they tended to operate in different combinations and in varying degrees of intensity. Certainly some assemblies lost their vitality or were simply no longer called, especially in the Spanish empire, but also in France, the German principalities and the Austrian-Habsburg dominions. Yet even here there was no uniform European picture. In Habsburg Hungary and the German principalities of Meckle-nburg, East Friesland, Saxony and Württemberg the Diets maintained an active and vigorous parliamentary tradition. And whilst the number of French provincial estates progressively diminished, as Dauphiné, Normandy and others ceased to be called, those in Languedoc, Brittany and Burgundy continued to control grants and collection of taxes and to attempt protection of the privileges and interests of their provinces. The case of Brittany illustrates the need to set aside the old images of a centralising French absolutism asserting control, in alliance with a bourgeoisie, over provinces and the nobility. It had three elites, noble, legal and commercial. The *grands* (nobles) and *sieurs* (rising lawyer elite) were interconnected rather than competitive. Through compromises with the crown they secured redress of local grievances, safeguarded their interests and provisioned the royal treasury. The system was one of mutual interdependence rather than of overweening royal authority, at least until the fiscal imperative began to change things in the 1620s–30s.[72]

At the opposite end of the spectrum from the 'failed' or defunct parliaments were those which grew politically from strength to strength, in the weak elective monarchies of the Holy Roman Empire and the 'noble nation' of Poland. At the same time, however, self-interest rendered them largely ineffectual. The imperial *Reichstag* and the Polish *Sejm* and *sejmiki* were all characterised by noble power. Emperors could achieve little from an assembly which was chiefly concerned with the rights and interests of the territorial princes and bishops and representatives of free cities who sat there.[73] In Poland the parliaments were a noble monopoly. From the end of the fifteenth century urban involvement in the *Sejm* was limited to Cracow, which had non-voting observer status. Noble monopoly, however, did not mean noble unity. In state and society there was often division and conflict between the greater (magnates) and lesser (*szlachta*) nobility. In order to counter such division and promote public agreement a growing emphasis was placed on the principles of *unanimity* and *unity*. The former required the consent of everyone in both houses of the *Sejm* to any proposed new law (*constitution*). In accordance with the *unity* principle one member's disapproval of a constitution rendered it void, together with others passed previously during that session. As the principles gained increasing acceptance, unproductive sessions became more frequent, especially after the union of Poland and Lithuania in 1569: eleven out of sixty-nine between 1572 and 1652. Then, in 1652, a Lithuanian member's written protest invoked the *unanimity* and *unity* principles, not just to veto a constitution, but to end the session. Everyone packed their bags and went home. This practice, known as the *liberum veto*, was regularly invoked thereafter, with paralytic effect on the national parliament. As in the Holy Roman Empire so in Poland-Lithuania, the political power of a parliament, as expressed in its membership, was no substitute for efficiency.

There were, however, more clear-cut success stories. The relatively young Swedish *Riksdag* began as an informal, often open-air assembly. By the mid-seventeenth century it had grown into a powerful consultative, law-making and taxing parliament with an unusual sense of community. Later in the century its promising future seemed to end with the Swedish absolutism of Karl XI and Karl XII, but it re-emerged with greater power in 1720.

None of these success stories, however, matches those of the Maritime Powers, the United Provinces and England. The Dutch regents and their assemblies played a vital part in establishing an independent republic, creating a fiscal-military state to protect it and (in 1648–50) success-fully preserving it from an Orangist threat. In England the civil war and revolution of 1642–60 laid the foundations of parliamentary supremacy. The second revolution of 1688–89, in which parliament played a central role, secured and confirmed that supremacy. Parliament resolved that King James II had 'abdicated', the throne was 'vacant' and that William of Orange was king.[74] It was appropriate that the house of Orange played such an important part in the Dutch war of independence from Spain and the English revolution of 1688–89, both of which were so vital in the parliamentary history of their respective countries. European parliaments had chequered fortunes. We need to keep in mind the English, Dutch and other examples treated above. Then it becomes clear that, when we look at early modern European history from the parliamentary perspective, 'the triumph of absolutism' is a phrase which needs to be significantly qualified, perhaps even set aside.

Notes

1 W.B. Patterson, *King James VI and I and the Reunion of Christendom* (Cambridge, 1997), pp. 155–8, 294–6 and n.7; D.L. Smith, *A History of the Modern British Isles, 1603–1707. The Double Crown* (Oxford, 1998), pp. 31, 36–9.

2 Patterson, *King James VI and I*, ch.6.

3 Smith, *Modern British Isles*, p. 33.

4 I.A.A. Thompson, 'Crown and Cortes in Castile, 1590–1665' *PER* 2, 1 (June 1982), p. 31.

5 See above p. 89.

6 J.M. Hayden, *France and the Estates General of 1614* (Cambridge, 1974), pp. 54, 62–3.

7 For discussion of the significance of the large number of king's officers returned to the third estate, see below, p. 133.

8   J. Miller, ed., *Absolutism in Seventeenth Century Europe* (London, 1990), pp. 4, 64; R. Mousnier, *The Institutions of France under the Absolute Monarchy, 1598–1789* 2 vols (Chicago, 1984), vol. 2, pp. 221–6; R. Bonney, *The European Dynastic States, 1494–1660* (Oxford, 1992), pp. 322–3; J. Russell Major, *The Monarchy, the Estates and the Aristocracy in Renaissance France* (London, 1988), VIII, pp. 258–9.

9   L.J. Reeve, 'The politics of war finance in an age of confessional strife: a comparative Anglo-European view' *Parergon*, New Ser., 14, 1 (1996), pp. 87–9.

10 Miller, ed., *Absolutism*, pp. 4–8; A.R. Myers, *Parliaments and Estates of Europe to 1789* (London, 1975), pp. 113–14; see below, pp. 131–2.

11 Bonney, *European Dynastic States*, pp. 327–8; P.T. Hoffman, 'Early modern France, 1450–1700', in P.T. Hoffman and K. Norberg, eds, *Fiscal Crises, Liberty and Representative Government, 1450–1789* (Stanford, CA, 1994), pp. 236–7, 239, 242–3. Reeve cites the crown's ordinary revenue in 1636 as 52 million *livres tournois*, of which 33.7 million was spent on war. Reeve, 'Politics of war finance', pp. 94–5; R. Bonney, *The Limits of Absolutism in Ancien Régime France*, XII (Aldershot, 1995), p. 116; J.B. Collins, *The State in Early Modern France* (Cambridge, 1995), p. 51; J. Russell Major, *From Renaissance Monarchy to Absolute Monarchy. French Kings, Nobles and Estates* (London, 1994), pp. 278–9, 297–9.

12 Fortea Pérez, pp. 118–20; see above, pp. 89–90; C. Jago, 'Review essay. Crown and Cortes in early-modern Spain' *PER* 12, 2 (Dec. 1992), pp. 181, 183–4; Miller, ed., *Absolutism*, pp. 75–6, 79–82; Reeve, 'Politics of war finance', p. 96; Thompson, 'Crown and Cortes, 1590–1665', pp. 34–7.

13 C. Jago, 'Habsburg absolutism and the Cortes of Castile', *AHR* 86, 2 (1981), pp. 311–17; ibid., 'Parliament, subsidies and constitutional change in Castile, 1601–1621' *PER* 13, 2 (Dec. 1993), pp. 123–37; Thompson, 'Crown and Cortes', pp. 32–3, 37–8.

14 I.A.A. Thompson, *Crown and Cortes* (Aldershot, 1993), VIII, p. 1.

15 Ibid., VIII, pp. 58–60, 64, 66.

16 I.A.A. Thompson, 'Castile: absolutism, constitutionalism and liberty', in P.T. Hoffman and K. Norberg, eds, *Fiscal Crises, Liberty, and Representative Government, 1450–1789* (Stanford, CA, 1994), pp. 189–95; Jago, 'Habsburg Absolutism', pp. 319–22, 324; H.G. Koenigsberger, 'Parliaments in the sixteenth century and beyond', in R.W. Davis, ed., *The Origins of Modern Freedom in the West* (Stanford, CA, 1995), pp. 276–7; Thompson, 'Crown and Cortes, 1590–1665', pp. 41–4; ibid., *Crown and Cortes*, IV, p. 66, VII, pp. 130–3, VIII, pp. 70–2; Jago, 'Crown and Cortes', pp. 190–1.

17 See above, p. 93.

18 X. Gil, 'Crown and Cortes in early modern Aragon: reassessing revisionisms' *PER* 13, 2 (Dec. 1993), pp. 112, 117–19, 121.

19 Ibid., pp. 120–1.

20 Joan-Pau Rubiés, 'Reason of state and constitutional thought in the crown of Aragon, 1580–1640' *HJ* 38, 1 (1995), pp. 20–1; Gil, 'Crown and Cortes', pp. 112– 15, 120–1; P. Sanz, 'The cities in the Aragonese Cortes in the medieval and early modern periods' *PER* 14, 2 (Dec. 1994), pp. 100–1; Thompson, *Crown and Cortes*, IV, p. 65.

21   A.J. Veenendaal, 'Fiscal crises and constitutional freedom in the Netherlands, 1450–1795', in Hoffman and Norberg, eds, *Fiscal Crises*, pp. 107–10, 133–4; Reeve, 'Politics of war finance', pp. 91–4; Koenigsberger, 'Parliaments in the sixteenth century and beyond', pp. 296–8.

22   Reeve, 'Politics of war finance', pp. 100–7.

23   S.R. Gardiner, ed., *The Constitutional Documents of the Puritan Revolution, 1625–1660* (3rd edn revised, Oxford, 1968), p. 83.

24   M. Roberts, *Gustavus Adolphus* (2nd edn, London, 1992), pp. 87–8; A.F. Upton, 'The Swedish *Riksdag* and the English Parliament in the seventeenth century – some comparisons', in N. Stjernquist, ed., *The Swedish Riksdag in an International Perspective* (Stockholm, 1989), p. 122; M. Roberts, ed., *Sweden as a Great Power, 1611–1697* (London, 1968), pp. 7–13, 150; M.F. Metcalf, ed., *The Riksdag: A History of the Swedish Parliament* (Stockholm, 1987), pp. 61–4, 68–71; Reeve, 'Politics of war finance', pp. 90–1. In most years between Gustav II's intervention in Germany in 1630 and the peace of Oliva (1660) which ended the northern wars, Sweden was at war, for example with Poland (1632–35, 1655–60), Denmark (1643–45, 1657–60) and the Habsburgs (to 1648 and 1658–60).

25   Roberts, ed., *Sweden as a Great Power*, p. 150.

26   Bonney, *European Dynastic States*, pp. 316–17; Jago, 'Habsburg absolutism', p. 307.

27   See below, Chapter 6.

28   Hoffman and Norberg, eds, *Fiscal Crises*, pp. 1–2.

29   J.A. Vann, *The Making of a State. Württemberg, 1593–1793* (London, 1984), pp. 89–96.

30   F.L. Carsten, *Princes and Parliaments in Germany* (Oxford, 1959), pp. 228–39.

31   Ibid., pp. 392–406; H.J. Cohn, 'Early modern German princes and their subjects' *European History Quarterly* 21 (1991), pp. 241–2.

32   Bonney, *European Dynastic States*, pp. 527–8.

33   Carsten, *Princes and Parliaments*, pp. 173–82.

34   F.L. Carsten, *The Origins of Prussia* (Oxford, 1954), pp. 205–22, 228, 251; H.W. Koch, 'Brandenburg-Prussia', in Miller, ed., *Absolutism*, pp. 134, 144–7.

35   A. Marongiu, *Medieval Parliaments. A Comparative Study* (London, 1968), pp. 212–13, 216–17; H.G. Koenigsberger, 'The Italian parliaments from their origins to the end of the 18th century', in *Politicians and Virtuosi* (London, 1986), pp. 45–6, 49–51.

36   Bonney, *European Dynastic States*, pp. 328–9.

37   E. Ladewig Petersen and Knud J.V. Jesperson, 'Two revolutions in early modern Denmark', in E.I. Kouri and T. Scott, eds, *Politics and Society in Reformation Europe* (London, 1987), pp. 486–98.

38   No longer, since 1627, including the peasantry.

39   Mousnier, *Institutions of France*, pp. 218–19, 221–8; G.A. Rothrock, 'Officials and king's men: a note on the possibilities of royal control in the Estates General' *French Historical Studies* 2, 4 (Fall, 1962), pp. 504–8; J.M. Hayden, 'Deputies and *Qualités*: the Estates General of 1614' *French Historical Studies* 3, 4 (Fall, 1964), pp. 513–14, 519–24.

40   See below, pp. 148–9; Metcalf, ed., *Riksdag*, pp. 73–5; M. Roberts, 'Queen Christina and the general crisis of the seventeenth century' *P&P* 22 (July 1962), pp. 36–59.

41 J. Miller, 'The Polish nobility and the Renaissance monarchy: the execution of the laws' movement: part one' *PER* 3, 3 (Dec. 1983), pp. 70–1, 74–9, 86–7; ibid., 'Part two' *PER* 4, 1 (June 1984), pp. 1–10, 18–19.

42 See below, pp. 143–4.

43 In 1621, for example, the entire committee of the articles consisted of men who were, according to Secretary Melrose, devoted to James's service. When it presented the Five Articles to the full parliament, 76 voted in favour but 48 against, with 18 abstaining. According to Julian Goodare, the division was clearly one between 'court' and 'country'. J. Goodare, 'The Scottish Parliament of 1621' *HJ* 38, 1 (1995), pp. 29–30, 32–45.

44 S.G. Ellis, *Tudor Ireland. Crown, Community and the Conflict of Cultures, 1470–1603* (London, 1985), pp. 257–8; see below, pp. 174–5.

45 D.L. Smith, *The Stuart Parliaments, 1603–1689* (Oxford, 1999), pp. 104–6; G.P.V. Akrigg, *Jacobean Pageant* (London, 1962), p. 48.

46 S. Vilfan, 'Crown, estates and the financing of defence in Inner Austria, 1500–1630', in R.J.W. Evans and T.V. Thomas, eds, *Crown, Church and Estates. Central European Politics in the Sixteenth and Seventeenth Centuries* (London, 1991), pp. 76–7.

47 Koenigsberger, 'Parliaments in the sixteenth century and beyond', pp. 283–4; G. Parker, ed., *The Thirty Years' War* (2nd edn, London and New York, 1997), pp. 14–15, 19.

48 Ferdinand claimed both kingdoms by inheritance. See map on pp. viii–ix.

49 Parker, ed., *Thirty Years' War*, pp. 4–8; Koenigsberger, 'Parliaments in the sixteenth century and beyond', pp. 283–5; J. Bérenger, 'The Austrian Lands', in Miller, ed., *Absolutism*, pp. 160, 164–7, 171–4; H.G. Koenigsberger, 'Composite states, representative institutions and the American Revolution' *BIHR* 62 (1989), pp. 139–40; R.J.W. Evans, 'Habsburg Monarchy and Bohemia, 1526–1848', in M. Greengrass, ed., *Conquest and Coalescence* (London, 1991), pp. 142–3.

50 Mousnier, *Institutions of France*, vol. 2, pp. 223–6. Although the third estate's assertion of full royal sovereignty over the Church was defeated by the joint resistance of clergy and nobility, Louis XIV secured its adoption in 1682.

51 Smith, *Stuart Parliaments*, pp. 117–19; Gardiner, ed., *Constitutional Documents*, pp. 90–1.

52 J. Morrill, 'A British patriarchy? Ecclesiastical imperialism under the early Stuarts', in A. Fletcher and P. Roberts, eds, *Religion, Culture and Society in Early Modern Britain* (Cambridge, 1994), pp. 214–21.

53 Ibid., p. 216.

54 Miller, ed., *Absolutism*, pp. 221–2.

55 Koenigsberger, 'Parliaments in the sixteenth century and beyond', pp. 273–4.

56 See above, p. 133 and below, pp. 148–9.

57 See below, Chapters 6 and 7.

58 H.G. Koenigsberger, 'Dominium regale or dominium politicum et regale: monarchies and parliaments in early modern Europe', in *Politicians and Virtuosi* (London, 1986), pp. 4–25. See Koenigsberger's critical analysis of attempts to achieve general explanations. I am in entire agreement, of course, with his contention that 'we should look for answers that go beyond the incidental, the detailed history of each country'.

59 See above, pp. 116, 118, 121, 130–2, 138–9.

60 C. Brady, 'England's defence and Ireland's reform: the dilemma of the Irish viceroys, 1541–1641', in B. Bradshaw and J. Morrill, eds, *The British Problem, c.1534–1707* (London, 1996), pp. 89–117.

61 R. Bonney, *Society and Government in France under Richelieu and Mazarin, 1624–61* (London, 1988), pp. 153, 172–3, 180, 182–5, 188, 191; ibid., *Limits of Absolutism*, IV, pp. 76, 81–2, V, pp. 367–80; J.L. Palos, 'The Habsburg Monarchy and the Catalan Corts: the failure of a relationship' *PER* 13, 2 (Dec. 1993), pp. 139–43; J.H. Elliott, *Imperial Spain, 1469–1716* (London, 1969), pp. 325–8; J.H. Elliott, *The Revolt of the Catalans, 1598–1640* (Cambridge, 1984), chs VIII, IX.

62 Koenigsberger, 'Parliaments in the sixteenth century and beyond', pp. 278–9; Elliott, *Revolt of the Catalans*, ch.XVI and pp. 539–41; ibid., *Imperial Spain*, pp. 334–50.

63 P. Cardim, 'Ceremonial and ritual in the Cortes of Portugal (1581–1698)' *PER* 12, 1 (June 1992), p. 13.

64 Smith, *Stuart Parliaments*, pp. 104–6.

65 J. Wormald, 'James VI, James I and the identity of Britain', in Bradshaw and Morrill, eds, *The British Problem*, pp. 148–71; J. Wormald, 'The creation of Britain: multiple kingdoms or core and colonies?' *TRHS*, 6th ser., II (1992), pp. 175–94.

66 J. Morrill, 'The British problem', in Bradshaw and Morrill, eds, *The British Problem*, pp. 27–32; M. Lynch, *Scotland. A New History* (London, 1994), pp. 247, 266–7.

67 A single coat of arms for England and Scotland might have given James VI and I some posthumous compensatory pleasure. J.R. Young, 'The Scottish Parliament, 1639–1661' PhD, University of Glasgow, 1993, Vol. 1, pp. 11, 28, 30–1, Vol. 2, App.1.

68 Ibid., Vol. 1, pp. 498–515; K.M. Brown, *Kingdom or Province? Scotland and the Regal Union, 1603–1715* (New York, 1992), pp. 144–5; Smith, *Modern British Isles*, p. 211; J. Barnard, 'Scotland and Ireland in the later Stewart Monarchy', in S.G. Ellis and S. Barber, *Conquest and Union. Fashioning a British State, 1485–1725* (London, 1995), pp. 259, 266; Young, 'Scottish Parliament', pp. 507, 511.

69 G. Parker, *Europe in Crisis, 1598–1648* (Brighton, 1980), pp. 141–5.

70 See above, p. 133.

71 A.F. Upton, 'Sweden', in Miller, ed., *Absolutism*, pp. 102–3, 107–9; Roberts, 'Queen Christina and the general crisis', pp. 38–45.

72 Koenigsberger, 'Dominium regale', pp. 3–4, 20; see above, pp. 126–7; J.B. Collins, *Classes, Estates and Order in Early Modern Brittany* (Cambridge, 1994), pp. 3–7, 23, 156–7, 179, 271–7, 279, 285–6.

73 R. Bonney, *The European Dynastic States, 1494–1660* (Oxford, 1992), pp. 319–20.

74 Smith, *Stuart Parliaments*, pp. 163–6.

PART TWO

The Characteristics of
Early Modern Parliaments

6

Representation and Membership[1]

The socio-political framework of parliaments

THOSE WHO were entitled to sit in parliament by virtue of election or selection, property qualification, social status or royal office did not, so far as we can tell, view the approach of parliaments with an air of excitement. In the normal course of events they did not anticipate that the forthcoming assembly would make the earth move and shake. Members did not ride up to early modern parliaments with their saddle-bags stuffed full of Declarations of the Rights of Man. Nor did they regard them as opportunities to demand the establishment of popular government or the implementation of democratic ideals.

On the other hand, grievances were commonly aired in the parliament-time, because their presentation and redress became and remained a common legitimate function of medieval and early modern European parliaments. But beyond this the men who sat in early modern representative assemblies would not go. It would not have occurred to them to do so. Democracy and popular government were not desired or contemplated objectives because their political (and therefore parliamentary) attitudes, beliefs and priorities were conditioned, even determined by the socio-political framework of their age:

1 Kings had the God-given right and duty to rule. Of course there were always exceptions: when sovereignty was vested in the provincial assemblies of the new Dutch state and when, for a decade (1649–60), England was a republic. Divine-right kingship, however, remained the European norm.
2 Nobles not only constituted the traditional warrior class. They also occupied a traditional role as the monarch's natural counsellors and 'a source of authority within society at large'.[2]

3 The prevailing concept of society was of one structured in social
   orders or 'estates'. It was a tripartite structure, consisting of those
   who prayed, fought or worked: clergy, nobility and the rest.

Conventional medieval and early modern thought, which embodied
these idealised images of rulers and the social orders, received corporate
expression in representative assemblies. A parliament was a royal institution, summoned by the monarch to assist in the business of government.
According to a generally accepted fiction, when one was called it was
the kingdom which was convoked.[3] In England, according to Thomas
Audley in 1542, Parliament represented the 'whole body of the realm';
in his draft parliamentary sermon in 1484 the bishop of Lincoln referred
to 'thys grete body of Englonde'; Henry VIII grandly pronounced in
1543 that during Parliament 'we as head and you as members are
conjoined and knit together into one body politic'; and in Elizabeth's
reign Sir Thomas Smith declared that 'Every Englishman is intended to
be there present, either in person or by [proxy]'.[4] It was the same everywhere. Medieval and early modern parliaments represented the whole
territory, whether it was a kingdom, duchy or county. In other words,
'deputies represented "the land", that is, a territory understood by its
inhabitants to be a *communis patria*'. Even when the Castilian Cortes was
reduced to thirty-six *procuradores* from eighteen cities it was called the
'kingdom', whilst the noble monopoly of Poland's *Sejm* was 'the noble
nation'. In Aragon, and in Naples, Sicily and Sardinia too, the king held
parliaments with 'all the inhabitants of the kingdom'; in Friuli members
were regarded as *electi pro patria* and in France the Estates-general
represented 'all the people' or 'all the subjects', and so on. Marongiu
offered a basically sound definition of such assemblies: '[P]arliament – or
the estates or *bracci* of parliament – formed a politically representative
body, representing the subjects in the structure of the State'.[5]

The place of nobles in parliaments reflected their position as
members of the social and political elite. Within and outside the assemblies they had the prestige and muscle denied to the lower orders or
third estate. This was reflected, for example, in the Swedish ordinance
for the house of nobility, which was issued in 1626. Its purpose was to
enhance the place of the noble estate by organising it into a hierarchy of
three grades: counts and barons; men of lower noble rank, but whose
forebears had served as councillors of the realm; and lesser nobles or
'gentry'. The estate's business was to be led by an officially appointed

speaker (*lantmarskalk*). 'Henceforth, the Nobility would clearly stand out as the leading Estate of the Riksdag; its character as a "public estate" was assured.'[6]

Not only in the *Riksdag* but in most assemblies, both general and regional, the nobles enjoyed a prominent, even dominant place, especially in the Bohemian *Sněm* and district Diets, the assemblies of the Austrian and German principalities, the imperial *Reichstag* and Poland's *Sejm* and *sejmiki*. In the Polish *Sejm*, the Diets of many German states and the Aragonese *Cortes* the greater and lesser nobility were separately represented. When the Polish *Sejm* became bicameral in the early sixteenth century, the magnates and *szlachta* virtually monopolised the senate and chamber. The bicameral Hungarian and Bohemian Diets were similarly recruited from magnates and lesser nobility. The English nobility might appear to be an exception. They shared the house of lords with the bishops (and, until the dissolution of the monasteries in the 1530s, some abbots too). The other chamber, the co-equal house of commons, was increasingly dominated by sub-noble country gentry who were returned not only for the shires, but also as carpet-bagging members for the towns, despite the existence of residential laws. Nevertheless, the nobles' continued prominence in Court, council, central and local government service and their many links of marriage, kinship and patronage with the commons' gentry ensured a sustained parliamentary influence.

The collective socio-political strength of the nobility, however, was not always transformed into an effective parliamentary force. The Polish *Sejm*, for example, was characterised by magnate-*szlachta* divisions. As illustrated in the Estates-general of 1614, the French nobility displayed neither leadership, organisation nor initiative. Frequently members of a highly competitive status group brought their external conflicts and rivalries with them into the assembly. In the Castilian Cortes they 'acted with a lack of procedural discipline that reflected their internal divisions and their political incoherence as an estate'. Often, however, many did not even bother to turn up. That was true of both English and Castilian nobles in the medieval parliament and Cortes. Although in England the lords' attendance dramatically improved from the time of Thomas Cromwell's ascendancy in the 1530s, that was not the case in Scotland. Apathy, disunity, lack of interest or organising ability: all or any of these could and sometimes did diminish or neutralise aristocratic power potential.[7]

Parliamentary structures

Parliamentary structures incorporated and reflected the organisation of European society into a hierarchy of estates. It was, as Koenigsberger writes, 'the crystallisation of powerful social groups into estates . . . which came to determine the form of representative assemblies'.[8] There was, however, no single, standardised form throughout Christian Europe. There were, for example, significant structural differences ranging from composite bodies, in which all sat together in one room, to four-chamber parliaments. There was also diversity in the groups actually represented, though these usually included the politically significant orders and, with the usual exception of the peasantry, those who paid taxes. The classic structure which had evolved in many medieval communities was the tricameral parliament, in which the three orders of clergy, nobility and third estate, sitting separately, were all represented. It existed, for example, in some of the dukedoms, lordships and other territories in the Netherlands, such as Artois, Brabant and Hainault; in Portugal, where the king called representatives of the clergy, nobles and people (*povo*); in Catalonia and Valencia; in Castile, until the gradual withdrawal of the first and second estates during the fifteenth century; and in Friuli in northern Italy. The parliament of colonial Sardinia had three *staments*: ecclesiastical, military (feudal lords) and 'royal' (consisting of cities, towns and villages on the royal demesne). It was an import, structurally modelled on the *brazos* of the Catalan Corts. Although the Sicilian *Parlamento* pre-dated that of Sardinia, from the thirteenth century, under the Crown of Aragon, it gradually acquired the characteristics and structure of the 'mainland' assemblies: three *bracci*, the ecclesiastical, military and domanial. The French Estates-general also consisted of three estates, but it was only from 1560 onwards that they sat separately.[9]

The Holy Roman Empire and the Habsburg territories (some within but others beyond the *Reich*) abounded in assemblies of all kinds and composition, ranging from the imperial Diet and the parliaments of principalities and ecclesiastical territories to *Landschaften*, urban and rural, of smaller areas. Variety rather than uniformity characterised such proliferation.[10] Nevertheless, especially at the beginning of the early modern period, the three-chamber parliament was much in evidence. The structure of the *Reichstag* reflected political rather than social organisation. So those ecclesiastics who sat there did so as territorial prince-bishops, rather than as churchmen, and three of them, the archbishops of Mainz, Cologne and Trier, were members of the college of electors who chose the emperor. Nevertheless, by the later fifteenth century the overall structure was tricameral: three colleges of electors, numerous territorial princes, many of whom were prince-bishops, and about sixty-five imperial free cities. The tripartite parliamentary organisation was repeated elsewhere in Germany in the majority of *Landtage* (assemblies) which had evolved in the principalities, though they followed the more normal estate pattern of clergy, nobility and towns. One common denominator was the parliamentary dominance of the landed lords: electors and territorial princes in the *Reichstag* and nobles in the assemblies of both German principalities and Habsburg hereditary lands.[11]

The classic tricameral estate structure, accommodating clergy, nobles and towns, was, as previously stated, not common to all European kingdoms, principalities, colonies and other territories. There were variations in both the structure and composition of late medieval parliaments and further changes would occur due to political, religious and social developments during the sixteenth and seventeenth centuries. Three assemblies, those of Aragon and Scandinavia, were unusual in each having four chambers. There were two *brazos* for the Aragonese noble estate. One accommodated the upper nobility and the other the *hidalgos* (lesser nobles) and *caballeros* (gentry). According to Xavier Gil, this marked the importance of the nobility in a society 'shaped by the trials of the Reconquest' of Aragon from Islam.[12] In the Swedish *Riksdag* and Danish *Rigsdag* the clergy, nobility and towns were supplemented by representatives of free, taxpaying peasantry. Furthermore, even as late as 1611 the number of Swedish parliamentary estates was uncertain and free miners, army officers and bailiffs were all possible additions.

At the other end of the spectrum was the unicameral assembly, exemplified by the Neapolitan and Scottish parliaments. Until the fifteenth century the assemblies of the kingdom of Naples consisted only of magnates and barons. Under Aragonese rule the towns were sometimes represented, but it was only during the reign of Ferdinand the Catholic (1479–1516) that all three estates of clergy, nobles and townsmen began to be summoned. They did not, however, sit and vote separately, but altogether as one body in a single chamber. Similarly, in the Scottish Parliament, officers of state, bishops and (until the Reformation) abbots, nobles and burgesses from thirty to forty (by 1603 fifty) royal burghs (which were directly under royal control) all sat and voted together in the same chamber. Clergy, nobility and burgesses constituted what was increasingly recognised as the three estates of Parliament, although this idea did not entirely replace the older concept of 'the community of the realm'. The three estates continued through the Reformation, despite the unprecedented attendance of about a hundred lairds (variously known also as gentry or barons of the shire). Over eighty also appeared in 1571–72, but they were still not accommodated within the three estates. Then an act of 1587 incorporated them when it created a system of representation by elected shire commissioners. Despite the decline in bishops' powers and numbers, due to the presbyterian Reformation, James VI prevented the demise of the clerical estate and resuscitated it. So from 1587 Parliament comprised four estates – clergy, nobles, burgh and shire commissioners – all of whom continued to assemble and vote together. From 1638 four estates became three when the episcopal office was abolished. In 1661, however, bishops and the clerical estate in parliament were restored.[13] When new seating arrangements were issued for the unicameral Parliament in the following year, their importance and status were acknowledged because 'non presume to sit upon the benshes save the nobilitie and clergie'. The single chamber structure continued until the Anglo-Scottish union of 1707 brought to an end the Parliament of Scotland.[14]

When that occurred, the Scots were given representation in the bicameral English Parliament, where, from the fourteenth century, the episcopate and peerage sat in the house of lords and representatives of English and (from Henry VIII's reign) Welsh shires and boroughs were elected to the house of commons. This continuity was broken only when there were experiments with nominated and unicameral assemblies following Charles I's execution in 1649. Tradition and conservatism, however, gradually reined in even the regicide regime of the 1650s. In 1657 the first bicameral protectorate assembly was a milestone on the path back to the parliamentary trinity of king, lords and commons. This became a constitutional reality at the Restoration in 1660.[15] The Irish Parliament of two houses was a colonial copy of the English model. That bicameral model, however, was not an English creation which was unique in Europe. Parliaments with a two-chamber structure were common. These might be the simple consequence of one estate's apathy, indolence, deliberate exclusion or voluntary detachment. In Piedmont, for example, the clergy was absent by choice, and so its bicameral form occurred by default.[16] In the French *pays d'états*, those provinces with their own assemblies, all three estates had originally attended. In many cases, however, individual estates, even entire assemblies, ceased to meet due to sheer lack of interest or the burdens involved. Elsewhere, in Bohemia, Poland and the eastern German principalities, upper clergy and nobles came together in one chamber, whilst lesser members of rural and urban elites formed another. In the sixteenth century, after the partition of Hungary caused by a Turkish invasion in 1526, a parliamentary assembly developed in the Habsburg-controlled western strip. As in England, the upper chamber consisted of prelates and magnates and the lower of representatives of the country gentry and towns. Russell Major argues that, as the English Parliament was not unique, the union of estates in a bicameral structure 'cannot be considered a fundamental cause of the triumph of constitutional government in England'. However, Koenigsberger's observation may be instructive: that it was in England, Poland and Hungary, which had such parliamentary structures, 'that the assemblies triumphed over the monarchy'.[17]

Changes in membership and structure

It is clear that one cannot write about an identifiable pattern of development in European parliamentary structures and composition. Some bore little or no relationship to estate representation. The Flemish assembly effectively consisted of three great cities – Bruges, Ghent and Ypres – and the wealthy region of the *Franc de Bruges*, between the coast and Bruges. The assembly of Holland comprised Amsterdam and five other cities, each with one vote and nobles with a single collective vote.[18] Furthermore, over the centuries membership and organisation of many European parliaments were altered by a range of historical developments, political, religious and ethnic, social and economic. A much-studied case is the detachment of the prelates and nobles from the medieval Cortes of Castile and, after their summons by Charles I in 1527 and 1538, a royal decision to end their participation in parliamentary meetings. This left a Cortes of thirty-six *procuradores*, representing eighteen cities (rising to forty and twenty-two respectively under Philip IV). It was not, however, a weak assembly and its position was strengthened by the *millones* arrangement, which placed the crown–Cortes relationship on a contractual basis. Individual nobles displayed a renewed interest in parliamentary meetings and, although the noble *brazo* was never recalled, in the seventeenth century some, including royal ministers and councillors, entered the Cortes through election as *procuradores*. Whatever their motives – royal control, personal, political or financial advantage – nobles became a regular element of the Cortes' membership. The increased power and importance of the Cortes as a consequence of the *millones* may be sufficient explanation for the aristocratic presence.[19]

The reappearance of individual Castilian nobles does not alter the fact that the Cortes had become and remained a unicameral assembly. The Württemberg estates experienced similar change. In the early sixteenth century the nobility refused to accept the duke's sovereignty. They seceded from the state and therefore from the assembly. The prelates ceased to attend as an estate when the Reformation occurred. Under Duke Christopher (1550–68) they asked to return and sit with the towns as they had done in the past. Thereafter the Diet consisted of a single deliberating chamber. It was composed of members of the urban elite and prelates who had become socially integrated with them. In many European medieval and early modern parliaments the clergy retained an important place: in the senate of the Polish *Sejm*, the English house of lords and as one of the four estates in the Swedish *Riksdag*. Elsewhere, especially in sixteenth-century Germany, the clerical estate was sometimes affected by the Reformation. Clerical estates, however, did not usually disappear from assemblies where they were retained by protestant rulers. Volker Press explains why: 'Protestant prelates, from now on more dependent upon the favour of the prince, proved to be instruments of princely influence on the diets'.[20] Of course there were, as usual, exceptions: so the Reformation did remove the first estate from the assemblies in Brandenburg, Prussia and Hesse.

Socio-economic change also had a widespread impact on parliamentary membership. The growth of urban population, economy and therefore taxable wealth made the representation of cities and towns increasingly important for rulers and ruled alike.[21] Economic growth also assisted social mobility, especially where, as A.F. Upton argues for Sweden-Finland, the 'structure was rigidly hierarchical, but it was not a closed hierarchy, all estates were open to recruitment from below'.[22] Men on the rise also became eligible for election to parliaments. In Scotland the lairds or barons of the shire became a fourth estate by the statute of 1587.[23] The shire seats in the English house of commons were too few to satisfy the appetite of the gentry. This was a numerous and multiplying social group. As Sir Thomas Smith observed in the 1560s, gentlemen 'be made good cheape in England. For whosoever studieth the lawes of the realme, who studieth in the universities, who professeth liberall sciences and, to be shorte, who can live idly and without manuall labour, and will beare the port, charge and countenaunce of a gentleman, he . . . shall be taken for a gentleman.' The parliamentary aspirations of this burgeoning, largely rural, land-based class were increasingly frustrated by the lack of seats. In Elizabeth I's reign, for example, there was an unchanging total of ninety knights of the shire, whereas the number of borough seats increased from 308 to 372. Since the fifteenth century, gentry had 'invaded' the boroughs, ignored the statutory residential qualification for membership and secured election to the commons. An attempt to remove the qualification failed in 1571 and the political nation continued to ignore its existence in practice. This may have been acceptable to the crown if, as Norman Ball argues, the new seats were intended to reinforce its managerial network in the commons in order to carry through a growing volume of business.[24]

Occupational escalators provided upwardly mobile access to parliament with its opportunities for public performance, profit and reputation, royal approval, favour and reward. This was especially true of lawyers. Their parliamentary services were highly valued: for example, the *licenciados* who advised and assisted the Castilian *procuradores*; the preponderance of ingratiating lawyers who, in their search for offices and promotion, often represented more than one town in the domanial house of the Sicilian *Parlamento*; the French lawyers who, for example, provided the president and clerks of the third estate at Pontoise in 1561; and the English common lawyers who drafted and scrutinised legislation, sat on many committees, spoke often in debate, hunted precedents and, but for the occasional exception, virtually monopolised the speakership of the house of commons.[25]

Not that the upward mobility, public prominence and importance of lawyers, facilitated particularly by the early modern state's demand for legal expertise, were widely welcomed. To some extent that was the consequence of an undying prejudice, summed up by an English gentleman, Thomas Wilson. He wrote in 1600 that the fortunate Isle of Anglesey boasted 'they never had lawyers nor foxes'.[26] In France the rise of third estate lawyers to occupy many places in the judiciary and to become *noblesse de robe* could have parliamentary repercussions if it appeared to diminish noble patronage prospects. Noble resentment was vocally expressed in the Estates-general of 1614–15, when only nineteen of the 190 deputies (or thereabouts) of the third estate did not hold administrative, judicial or financial offices. Whether or not these royal officials were 'king's men', they and their kind were the villains targeted by the nobility who demanded a large and specified share of central and regional offices. The third estate hit back. It demanded an end to royal pensions for nobles whose 'loyalty and service were in fact the king's natural due' and should not require reward. An attempted conciliation by the third estate went disastrously wrong when its spokesman told the nobility that it 'must recognise the Third Estate as its brother'. The *gentilshommes*' furious response was that 'We do not want to be called brothers by cobblers and bootmakers'. The clash of orders and their deference to the king as arbiter contributed to an unproductive session and it illustrates the possible parliamentary consequences of upward mobility.[27] As usual, however, there was a gap between prejudice and reality, because, as we have seen, some of the *noblesse de robe* were, in origin, *noblesse de race*. Functional mobility and compatibility, rather than hostility and separateness between sword and robe, characterised areas as far apart as Brittany, Provence and Aix. Old and new squabbled over the robe's social pretensions and the sword's hunger for more offices, but they also intermarried and had a common outlook and purpose.[28]

The nearest to a peasant in the Estates-general of 1614–15 was Constantin Housset, who, according to Mousnier, '*may* have been a wealthy plowman'. It has already been observed that, in some other parliaments such as West Friesland, Scandinavia and Alpine Switzerland and Tyrol, a peasant elite was represented and it constituted an active and important component. This was, to some extent, because of its economic importance and the recognition of its place as a free, land-holding, taxpaying group in the community. These characteristics, however, are not sufficient to explain the phenomenon of peasant representation. According to Blickle, it was, in two important instances, the existence of an 'autonomous community', which evolved because of the isolation imposed by physical geography. So from the thirteenth to the fifteenth century there developed peasant assemblies in 'largely self-governing communities' in the inner Swiss valleys.[29] In Sweden, a land of dense forests and difficult communications between settled areas, the peasantry were present and politically active in both local assemblies and provincial gatherings. As the national parliament, the *Riksdag*, developed, they were a component part. When an independent Sweden and national monarchy emerged they were there too, at Vasteras, the first great Vasa assembly, in 1527. Peasant representation at all levels was, as Erik Lönnroth argues, 'a reflection of the social reality'. Isolation, distance and the terrain gave the peasants 'real power, and to a certain extent [they] knew how to use it'. They proved incapable of concerted organised action across the country, but at least they had the capacity and opportunity to participate fully in law-making, to approve taxation and to press for redress of grievances in the *Riksdag*.[30]

Sweden and Switzerland had 'one thing in common: the stability of peasant representation, based on their institutions of political communities in the provinces (Sweden) and the rural republics (Switzerland) . . . [N]owhere else in Europe did political participation reach as broad a segment of the population'. Nevertheless the peasantry were the lowest estate and therefore a politically vulnerable one. In Sweden they were all tenants of the crown or nobles. The majority were tenants at will, whereas a minority were taxpaying peasants who had guaranteed tenure so long as they met their financial obligations of taxes and fixed dues. This virtual freehold, however, came under threat due to royal policy in Queen Christina's reign.[31] That threat was mitigated by the united protest of the non-noble estates in the *Riksdag*. In contrast, the Danish peasantry became the political victim of crown and nobility. Their membership of the *Rigsdag* was ended in 1627, partly because their interests were regarded as adequately represented by the nobles.[32] Elsewhere peasants were usually excluded, as individuals or estates, on the grounds of inferiority, unfitness or subjection. None of the Italian parliaments included peasants, who were viewed collectively as the lowliest estate. The *Complaynt of Scotland*, a Scottish version of a French political allegory, which appeared in 1550, really says it all. It instructed the peasant that he had no political role because, as 'your hart is ful of maleis, ignorance, variance and inconstance', he needed to be kept in a state of 'subjectione'.[33]

The conservative characteristics of representation

The exclusion, removal or withdrawal of a particular estate usually occurred within an enduring parliamentary structure. Changes in the organisation and membership of early modern parliaments did not indicate a shift away from a powerful social conservatism. Even during the British political revolution that conservatism prevailed. In 1639 the bishops were expelled from the Scottish Parliament but the other traditional elements – nobles, gentry and burghs – remained until the Cromwellian conquest of Scotland, in 1651, ended its life. Nor did political relationships change significantly in the 1640s. Political 'parties' in particular were determined not only by their positions on major issues, but also by traditional kinship and blood ties. The organised, radical Leveller movement, which was influential amongst rank-and-file soldiers in the victorious English parliamentary army, sought a one-chamber assembly chosen by universal male suffrage. In a range of pamphlets and proposals, especially the *Agreements of the People* (1647–49), they publicised their proposals and offered a blue-print of the parliament which they sought. At the Putney debates, when the generals met the radicals and discussed their proposals, the gulf was clearly unbridgeable: on the one hand, the radicals' assertion that 'every man that is to live under a government ought first by his own consent to put himself under that government' and, against that, General Ireton's contention that only those with 'a permanent fixed interest in the kingdom' should be able to vote. Ireton's view prevailed when, for example, the county franchise for the Protectorate Parliaments was limited to those 'seised or possessed to his own use, of any estate, real or personal, to the value of £200'. Although Oliver Cromwell was a political revolutionary, he expressed a view shared by his royalist opponents when he insisted 'that men that have no interest but the interest of breathing shall have no voice in elections'.[34]

Although neither in time of political stability nor revolution did the English parliament have an estate structure, it did, in common with other European assemblies, represent elites: ecclesiastical, noble, professional and official, urban economic and rural sub-noble. Both in the British Isles and on the continent the actual parliamentary membership was not determined by democratic or popular mechanisms. Members of ecclesiastical and noble elites were usually summoned individually by royal writ: for example, English prelates and peers and, until the dissolution of the monasteries, *some* abbots and priors; the Sardinian military *brachium*, prelates and fully empowered procurators of other Church bodies such as cathedral chapters; and, in accordance with the Swedish *Form of Government* (1634), 'all counts, barons, knights and esquires . . . who are come to full age'.[35] And, if they were not too numerous, elites might attend in their entirety, as in England, the smaller German states and Sweden. In contrast, the size of the French ecclesiastical establishment and nobility necessitated elections by the two orders through assemblies in each *baillage* or *sénéchaussée*. It was only in such cases that there was an element of choice in the decision who should attend. On the other hand, when all members of an elite were traditionally summoned, it became more and more difficult for monarchs to single out for exclusion a fit, sane adult noble. As the English lord chancellor observed to Viscount Lisle in 1536, 'it ys the order that every nobilleman shuld have his wrytt of somonz of a parlament'.[36]

Representatives of the third estate were chosen by election or selection, not summoned from above. That did not, however, preclude electoral influence, management, even control by the crown. Even when elections were free from royal interference, they could hardly be described as 'popular'. This was particularly true of cities and towns, where the relatively open medieval urban government gradually became more restricted and exclusive. In the fourteenth century, when many Castilian cities became subject to closed corporations of municipal councillors (*regidores*), their *procuradores* in most cases came to be selected, in a variety of ways, by a narrow electorate. Then, in the following two centuries, a series of agreements, designed to ease the internal conflicts between the competing factions, interests and lobbies which divided the cities, shared out or rotated the *procuradores* between them.[37] Urban representatives in Italian parliaments too were not usually elected but appointed by city councils from amongst their own members or officers or local dignitaries.

It was in the Netherlands, however, that oligarchic management of local administration and of both provincial and general representation was most successful and complete. Even before the sixteenth-century Dutch 'revolution' the urban elites had established control not only in their towns but also, by adherence to the delegate principle, of business in the States-general and provincial states. During and after the long and bloody process of what became a war of independence, the patrician class or 'regents' of the rebellious Dutch cities established an increasingly exclusive control of the new state. The real power-base of the United Provinces and its assemblies resided in the closed town councils (*vroedschappen*), to which members of the assemblies, as delegates, could always refer back for further advice and instructions. In numerical terms, some 2,000 families controlled central, provincial and local government and parliaments, and during the seventeenth century they became grander and more remote as the gulf between them and the citizenry steadily grew.[38]

There was, of course, some diversity in the municipal power structure, franchise and elections across Christian Europe. Borough representation in the English Parliament encapsulates that diversity. Two of London's four members – invariably an alderman and the recorder – were chosen by the City's aldermen, a tight group of twenty-six. The other two, 'junior', members, who from 1571 included the lord mayor's remembrancer (secretary), were elected by 'the immense multitude of the commons of the city'. Other parliamentary boroughs had a wide franchise too, yet the system defies generalisation. Bristol and Exeter had relatively large electorates. In Bristol the mayor, aldermen, common councillors, forty-shilling freeholders and chief merchants had the vote, but in Exeter the franchise extended to all freeholders. In contrast there were (1) the many corporate boroughs, in which, like Castilian, Italian or Dutch cities, a closed corporation of mayor, alderman and common council resolved everything, and (2) the proprietary boroughs, where the owner, a Lord Mountjoy, a Dame Packington, or Dame Copley wrote in his or her choices on the electoral return. The possible political value of this is illustrated by the threat of Stephen Gardiner, who, as English bishop of Winchester, controlled the election of members for the episcopal boroughs of Downton, Hindon and Taunton. Gardiner was imprisoned in the Fleet when the first Edwardian Parliament was called in 1547. He wrote to Protector Somerset that 'If it should be of anye man through polecy to kepe me from the Parliament, it were good to be remembred whether mine absence from the upper house, with the absence of those I have used to name in the nether house, wil not engender more cause of objection, if oportunitye serve hereafter, then my presence with such as I should appoynte were there'.[39]

Despite the diversity illustrated in urban franchises and elections, it remains clear that parliamentary representation was predominantly influenced, if not determined, by royalty, elites and wealth. The franchise was commonly property-related and influenced by hierarchy. The electorates tended to be narrow. The Portuguese Cortes displayed all those characteristics. When the crown ordered each municipality to *elect* 'two of the most respectable members' of the local elite, they were in practice *selected*. Rank was important both in the selection process and in the third estate's seating arrangements in the Cortes. Although inflation increased the number of forty-shilling freeholders who thereby qualified for the rural vote in early modern England, that property franchise remained intact until the reform act of 1832. Furthermore, selection was also a part of the shire election process, although its extent, significance and relation to contemporary notions of represent-ation are subjects of recent debate.[40] As in England, French rural suffrage too increased during the sixteenth and seventeenth centuries, especially in northern France. Efforts were made to increase electoral attendance, *curés* were called and the peasantry were consulted. To some extent this may be explained by a more literal application of the *quod omnes tangit* principle. Of more practical significance, however, was probably the struggle for local dominance in towns and *baillages* between the old-established municipal patricians and local royal officers. The latter sought not to promote greater public involvement for the greater good, but to exploit an enlarged electorate to win support and advance their position.[41] Wherever one looks, no matter what the size and composition of the electorate was, elections to the third estate or the lower chambers of parliaments were open to exploitation.

In such a system carpet-bagging was a common characteristic. It could be an innocuous, indeed beneficial practice, providing small communities with the kinds of contact, bill promotion skills and arts of vocal presentation which local men lacked. Furthermore, as Thomas Norton argued in the English house of commons in 1571, during a debate on a bill which proposed to end the fifteenth-century statutory residential qualification for parliamentary burgesses, it could also benefit the realm: 'the choyce shoulde bee of such which were able and fitt for soe greate a place, without respect or privilege of place . . . Withall hee argued that the whole body of the realme and good service of the same was rather to bee respected then the private regard of place or privi-ledge of any person.' This national perspective accorded with that of Sir Thomas Smith, Elizabeth's secretary of state, who wrote that the Parliament of England 'representeth and hath the power of the whole realme both the head and the bodie. For everie Englishman is entended to bee there present, either in person or by procuration and attornies . . . And the consent of the Parliament is taken to be everie mans consent.' Against this national perspective, however, were set local rights and interests. One member asserted that 'to choose of their owne it is a liberty, noe burthen; to loose then their liberty I thinke it a badd commodity'. Another member, James Warnecombe, spelt out the bill's danger: if it passed, 'lordes' letters shall from henceforth beare all the sway'. In practice, as we have seen, the residential qualification was to a large extent ignored.[42]

In England most non-resident parliamentary burgesses were not royal nominees, though some were elected in response to the requests of privy councillors, royal officials, nobles or other powerful men. Elsewhere, however, the absence of required residence was sometimes exploited, especially, though not only, by royal governments. Members of the Sicilian domanial *brazo* were often chosen by the viceroy and usually included nobles, carpet-bagging lawyers and, in regular breach of a 1348 law, royal officials. Royal intervention and manipulation were also longstanding characteristics of selection to the Castilian Cortes and they were prominent concerns of the *Comuneros* in 1520. For the rest of the sixteenth century such interference seems to have been insignificant, but it was very vigorous in the following century, especially during the duque de Lerma's ministry (1598–1618). The crown's creation and sale of many new municipal offices, which gave the occupants' electoral rights, enabled councillors of state, household officials and even ministers, such as Lerma and, under Philip IV, Conde Duque de Olivares, to represent, Castilian cities as *procuradores*. It also facilitated the election of carpet-baggers' who sat for different cities in different Cortes' and of grandees who, in the seventeenth century, displayed a growing and active interest in parliamentary elections and service. The result, Thompson writes, was that the cities 'had lost not only the power to elect their representatives, but also the power to control them'.[43]

Of course, when pressing circumstances seemed to demand it, governments could resort to blatant manipulation, though this might backfire and imperil the fulfilment of the purposes for which the body met. When Elizabeth I's governor, Sir Henry Sidney, called the Irish Parliament in 1569 he secured the return of non-resident Englishmen for borough seats. It might be argued that Sidney was simply following English parliamentary practice, but the Irish statute requiring residence had been confirmed by the Irish Parliament as recently as 1542. Furthermore, as John Hooker, one of those non-resident burgesses, wrote, '[S]ome beinge shiriffes of countyes and some maiors of townes had named and apoynted themselffes'. Burgesses were also returned for non-corporate towns, which were not entitled to their own representation. When the lower house met, 'These [matters] were had yn greate questyon and miche stomake[dyd] growe thereof' and continued from 25 to 29

January. When the judges were consulted, the return of self-selected sheriffs and mayors and the non-corporate towns' burgesses was annulled but, despite the statute to the contrary, non-resident members retained their seats. The anger of the Anglo-Irish was not assuaged and, in the disturbed session which followed, much of the government's programme was not fulfilled.[44]

Nevertheless the English monarchy and its Irish governors did not give up. European rulers were particularly active and rigorous in electoral intervention and management if the objective was religious or ethnic exclusiveness. In Ireland it was both. Henry VIII had already secured the removal of the third house of clerical proctors in 1537, in order to strengthen his hand to ensure the enactment of anti-papal legislation. In Elizabeth's reign protestant bishops ensured a government majority in the lords. Although Sidney's attempt to achieve the same in the commons was not successful in 1569, more drastic measures in the following reigns were. Eighty-four new parliamentary boroughs, which were either villages or sites for plantation settlements, returned pro-testants to James I's only Irish Parliament in 1613. The effect was to turn the longstanding catholic Anglo-Irish majority into a minority and transform the Parliament into a colonial assembly. Thomas Wentworth, Charles I's governor during the 1630s, obtained the king's permission to reduce the number of boroughs returning catholics. He was motivated in this by both ethnic and religious hostility: 'We might well overthrow at least twenty of these old corporations who all sent [to Parliament], and so will still, mere Irish and papists, the most obstinate senseless creatures I am persuaded of the world.' He did not achieve his target but at least seven were disfranchised.[45] Legalistic though early modern rulers were, ethnic or religious hostilities, as in Ireland, could set aside rights, liberties and privileges. This is, for example, also evident in the religious uniformity imposed on estates in the German principalities and some Habsburg territories, such as Bohemia, and, one might add, in the English Parliament after the Elizabethan Settlement.

Notions of representation

Although European representation tended to be elitist and was certainly not, in any sense, democratic, there were clear contemporary notions of representation and in what sense parliaments were representative institutions. Michael Metcalf identified several criteria for 'a representation by estates': that it represented the whole realm and all free estates, that they were independent of each other and that the parliament had 'specific tasks in the life of the polity'. Many European assemblies did not satisfy all of these criteria, but there was one common characteristic: that they represented the entire community. This might not translate into the community's consent to new laws and taxes where autocratic monarchy or *dominium regale* existed and to which much of early modern Europe was subject. Where, however, limited monarchy or *dominium politicum et regale* existed, as in the British Isles and Poland-Lithuania – to which one must add the Dutch parliamentary republic – such assent by the whole community was a political reality. Whether, in practice, *quod omnes tangit* was an observed principle or just a nice-sounding platitude, it embodied the concepts of representation and consent. These were conventionally expressed in images of the body politic, nowhere more so it seems than in England, by Henry VIII, Thomas Smith, the lawyer Edward Coke and, in 1621, James I amongst others. The crucial point was not the imagery but the acknowledgement that Parliament stood for the community, the realm, all the people. So, again in England, Chief Justice Fortescue (in the fifteenth century) and Lord Keeper Coventry (in 1628) referred to Parliament as 'the whole kingdom'.

This shared conception of parliament did not mean, however, that ruler and ruled valued it in the same way. As we know, princes called it for advice and, when necessary, for laws and taxes. Whilst the necessity, indeed desirability of co-operation with government was not normally questioned, representatives were bound to be concerned also about the liberties and privileges not only of the whole community, but of particular localities, social orders and economic interests too. Marongiu summarised it thus: '[A]lthough there was no element of popular choice or election, parliaments represented the community and expressed if not the will, at least the interests of subjects . . . [I]n this respect parliamentary assemblies were representative.'[46]

During the early modern period, the powers accorded to members of some of those assemblies by their electorates became an increasingly sensitive, even contentious, matter. For a variety of reasons, including sheer financial necessity and the influence of Bodinian sovereignty theory, the parliamentary expectations of rulers tended to increase. For centuries English representatives had exercised *plena potestas*, the right to make decisions without first consulting their electorates. Aggressive and financially needy monarchs, however, could exploit this to isolate members and, by coercion or seductive *douceurs*, secure their consent to taxation. The Habsburgs demanded that deputies come with *plena potestas*, for example in Castile, the Low Countries and Sicily, whilst Sigismund I (1506–48) attempted to achieve the same in Poland. Many of the communities represented by parliaments, however, clung tenaciously to the principle of delegacy: their representatives were given strict instructions, which they could not exceed in their parliamentary dealings. Any royal request not covered by those instructions required the deputies to return home for advice and further directions. There were various outcomes to the protracted struggle over the powers of deputies. The delegate principle had been upheld by Castilian *procuradores*, despite royal pressure, since the thirteenth century. It was not until the Cortes of 1632 that they succumbed to royal pressure and made decisions on tax grants without reference back to the cities.[47] In contrast delegacy in the Low Countries was not just a tactical weapon deployed against aggressive monarchy, but a symbol of the urban particularism which dominated political life. Members' first loyalty was not to the Burgundian dukes, Habsburgs or Castile but to their cities. So delegacy survived Habsburg rule and continued in the Dutch republic.

Delegacy was one particular expression of the deputies' defence of localities, social orders and economic interests. Parliaments were not just occasions for airing grievances, but for organising defences: of the French nobles' right to pensions and offices (1614–15);[48] of the rights of the Swedish peasantry against noble encroachments (in 1650); of the Church's liberties (during the Reformation); and of the Holland estates against harmful economic policies and Brabant's against threats to revoke their privileges, both under Emperor Charles V. There was, however, a natural (albeit not rigid) distinction between central parliaments and regional or local assemblies. At the national level, defence of interests could be diluted by the persuasive presence of king and Court. It could be intimidating, enable direct royal coercion and at the same time hold out the seductive prospect of royal favours and advancement. The Castilian *Comuneros* of 1520 expressed grave concern about this. Regional and local parliaments, firmly anchored in home territory, were liable to be bolder and more tenacious in defence. French provinces with effective estates which controlled money grants, such as Brittany, Burgundy and Languedoc, were less burdened with direct taxes than most others, even during the financially insatiable Thirty Years' War, although this is not to deny a dramatic increase in absolute terms. The Languedoc assembly, in which the cities and towns were numerically preponderant from the fifteenth century onwards and in which voting was by head not by estate, was a kind of model of local representation. It had a major role in provincial administration and transacted a wide range of business. It controlled the collection of taxes and presented grievances when it met. It also attached conditions to tax grants: in 1523, during the reign of the financially needy Francis I, for example, it required that the amount voted would be spent on Languedoc's defence and other needs. It was not, however, genuinely representative, it did not constitute a provincial government and its rivalry with the provincial *parlement* prevented solidarity against royal demands in the seventeenth century. This was equally true of Brittany.[49]

Such local or regional assemblies usually focused on parochial priorities and operated independently of other parliaments within a composite monarchy. There were, however, notable exceptions. One which springs readily to mind was the Netherlands. Another, to which less attention has been given, was the *Confoederatio Bohemica* of 1619. This was a draft federal constitution, achieved by the estates of the crown 'Lands' of Bohemia, Moravia, Silesia and Upper and Lower Lusatia. Its purpose was to protect the political and religious liberties of each crown 'Land' on the basis of equality. The fact that the Habsburgs won and the federation lost does not diminish its significance as 'a notable alternative form of state-building' in early modern Europe.[50]

So local, regional and national assemblies, working alone or in collaborative ventures, had, as a common concern, the protection of the interests, rights and liberties of their communities. This is not to deny or ignore their willingness to serve the interests of God's anointed with advice and *auxilium*. Representative assemblies were generally of value to both rulers and ruled. This does not mean, however, that members of early modern parliaments rushed to the capitals of Europe full of excitement and eager anticipation, demanding frequent, even annual assemblies. Nor did monarchs hunt around for excuses to call them. They were expensive to stage, especially if, as in England, many nobles and others, their gentleman-servants and horses were entitled to *bouge* of Court – accommodation, stabling and rations – for the duration of the Parliament. Public displays and entertainments added to the bill.[51] Expenditure escalated when rulers in composite monarchies were obliged to travel long distances with their Courts in order to preside at parliamentary gatherings. This contributed to the medieval French crown's abandonment of separate general assemblies of Languedoil and of Languedoc. The Spanish King Charles I and his successors found the Cortes of the eastern kingdoms equally unrewarding occasions. They had to attend in person if they sought a *donativo* (subsidy). The costs involved were considerable, whilst the amounts voted were modest, tended to remain static in amount during the sixteenth century and were always difficult to collect.[52]

The occasion of parliaments: burdens and benefits

Parliaments were, of course, sometimes an unavoidable necessity and they could bring substantial benefits to a ruler, as they undoubtedly did, for example, to Henry VIII of England and Gustav Vasa of Sweden. They also provided opportunities for individuals and communities to seek a variety of benefits. That does not mean, however, that they were universally popular. Herman Schück describes the early seventeenth-century Swedish *Riksdag*, already established as an important fact of political life, as 'mistrusted among "the higher estates" as an instrument of the royal power [and] disliked among "the lower estates" as a burden and source of discomfort'.[53] Parliaments meant taxes and so they were unpopular with non-voters and electors alike. They were no more popular with many of the deputies, who were responsible for legally binding their constituents to pay up. Evidence survives that members of the English commons, Swedish *Riksdag* and other assemblies did not relish the prospect of justifying to their neighbours the latest imposition. Furthermore, parliaments disrupted normal life. Although Dutch delegates frequently journeyed back and forth to consult their electors, they travelled in relative comfort along the canals and rivers, but it was a different matter, tedious and sometimes dangerous, across Castile or going up to Paris. When deputies arrived, they had to endure cramped lodgings and inflated prices in cities swollen in numbers by the occasion of a parliament. There was also an increased danger of violence and, as the two sessions of 1625 in overcrowded London and Oxford illustrate, of bubonic plague. When the Elizabethan bishop, Parkhurst of Norwich, wrote at the conclusion of a session that he and other members of the house of lords were glad to go home, being 'thoroughly tired of the

City', he must have been echoing a common contemporary view across many countries.[54]

Localities were also burdened with wage bills. Some Neapolitan towns cut costs when they chose to be represented by nobles rather than paid deputies. The Castilian cities, in contrast, were faced with varying but significant increases in expenditure. From the 1570s on, the life of individual Cortes increased from less than twelve months to two years or more and from the 1590s *procuradores* sometimes served in Cortes which spanned four, five or six years.[55] Wage bills escalated and pay was often in arrears. In Sweden too meetings of the *Riksdag* were not popular because of the time and money involved. In such disparate communities as some Scottish burghs and some Breton towns a similar attitude prevailed and members were not sent.

The failure of the social orders and communities to ensure adequate representation was not the only consequence of common and widespread public lack of interest or enthusiasm and dislike of the burdens which parliamentary meetings engendered. In Sicily not only did some cities obtain or, as Palermo and Messina did, sometimes claim the right not to send representatives, but also some of the prelates were absentee foreigners, whilst others, and Sicilian nobles like their Catalan counterparts, were permitted to send proxies.[56] There were similarities in some of the French provincial estates. The attempt of Louis XIII's chief minister, Cardinal Richelieu, to manipulate the Breton estates was aided by the fact that some of the ecclesiastics were non-native and so uninterested. Furthermore, the recently granted right of all Breton nobles to sit had not received an enthusiastic response. On the other hand, nobles' attendance had markedly increased from 1576, when they assumed control of the assembly, and in the seventeenth century tax-conscious towns' representation did likewise.[57]

There is nevertheless evidence that representation was often regarded as neither privilege nor right but as an obligation to be avoided. When members, especially of the first two estates, were individually summoned or communities dutifully elected or selected deputies to represent them, those called or chosen frequently failed to fulfil the duty assigned to them. Apathy and indifference, expressed in absenteeism, was a commonplace occurrence. Specific studies and surviving evidence have shown this to be the case amongst prelates and nobles, for example in Scotland and England, the Low Counties, France and Scandinavia. Even the elections of shire commissioners by Scottish lairds and of French nobles at *baillage* assemblies were poorly attended, although the turnout at French elections did improve in the seventeenth century. James VI of Scotland took a decidedly dim view of Scottish noble absenteeism and he reprimanded the English house of lords for one day's lapse in 1610. In fact he was less than just to the English nobility. Although they shared with their Scottish, Castilian and French counterparts a lamentable attendance record in medieval parliaments, absenteeism noticeably diminished during the 1530s. Thereafter attendance ran at a more respectable level, although there were always a considerable number of both licensed and unlicensed absentees.[58]

Nobles often took advantage of the parliament-time to visit the capital and the ruler's Court, to socialise and self-indulge, but not necessarily to attend the assembly. In 1617 Gustav Adolf's Chancellor, Axel Oxenstierna, complained to the *Riksdag* that many of his fellow-nobles, 'when matters of the greatest consequence are under discussion, hold dinner parties, or themselves go to dinner with someone else, and thereby waste time, and fail to take the business seriously, but rather hold it of small account'. A darker example of noble priorities occurred in London when the fourth Baron Latimer's absence from Parliament in 1558 followed the attempted rape of his landlady and her death, which were 'to grete a vellany for a noble man'.[59]

Absenteeism during sessions was not confined to ecclesiastics and nobles. It was prevalent amongst all three estates in parliaments as far apart as Finland, where problems of distance, communication and climate discouraged attendance at the Swedish *Riksdag*,[60] and Brabant. And Sir David Lindsay, the Scottish poet, wrote of his own national Parliament that 'the thrie estaits gang all backwart'.[61] Absenteeism was countered in some parliaments by roll-calls and the threat or imposition of fines; in Aragon the parliamentary response to the problem was to establish a required quorum for each estate at the start of the session. Non-attendance was sometimes most serious, even endemic in the third estate. Aragonese urban attendance was often poor, and it was unusual for more than twelve of the twenty-two members of the Dutch States-general to be present. English lawyer-members were particularly notorious absentees because they preferred to wax fat on fees in the law-courts next-door to the commons. Thomas Norton advised an Elizabethan privy councillor that, to get rid of contentious bills in the lower house, they should be sent to bill committees full of lawyers, who were preoccupied elsewhere: 'the longer it wilbe ere the matter come in againe'. The time-conscious

Norton was also cynical about parliamentary novices who 'are comonlie most adventurous and canne be gladdest of large parleamentes to learn and see fashiones'.[62]

It should be added that the European picture was not one of unalloyed apathy and, in any case, times were constantly changing. There were high attendance levels in the later fifteenth-century Irish Parliaments, which then reflected broad Anglo-Irish interests and not just those of the Pale. In Scotland levels improved in the seventeenth century as the Parliament became more active and influential. Indeed, Keith Brown paints an attractive picture of Edinburgh in the parliament-time, when it was 'filled to overflowing with noblemen and their attendants, taverns and coffee houses became impromptu debating chambers, covert literature circulated, merchants did profitable business and crowds were drawn to the spectacle'. And, despite the usual depressing images of French representative institutions, the deputies of the third estate at Pontoise in 1561 toiled away diligently from 6 am each day, including Sundays and feast days. Indeed it was around this time – in 1560, 1561, 1576 – that, after an abeyance of over half a century, demands for more frequent and regular meetings of assemblies, even without royal summons, were voiced by nobles and the third estate: for the Estates-general every ten, five or two years, a greater role for provincial estates and annual sessions of local estates. It hardly suggests antipathy or a lack of interest. The variegated European picture, however, cannot hide the widespread lack of interest or enthusiasm, a circumstance with which we are so familiar today. 'Few parliaments' was the ideal and kings such as Henry VII of England and Gustav Adolf of Sweden sought popularity by promising just that.

The royal officers who were responsible for the organisation, staging and management of parliamentary gatherings must have responded warmly to such a promise. They were beset with problems caused by the shortcomings and, at times, difficult behaviour of deputies. In the English commons they chattered, hawked, spat and hissed, and in speech they could be garrulous to a fault. They could speak in unseemly fashion as Sir Robert Cecil noted when, in 1601, he accused members of language 'fit for a grammar school'. Often they displayed ignorance. In 1584 William Fleetwood, the experienced recorder of Elizabethan London, described 'the knights and burgesses, out of all order, in troops standing upon the floor, making strange noises, there being not past seven or eight of the old Parliament'.[63] Worse still was the handicap of illiteracy amongst peasant members of the Swedish *Riksdag*. In 1617 there was official concern that 'the Commonalty, when the points in the King's Proposition are communicated to them, tend to run around for scriveners, and maybe (as has happened in the past) hit upon a bunch of spies and intriguers to write their answer for them'. The result was that, as we are told, 'the enemy' in Poland obtained knowledge of the Swedish king's parliamentary proposals.[64]

Even seating arrangements had a potential for trouble in an age when great importance was attached to rank, order and precedence. The English house of lords could spend much time in discussion, consultation and genealogical searches in order to determine whether Lord A should sit above or below Lord B and whether Baron C should take his place as 23rd or 27th junior peer. If, however, seating was not organised at all, 'disorder and confusion' could occur, as in Sweden. In 1617 Chancellor Oxenstierna painted a graphic picture of the way members of one estate 'run in and out among members of the others in places where business is to be done'. The estates became intermingled and indistinguishable, one from the other: 'here stands a nobleman, there a priest, here a burgher and there a peasant, all mixed up together'. Order was replaced by social anarchy, so that 'persons who ought to have been at the far end of the room have the foremost seats' and vice versa. He lamented how the disorder was contemptible and humiliating abroad, where they laughed at it and derided it. Even worse, those dreadful Polish spies were able to infiltrate the meetings.[65] Doubtless they were the agents of Sigismund Vasa, king of Poland, who seems to have been the early modern Swedish equivalent of a Soviet bogeyman. Everywhere princes, their councillors and bureaucrats must have walked with a lighter step after the closing ceremonies of parliament.

Nevertheless monarchs would not have continued to summon them if they did not fulfil needs which could not be satisfied elsewhere.[66] The usual and obvious benefits were advice, money and laws. In addition, a meeting might be the occasion for celebrating the commencement of a new reign and the recognition or legitimisation of the ruler's authority.[67] Parliament-time was also seen as politically useful and socially attractive. It was an important 'point of contact' between rulers and elites; it provided members with opportunities to conduct personal and public business; and it enabled them to socialise, sometimes to excess. So Madame de Sévigné dismissed the occasion of the Breton estates in 1671 as no more than 'everlasting games, eternal balls, a great show'.[68]

Where, as in French *pays d'états*, some German principalities, the Aragonese kingdoms and the United Provinces, taxation management was in the hands of assemblies or their permanent committees, the social dominance of elites was strengthened. And in one particular respect considered elsewhere, the presentation of grievances, parliaments were valued not only by elites but also by the wider community. Right across Europe parliaments presented petitions for redress. The prospects of their success were often slender and the principle of 'redress before supply' (of money) rarely applied.[69] Nevertheless, it illustrates that there were perceived credits as well as debits in the early modern parliamentary ledger.

Control mechanisms: the arts of management and manipulation

In order to fulfil their parliamentary objectives and to do so quickly and with a minimum of fuss, rulers attempted to secure the willing co-operation and consent of their representative assemblies. This was often a difficult task, but not necessarily because of resistance to government policies and proposals. No early modern European assembly was under greater financial pressure than the Cortes of Habsburg Castile. Yet the cities who chose the *procuradores* and bore that financial burden were devoted to the monarchy and to its service. Nevertheless, the membership of European parliaments displayed a variable interest in the needs of rulers and an equally varying willingness to accept their policies, priorities and demands. Disapproval might be expressed simply by withdrawal: Castilian and Low Countries' deputies could use their *poderes* (cities' instructions) to justify this; Claude Berard of Provence publicly announced his departure from the Estates-general in 1561 because matters under consideration were not covered by his constituents' instructions; in 1613 Anglo-Irish peers demonstrated displeasure when they publicly withdrew from the Irish Parliament; and, in discreet contrast, some English peers and over 100 knights and burgesses quietly and tactfully left the Marian Parliament of 1554–55 to avoid involvement in a controversial royal bill. Of course members could openly criticise or resist their governments, especially in some German assemblies, over partition or religious change. When he dissolved the turbulent English Parliament of 1628–29 the admittedly over-reactive

Charles I denounced those members who had resisted his requests, 'wasted much time . . . blasting our government . . . [and sought] to erect an universal over-swaying power to themselves'.[70] Government–opposition disagreement could even lead to violence. When, in a dispute over the Irish commons' speakership in 1613, the Anglo-Irish placed their candidate in the chair, government supporters lifted up the official nominee and dropped him on to the incumbent's lap, thereby injuring his dignity and possibly more. A struggle for the chair ensued.

Opposition could be dealt with in a variety of ways. It could be headed off by manipulating or tinkering with the electoral system, as, for example, in Ireland, Castile, Sicily and French *pays d'états* such as Brittany.[71] *Douceurs*, such as *mercedes* (royal gifts and favours) to susceptible Castilian *procuradores*, could transform potential troublemakers into devoted loyalists, as the *Comuneros* complained in 1520. The royal viceroy in Sicily recommended honours and offices to make deputies obliged or personal letters from the king to stroke their egos. The Dutch rebel leader, William of Orange, reputedly managed the States-general through five or six deputies who were the recipients of his pensions, gifts and hospitality. Blatant intimidation and chicanery might even be employed. In the single-chamber Scottish Parliament members voted 'Agree' or 'Disagree' under the careful scrutiny of the king's secretary. David Calderwood wrote in 1621 that 'It came to pass that the wide opening of the mouth at A, the second syllable of 'Disagree', did eat up the first syllable, especiallie in these who did speak with a low voice, being threatened . . . with menacing eyes and looks of the [King's] Secretary, and so the negative were noted as affirmative'. The French crown was prepared not only to intimidate but to punish. When in 1671 members of the estates of Provence resisted yet another increase in the royal tax demand, Louis XIV ordered 'ten of the worst-intentioned deputies' into exile. That was enough to end parliamentary resistance.[72]

Criticism, opposition and deliberate lack of co-operation were not the only official concerns. Deputies in many parliaments were simply ignorant of the workings and financial needs of government. They and their governments also had competing priorities. Although representative assemblies had originated as institutions to service rulers, they had, as we have seen, acquired over time a wider range of functions. By the sixteenth century they provided the opportunity to resolve grievances and, in some cases, to secure beneficial laws. These, however, were time-consuming exercises. Furthermore, all parties to a parliament preferred to keep sessions as short as possible. So official programmes could find themselves in competition with the advancement of social, economic, local, ethnic, religious or other interests. Thomas Norton, the Elizabethan 'Parliament man', advised that, to achieve short sessions 'then is it good to abridge the thinges that lengthen the session', especially 'privat bills of singular p[er]sons . . . bills of occupation, misteries and companies . . ., [m]atters of Longe Argument [and] Delaying of the principall thinges for w[hi]ch the Session is called'.[73] Norton was writing in an English context, but his arguments could have applied to many parliaments.

One device which could facilitate shorter and fewer parliaments was the standing committee. There were, however, other simple alternatives to the staging of a parliament, with all its attendant inconvenience and the labour, cost and time involved. Kings of Scotland, for example, could call conventions of estates or nobility, which, with a relatively small membership and sitting briefly, could legislate and vote taxes. French monarchs sometimes called assemblies of notables in preference to the Estates-general, as in 1566, 1583, 1596, 1617 and in 1626–27 when they considered significant royal reform proposals. Indeed, this was the very purpose of such assemblies. Like the Estates-general, their role was consultative, but that is where the similarity ended. They were not representative assemblies but officially selected groups of grandees, bishops, judges and other members of elites whose function was to formulate and sanction reform packages. Occasionally they had some success but usually they were ineffective.[74] Whether princes continued to meet full parliaments, or they preferred one of the alternatives, the occasion was a coming together of the needs of the ruler and, in some sense, however attenuated, the interest of the community.

Notes

1. Political participation by representative bodies existed at all levels – national, provincial/regional and also local – as demonstrated in, for example, K. Krüger, 'Regional representation in Schleswig and Holstein: a special type of early modern political participation' *PER* 7, 1 (June 1987), pp. 33–9. This study, however, confines itself to representation in national and major internal assemblies.

2. H.M. Scott, ed., *The European Nobilities in the Seventeenth and Eighteenth Centuries*, 2 vols (London, 1995), Vol. 1, pp. 9–11.

3. A. Marongiu, *Medieval Parliaments. A Comparative Study* (London, 1968), pp. 223, 226.

4   S.E. Lehmberg, 'The role of parliament in early modern England – a recon-
    sideration', in N. Stjernquist, ed., *The Swedish Riksdag in an International Perspective*
    (Stockholm, 1989), p. 81; G.R. Elton, '"The Body of the Whole Realm": parliament
    and representation in medieval and Tudor England', in *Studies in Tudor and Stuart
    Politics and Government* 2 vols (Cambridge, 1974), Vol. 2, pp. 32, 36; A.R. Myers,
    'Parliament, 1422–1509', in R.G. Davies and J.H. Denton, eds, *The English
    Parliament in the Middle Ages* (Philadelphia, PA, 1981), p. 149.

5   Marongiu, *Medieval Parliaments*, p. 226; T.N. Bisson, 'The origins of the Corts of
    Catalonia' *PER* 16 (1996), pp. 34–5; J.D. Tracy, *Holland under Habsburg Rule, 1506–
    1566. The Formation of a Body Politic* (Oxford, 1990), pp. 34–5.

6   M.F. Metcalf, ed., *The Riksdag: A History of the Swedish Parliament* (Stockholm, 1987),
    p. 69.

7   R.J.W. Evans and T.V. Thomas, eds, *Crown, Church and Estates. Central European
    Politics in the Sixteenth and Seventeenth Centuries* (London, 1991), pp. 30–1, 71, 81–2,
    137; J.M. Hayden, 'Deputies and *Qualités*: the Estates General of 1614' *French
    Historical Studies* 3, 4 (Fall, 1964), pp. 511–12, 514; P. Croft and I.A.A. Thompson,
    'Aristocracy and representative government in unicameral and bicameral institutions.
    The role of the peers in the Castilian Cortes and the English Parliament, 1529–1664',
    in H.W. Blom, W.P. Blockmans, H. de Schepper, eds, *Bicameralisme* (The Hague,
    1992), pp. 64–5, 66 and n.7, 74; M.A.R. Graves, *The House of Lords in the Parliaments
    of Edward VI and Mary I* (Cambridge, 1981), pp. 58–94.

8   H.G. Koenigsberger, 'Parliaments and estates', in R.W. Davis, ed., *The Origins of
    Modern Freedom in the West* (Stanford, CA, 1995), p. 160.

9   R. Bonney, *The European Dynastic States, 1494–1660* (Oxford, 1992), p. 317; P.
    Cardim, 'Ceremonial and ritual in the Cortes of Portugal (1581–1628)' *PER* 12, 1
    (June 1992), pp. 4, 7; Marongiu, *Medieval Parliaments*, pp. 139–44, 157–65; J. Russell
    Major, *The Monarchy, the Estates and the Aristocracy in Renaissance France* (London,
    1988), VIII, pp. 256–7.

10 V. Press, 'The system of estates in the Austrian hereditary lands and . . . Empire. A
    comparison', and A. Kohler, 'Ferdinand I and the Estates, 1521–64', both in Evans
    and Thomas, eds, *Crown, Church and Estates*, pp. 2, 4–10, 48.

11 However, the attempt by some nobles in 1547 to reinforce their position further,
    by securing the exclusion of the third estate from the Bohemian *Sněm*, failed
    because they did not win King Ferdinand's support.

12 X. Gil, 'Crown and Cortes in early modern Aragon: reassessing revisionisms' *PER*
    13, 2 (Dec. 1993), p. 111.

13 Marongiu, *Medieval Parliaments*, pp. 148–55; J. Goodare, 'The Estates in the Scottish
    Parliament, 1286–1707', in C. Jones, ed., *The Scots and Parliament* (Edinburgh, 1996),
    pp. 7, 11–17, 19–20, 21–4, 26, 27, 31–2; J.M. Goodare, 'Parliament and society in
    Scotland, 1560–1603' PhD, University of Edinburgh, 1989, pp. 58–62; K.M. Brown,
    Kingdom or Province? Scotland and the Regal Union, 1603–1715 (New York, 1992), p. 15.

14 Goodare, 'Estates in the Scottish Parliament', p. 27.

15 I. Roots, '"The Other House": bicamerism in the Protectorate Parliaments', in
    Blom et al., eds, *Bicameralisme*, pp. 249–53.

16   H.G. Koenigsberger, 'The Italian parliaments from their origins to the end of the 18th century', in *Politicians and Virtuosi* (London, 1986), pp. 54–5.

17   J. Russell Major, *The Estates General of 1560* (Princeton, NJ, 1951), p. 91; H.G. Koenigsberger, 'Dominium regale or dominium politicum et regale: monarchies and parliaments in early modern Europe', in *Politicians and Virtuosi* (London, 1986), pp. 6–7.

18   H.G. Koenigsberger, 'The beginnings of the States General of the Netherlands' *PER* 8, 2 (Dec. 1988), p. 104.

19   I.A.A. Thompson, 'Castile', in J. Miller, ed., *Absolutism in Seventeenth Century Europe* (London, 1990), pp. 80–1; I.A.A. Thompson, *Crown and Cortes* (Aldershot, 1993), VIII, pp. 14–17; IX, pp. 77–8; ibid., 'Crown and Cortes in Castile, 1590–1665' *PER* 2, 1 (June 1982), pp. 32–3, 41 n. 68.

20   Press, 'The system of estates', in Evans and Thomas, eds, *Crown, Church and Estates*, pp. 2–3; F.L. Carsten, *Princes and Parliaments in Germany* (Oxford, 1959), pp. 23–5, 161–2; Koenigsberger, 'Dominium regale', p. 11; F.L. Carsten, *The Origins of Prussia* (Oxford, 1954), p. 165.

21   See e.g. P. Sanz, 'The cities in the Aragonese Cortes in the medieval and early modern periods' *PER* 14, 2 (Dec. 1994), and Bisson, 'Corts of Catalonia', pp. 40–4.

22   A.F. Upton, 'Sweden', in J. Miller, ed., *Absolutism*, p. 103.

23   See above, p. 164.

24   Sir Thomas Smith, *De Republica Anglorum*, ed. Mary Dewar (Cambridge, 1982), pp. 71–2; N. Ball, 'Representation in the English House of Commons: the new boroughs, 1485–1640' *PER* 15 (1995), pp. 117–24.

25   J. Russell Major, 'The third estate in the Estates General of Pontoise, 1561' *Speculum* 29 (1954), pp. 466–7; Lehmberg, 'Role of parliament', in Stjernquist, ed., pp. 84–5; D. Mack Smith, *A History of Sicily*, 3 vols (London, 1968), Vol. 1, pp. 125–6.

26   F.J. Fisher, ed., Thomas Wilson, *The State of England, 1600, Camden Miscellany* 16, 3rd ser., 52 (1936), p. 25.

27   G.A. Rothrock, 'Officials and king's men: a note on the possibilities of royal control in the Estates General' *French Historical Studies* 2, 4 (Fall, 1962), pp. 505–7; J.M. Hayden, 'Deputies and *Qualités*: the Estates General of 1614' *French Historial Studies* 3, 4 (Fall of 1964), pp. 513–14; R. Mousnier, *The Institutions of France under the Absolute Monarchy, 1589–1789* 2 vols (Chicago, 1984), Vol. 2, pp. 218–19, 221–3.

28   M.P. Holt, ed., *Society and Institutions in Early Modern France* (London, 1991), pp. xv–xvi, 59–60; J. Russell Major, *From Renaissance Monarchy to Absolute Monarchy. French Kings, Nobles and Estates* (London, 1994), pp. 328–9; Mousnier, *Institutions of France*, Vol. 2, pp. 218–19, 221–8.

29   Mousnier, *Institutions of France*, p. 219; P. Blickle, 'Peasant political representation in Sweden and Switzerland – a comparison', in Stjernquist, ed., *Swedish Riksdag*, pp. 27–30.

30   Erik Lönnroth, 'Regional and national representation. The problems of communication in olden times', in Stjernquist, ed., *Swedish Riksdag*, pp. 88–90; Metcalf, ed., *The Riksdag*, pp. 41–2.

31 Blickle, 'Peasant political representation', p. 32; Upton, 'Sweden', in Miller, ed., *Absolutism*, pp. 100–3.

32 Myers, *Parliaments and Estates*, p. 28.

33 Goodare, 'Estates in the Scottish Parliament', pp. 16–17.

34 D.L. Smith, *A History of the Modern British Isles, 1603–1707. The Double Crown* (Oxford, 1998), pp. 155–6; S.R. Gardiner, ed., *The Constitutional Documents of the Puritan Revolution, 1625–1660* (3rd edn revised, Oxford, 1968), p. 411; J.R. Young, 'The Scottish Parliament, 1639–1661' PhD, University of Glasgow, 1993, Vol. I, pp. 7–10, 16–17; Vol. II, App. 2, 6, 10, 43.

35 Marongiu, *Medieval Parliaments*, pp. 139–42; M. Roberts, ed., *Sweden as a Great Power, 1611–1697* (London, 1968), p. 25.

36 J.G. Nichols, ed., *The Chronicle of Calais in the Reigns of Henry VII and Henry VIII*, Camden Society, 35 (1846), p. 166.

37 Thompson, *Crown and Cortes*, VIII, pp. 5–7.

38 Bonney, *European Dynastic States*, p. 329; A.J. Veenendaal, 'Fiscal crises and constitutional freedom in the Netherlands, 1450–1795', in P.T. Hoffman and K. Norberg, eds, *Fiscal Crises, Liberty and Representative Government, 1450–1789* (Stanford, CA, 1994), pp. 109–10, 133–4; H.G. Koenigsberger, *Estates and Revolutions* (Ithaca, NY, 1971), pp. 206–8; J.H. Grever, 'Unicameral and multicameral assemblies during the time of John de Witt', in Blom et al., eds, *Bicameralisme*, pp. 189–93, 197–8, 203, 206.

39 J.A. Muller, ed., *The Letters of Stephen Gardiner* (Cambridge, 1933), p. 424; P. Williams, *The Later Tudors. England, 1547–1603* (Oxford, 1995), p. 137; P.W. Hasler, ed., *The House of Commons, 1558–1603* 3 vols (London, 1981), vol. I, pp. 50–3, 146, 201–2.

40 Cardim, 'Ceremonial and ritual', p. 8. For a useful, concise assessment of the 'election/selection' debate, see N.L. Jones, 'Parliament and the governance of Elizabethan England: a review' *Albion* 19, 3 (Fall, 1987), pp. 335–8.

41 J. Russell Major, 'The electoral procedure for the Estates General of France and its social implications' *Humanistica* 10 (1956), pp. 137–46.

42 T.E. Hartley, ed., *Proceedings in the Parliaments of Elizabeth I*, Vol. I, *1558–1581* (Leicester, 1981), pp. 225–9; Smith, *De Republica Anglorum*, p. 79; J.H. Hexter, ed., *Parliament and Liberty* (Stanford, CA, 1992), pp. 88–90; D.M. Dean and N.L. Jones, eds, *The Parliaments of England* (Oxford, 1990), pp. 2–4.

43 Thompson, *Crown and Cortes*, VIII, pp. 12–20, 55–6; Mack Smith, *Sicily*, pp. 125–6.

44 S.G. Ellis, *Tudor Ireland. Crown, Community and the Conflict of Cultures, 1470–1603* (London, 1985), pp. 257–9; C.L. Falkiner, 'The Parliament of Ireland under the Tudor sovereigns: supplementary paper', *Proceedings of the Royal Irish Academy*, 25, Section C, no.10 (1905), pp. 563–6.

45 Ellis, *Tudor Ireland*, pp. 194–5; T.W. Moody, F.X. Martin, F.J. Byrne, eds, *A New History of Ireland*, 10 vols (Oxford, 1978), Vol. 3, pp. 213–14; B. Fitzpatrick, *Seventeenth Century Ireland. The War of Religions* (Dublin, 1988), pp. 47–8.

46 See above, p. 160; Metcalf, ed., *The Riksdag*, p. 58; G.R. Elton, *The Tudor Constitution* (2nd edn, Cambridge, 1982), p. 277; Marongiu, *Medieval Parliaments*, pp. 223–5, 228; Hexter, ed., *Parliament and Liberty*, pp. 86–8; Koenigsberger, 'Parliaments and estates', pp. 135, 150–1, 157.

47   Thompson, *Crown and Cortes*, VIII, pp. 20–33.

48   See above, pp. 167–8.

49   Koenigsberger, *Estates and Revolutions*, pp. 169–75; G. Griffiths, *Representative Government in Western Europe in the Sixteenth Century* (Oxford, 1968), pp. 234–6, 298–301; Bonney, *European Dynastic States*, pp. 327–8. Francis was driven not by autocratic ambition but by frequent financial short-falls. Major, *From Renaissance Monarchy to Absolute Monarchy*, pp. 25–9; R. Bonney, *The Limits of Absolutism in Ancien Régime France* (Aldershot, 1995), I, pp. 112–13.

50   J. Bahlcke, 'Modernisation and state-building in an east-central European Estates' system: the example of the *Confoederatio Bohemica* of 1619' *PER* 17 (Nov. 1997), pp. 65–73.

51   For the elaborate preparations and costs of staging an early Stuart parliamentary session see E.R. Foster, 'Staging a parliament in early Stuart England', in P. Clark, A.G.R. Smith, N. Tyacke, eds, *The English Commonwealth, 1547–1640* (Leicester, 1979), pp. 129–46.

52   E.g. Catalonia, see J.L. Palos, 'The Habsburg Monarchy and the Catalan Corts: the failure of a relationship' *PER* 13, 2 (Dec. 1993), pp. 145–6 and n.32.

53   H. Schück, 'Early Swedish representation: instrument or opponent of the government?' *PER* 8, 1 (June 1988), p. 29.

54   Croft and Thompson, 'Aristocracy and representative government', in Blom et al., eds, *Bicameralisme*, pp. 66–7; H.G. Koenigsberger, 'Parliaments in the sixteenth century and beyond', in Davis, ed., *Origins of Modern Freedom*, p. 276.

55   Koenigsberger, 'Italian parliaments', p. 46; Thompson, *Crown and Cortes*, VIII, pp. 59–61.

56   So, in 1556, for example, only 26 out of 120/130 nobles and ecclesiastics turned up. Koenigsberger, 'Italian parliaments', p. 41; Mack Smith, *Sicily*, pp. 124–6.

57   K.M. Dunkley, 'Patronage and power in 17th century France: Richelieu's clients and the Estates of Brittany' *PER* 1, 1 (June 1981), p. 4; J.B. Collins, *Classes, Estates and Order in Early Modern Brittany* (Cambridge, 1994), pp. 161–3.

58   Major, 'Electoral procedure', p. 144; Brown, *Kingdom or Province?*, pp. 14–15, 44; Croft and Thompson, 'Aristocracy and representative government', in Blom et al., eds, *Bicameralisme*, pp. 65–6 and n.7; J. Wormald, *Court, Kirk and Community: Scotland 1470–1625* (London, 1981), pp. 156–7.

59   Roberts, ed., *Sweden as a Great Power*, p. 12; Graves, *House of Lords*, pp. 87, 263 n.230.

60   In 1615, Finland's own assembly, the *Lantdag*, was convened by Gustav Adolf. J.-M. Jansson, 'The Finnish Riksdag – a common heritage', in Stjernquist, ed., pp. 44–5.

61   E. Lousse, 'The Estates of Brabant to the end of the fifteenth century: the make-up of the assembly', in P. Mack and M.C. Jacob, eds, *Politics and Culture in Early Modern Europe* (Cambridge, 1987), pp. 95–9; Goodare, 'Parliament and society', p. 5.

62   B.L. Harleian MS 253, fols 32, 35.

63   Brown, *Kingdom or Province?*, p. 14; Major, *Renaissance Monarchy to Absolute Monarchy*, pp. 113–14; B.L. Lansdowne MS 41, f.45; Major, 'The third estate of Pontoise', p. 469.

64 This reflected the 'Cold War' mentality of the government, which was constantly nervous about Sigismund, ex-king of Sweden and now Poland's elected monarch, Roberts, ed., *Sweden as a Great Power*, p. 12.

65 Ibid., p. 11.

66 See below, Chapter 7.

67 See below, pp. 202, 207.

68 Metcalf, ed., *The Riksdag*, p. 66.

69 See above, p. 162 and below, pp. 198–200.

70 Thompson, 'Castile', in Miller, ed., *Absolutism*, pp. 75–6; Major, 'The third estate of Pontoise', pp. 472–3; Graves, *House of Lords*, pp. 197–8; Gardiner, *Constitutional Documents*, pp. 85, 95.

71 Dunkley, 'Patronage and power', pp. 4–12.

72 Koenigsberger, *Estates and Revolutions*, p. 200; R.S. Rait, *The Parliaments of Scotland* (Glasgow, 1924), p. 407; R. Mettam, ed., *Government and Society in Louis XIV's France* (London, 1977), pp. 51–2.

73 B.L. Harl. MS 253 f.33.

74 E.g. those attending conventions in 1561, 1564, 1565 ($\times$ 2) and 1566 = 30, 13, 38, 30 and 25. Goodare, 'Parliament and society', pp. 480–502; Major, *From Renaissance Monarchy to Absolute Monarchy*, pp. 112, 133, 174, 223, 225–30, 232; R. Bonney, *Society and Government in France under Richelieu and Mazarin, 1624–61* (London, 1988), pp. 7, 87, 93–4; J.B. Collins, *The State in Early Modern France* (Cambridge, 1995), pp. 22, 47–9.

7

Business and the Manner
of its Transaction

Taxation

THE NATURE AND range of parliamentary business and functions were,
to a large extent, determined by the origins of representative
assemblies as royal institutions and by acceptance of the principle *quod
omnes tangit*. Parliaments were in a sense curial enlargements: so *consilium*, a
vital function of royal councils, was also a parliamentary duty, although
time transformed it into a right. Throughout the medieval and early
modern history of the French Estates-general 'counsel', not 'consent', was
its crucial function. In the same way parliamentary *auxilium*, especially
financial assistance in the form of grants of taxation, betrays the royal
origins of assemblies. It became increasingly important as the domain-
state was replaced by the fiscal or tax-state. The financial role of the
French Estates-general was only one of recommendation, not consent.
Many parliaments, however, obtained not only the right of consent but
also control of the assessment, collection and administration of taxes.
Those of the pre-revolutionary Netherlands in the 1550s, the post-
revolutionary southern Netherlands, the provinces in the loose-knit
Dutch United Provinces and sixteenth-century Hungary also controlled
spending; the Württemberg Diet did so from the 1550s; and, after the
second English Revolution (1688–89), Parliaments established firm
control over appropriation of supply.[1] The Cortes of the three eastern
Spanish kingdoms voted, collected and administered revenue and the
fiscal importance of Aragon's assembly was not diminished by the crisis of
1592.

Function, however, should not necessarily be equated with power,
as the financially hard-pressed parliaments of Naples, Sardinia and
Sicily were well aware. Whatever other functions the parliaments of the
Habsburg composite monarchy performed, they paled into insignifi-
cance alongside the taxative role. This was true of post-1580 Portugal,

the Caroline and Philippic Netherlands and, above all, of the Castilian Cortes. Although Spanish kings had non-parliamentary tax alternatives, such as the lucrative *alcabala* (sales tax), the autonomy and decentralisation which characterised the fiscal system gave the Cortes a crucial position in the management of both *alcabalas* and *servicios*. In the late sixteenth and early seventeenth centuries, the *millones* extended its role and control, until Philip IV circumvented it and finally ended its existence. The key to the Castilian Cortes' financial role lies in the contrast between the maximisation of royal power at the centre and the flimsy framework of royal authority in the localities.[2] This was equally true in France, where provincial estates voted and usually collected the taxes in more than half the kingdom.[3] The fragmented nature of the French polity effectively limited royal power and made the fiscal functions of the provincial estates vital to the crown's financial well-being. The importance of their role did not diminish during the seventeenth century, but their number did, whilst taxes increased as the crown became more effective in reducing the survivors to obedience.[4]

Not just in France and the Spanish empire but throughout Christian Europe parliaments were most valued by monarchs for their financial 'servicing'. The German estates in the sixteenth and seventeenth centuries were vital for that very reason. Indeed *Landtage sind Geldtage* [Parliaments are financial assemblies] was a contemporary saying.[5] Although some, such as Bavaria, fell under ducal control in the seventeenth century, many continued to control the mechanisms of consent and fiscal management. The regional representatives of Schleswig-Holstein, for example, provided prompt taxes and in return retained fiscal autonomy in tax administration. Württemberg, a kind of role model in this respect, derived its financial responsibility and power from an arrangement between duke and estates in 1514. The duke was expected to 'live of his own' and the estates accepted liability only for his debts – at least until 1638 when it voted taxes to supplement his current income. Eastwards beyond the Empire, in Poland and the Habsburg hereditary lands, parliaments exercised similar financial responsibility and managerial control. In Bohemia the Diet's power to assess and collect taxes – and pass the burden to the peasants – actually increased after the unsuccessful rebellion of 1620.[6]

One way in which assemblies could safeguard their financial role and maintain a degree of princely dependence was by granting taxes which were temporary or periodic and so required parliamentary renewal. The Castilian Cortes granted the traditional *servicio* and the *millones* for fixed periods. English and Scottish monarchs received permanent customs dues, and in England (until Charles I) Parliament voted each new monarch tunnage and poundage (additional dues) for life. Direct taxation, however, was always for a limited period. The grant of four fifteenths and tenths to Henry VIII in 1540, for example, was paid in four annual instalments and the subsidy of 1542–43 was payable 'by the space of three yeres'. Eighty years later Charles I's urgent war subsidies, obtained in the session of June–July 1625, were to be paid in two instalments: before 20 October 'next coming' and by 20 April 1626.

As the previous pages demonstrate, two ingredients determined the nature of a parliament's financial function: first, the extent to which it exercised, in practice and in law, the right of consent to taxation; secondly, the extent to which it controlled or at least participated in the assessment, collection, administration and appropriation of the voted taxes. It is evident that, as in most things, there was geographical variety. And, as usual, we also have to take into account changes over time. The Scottish Parliament is a case in point, because its record as a taxing-body is a commentary on a common early modern European phenomenon: the shift in royal funding from a domanial to a tax base. There is some evidence of this in the reign of James VI, especially from the 1580s, even though, until the Revolution, Scottish taxation was feudal and based on a very old customary assessment system. During the previous twenty years parliaments and conventions had voted sums ranging from £4,000–£12,000. Then in 1581 a convention levied £40,000 to counter a military assault from 'sindrie partis of Europe'. Thereafter the sums voted varied between £15,000–£20,000, £40,000 and, in 1588 and 1594, £100,000. In 1621, despite fierce opposition, James's government secured the largest recorded ordinary tax to date and a new tax on annual rents. The archaic tax structure and the antiquated assessment system remained, however, until they were replaced during the Civil War and Revolution. At the Restoration the Scottish Parliament voted Charles II an annual income, equivalent to £40,000 sterling, for life. And shortly afterwards the recent innovation in tax assessment, based on valued rent, was adopted. So within a century a new fiscal system, in which Parliament had an increasingly central role, was created. It was not of course an isolated phenomenon. Fiscal modernisation also occurred, for example, in England and the pioneering Netherlands, in both of which representative assemblies were institutionally and politically much stronger and were the chief instruments of change.[7]

The taxative function made the early modern centuries a time of both opportunity and danger for representative assemblies. The states' financial needs made them more important and valued, but they might become hindrances which had to be overcome or set aside. The advent of absolutism, for example, in Denmark and Piedmont, or their failure to fulfil rulers' growing expectations, as in France and Naples, could render them ineffective or lay them to rest. The Swedish *Riksdag*, a parliamentary latecomer, experienced the gamut of political fortunes. For long its tax role, especially in relation to the *landsting* (provincial assemblies), was uncertain. Although Karl IX used it to authorise levies, Gustav Adolf's accession charter (1611) was vague on the subject. Its taxing authority was finally acknowledged during Queen Christina's regency in the 1630s, but that was undermined by the advent of absolutism in 1680. For good or ill, financial assistance was the most important service rendered by parliaments to princes.[8]

Legislation

Legislation, like taxation, was one of those functions which derived from the royal origins of representative assemblies. Not all early modern assemblies retained the right to enact laws in conjunction with the ruler or indeed had ever enjoyed that right. In Castile it was a presumption of Roman civil law that legislation was a royal prerogative.[9] Likewise in France the king made laws independently. However, they then had to be registered by the Paris *parlement*, the court of appeal, whose magistrates had the right to raise objections to the legislation before registration. In Sicily too the king or his representative, the viceroy, could legislate without reference to the *Parlamento*, whose law-making role was confined to the presentation of petitions. He often rejected them, whilst those which were accepted were not necessarily observed or enforced.[10]

Castile, France and Sicily were exceptions, not the norm. Many European assemblies, as curial extensions, exercised judicial functions, amongst them those in Britain, Aragon, Poland and Friuli. So they received and adjudicated upon petitions from the rulers' subjects. In the course of time, however, parliaments moved from judicial process to legislation in order to deal with petitions and grievances and to respond to urgent and important concerns of both ruler and subjects. Spanish kings could obtain laws in their Aragonese kingdoms only with the consent of the Cortes. Sessions invariably ended with the declaration of new laws and taxes before the king and estates in plenary session. To contemporaries, such as the chroniclers Blancas and Martel (writing in 1585 and 1601 respectively), legislation was the most important function of the Aragon Cortes. Nor was it significantly impaired by the 1592 crisis.[11] In Ireland the parliament rolls of 1462–81 illustrate how subjects as well as rulers sought and obtained benefits from an assembly: of the 809 recorded acts, 155 concerned the whole lordship and the rest apparently originated in private petitions which related to communities within *and* beyond the Pale. From 1494, however, its value declined. Before then Irish Parliaments had been almost annual events, but from then until the end of the Tudor dynasty in 1603 there were only twelve. Furthermore, Poynings' Law, enacted in 1494 to curb the activities of the Tudors' Anglo-Irish governors, required the prior approval of king and council in Whitehall for any bill before it could be submitted to the Parliament in Dublin. The constraints which this imposed, together with infrequent sessions, reduced it to an occasional instrument in the service of the English administration.[12]

In contrast, legislative business grew in importance in the parliaments of both Scotland and England. Scottish acts tended to be textually brief, narrow in coverage and deal with just a few specific points.[13] On the other hand, the legislation during the fifteenth to seventeenth centuries covered a wide range of subjects including the economy, social policy, national defence, the royal patrimony and admin-istration of justice. The institution's judicial significance was reflected in the parliamentary committee which, in James V's reign for example, was actively concerned with criminal matters between sessions, and of course, as the highest court of the land and the law-giver, in the 'immense amount of law' which it enacted.[14] For example, under James VI, 74 acts were passed in 1585, 136 in 1587, 182 in 1592, 95 in 1597, 64 in 1609, 75 in 1612 and 114 in 1621. The 100 statutes of 1594 included acts on ministers, bishops, the Sabbath and kirks, law courts and the offences of patricide, fraud, slander, theft and usury, wine, wildfowl and salmon and more than forty beneficial measures for individuals and localities.[15] Furthermore, after the Scottish Reformation parliament dealt with vital matters of Church–state relations in the 'Black Acts' of 1584. At the same time, the acts of conventions were ceasing to have the authority of statute which was emerging as the supreme law, superior also to the precedents of the court of session, the supreme civil court. So in 1661 it required statute to annul the enactments of the 'rebel' Parliaments of the 1640s.[16]

Within contemporary England the 'rise' of statute was swift, even dramatic. Until the 1530s its scope was limited by property rights and matters spiritual, both of which were deemed to be beyond its competence. Between the 1530s and 1559 parliamentary legislation demolished those limitations. Statute became supreme and omnicompetent. In consequence, Parliament became a popular resort for the state, localities, interests and individuals[17] to seek legislative solutions and benefits. Nevertheless, in the output of acts the early modern English legislature could not match the Scottish record.[18]

Many of those medieval continental assemblies which had exercised extensive legislative authority continued to do so in the sixteenth and seventeenth centuries. They included some of the *Landtage*, for example in Saxony, and the diet of Habsburg Hungary. The Polish *Sejm* was able to control the initiation of legislation by the promulgation of the constitution *Nihil Novi* in 1505. In contrast, the Bohemian *Sněm* lost the right to initiate legislation in 1620. The assemblies of the Low Countries before the revolution and in the revolutionary state of the seven Dutch provinces were actively concerned with the management and regulation of economic affairs. In yet another contrast, in 1632 the Swedish *Riksdag*, parliament of another relatively recent independent state, still had no legislative monopoly, much was enacted by royal ordinance and it had to petition for permission to initiate. Its legislative power was not fully established until the mid-seventeenth century. And that continued only until the 1680s, when the *Riksdag* virtually abdicated its role. As so often, diversity was the consequence of circumstances peculiar to a particular society.[19]

Privilege, protection and the presentation of grievances

On the other hand, the legislative function does indicate a characteristic common to many European assemblies. This is especially true of those which enacted laws for the community and specific interests within it as well as for the state. 'Private' legislation is indicative of the way in which parliaments became a two-way process. Representative assemblies developed their own agendas which encompassed safeguards as well as services, and protection of the community as well as provision for the ruler. Those in the Netherlands typified the fullest development of this in the commonest form of late medieval state, *dominium politicum et regale*: new rulers had to promise on oath to uphold the provinces' privileges, make no laws which breached them and levy no taxes without their consent. Whether or not they sought *consilium* they were expected to listen to advice on those matters which the estates regarded as important. This was not, however, something unique to the Low Countries. Most European Christian rulers swore to recognise and observe existing geographical, social and economic privileges, liberties and immunities.[20]

Parliaments or (where they existed) permanent committees tended to become the watchdogs of privilege and also instruments for its extension. Their members were often particularly sensitive to breaches of their privileges (especially freedom from arrest and free speech) and of institutional liberties which developed over the course of time. When King James I of England insisted that parliamentary free speech was limited and dependent on royal grace, he provoked the famous commons' protestation of 1621. And when Charles I arrested two members of the lower house in 1626, for words uttered there, all business in the commons ceased by way of protest. It was not solely a matter of power politics, but also an issue of principle and even a concern for efficiency. This was evident in a protest speech delivered by a member of the Swedish *Riksdag* in 1680: 'What is spoken, without any malice, with good intention and for a good purpose . . . should in no way be taken badly at once: everyone is understood to have freedom to speak here . . . [N]o one should be subject to suspicion.'[21] The crucial question of course was the extent of that freedom. Was free speech absolute and unqualified? Or was it limited in content, to matters placed before them, and in honesty and directness by due deference to the ruler and the avoidance of 'licence'. The latter was usually the case.

Despite such constraints the occasion of a parliament provided a legitimate opportunity for the articulate spokesmen of a community – from Polish *szlachta* to English knights and burgesses – to air discontent, present grievances and investigate ministerial misconduct.[22] Furthermore, the resolution of grievances was a generally unquestioned parliamentary function with its allotted places in the parliamentary timetable and order of business. So 'as is the custom of parliament' examiners of grievances were named to investigate and settle them, before the assemblies of the Aragonese kingdoms and Sardinia proceeded to other business. Naples had a similar set procedure, whereas the Castilian Cortes presented its petitions at the end of the session. The business of the Swedish *Riksdag* often commenced with a reading of the government's response to the grievances presented at its previous meeting. During the session a list of general grievances was compiled from the commonest complaints of each estate. Then in the seventeenth century it became customary for the four estates to present their general grievances towards the end of the session and for the government to answer them when it had ended. Most European rulers accepted the consideration of grievances as an expression of their duty to dispense justice. So Hungarian *postulata et gravamina*, the French Estates-general's *cahiers de doléances*, Portuguese and Castilian *capitulos*, Sicilian and Piedmontese *capitoli* and the *gravamina* of the Diet of Hesse were duly presented for royal scrutiny.[23]

In some cases, there was a reciprocal link between *capitoli* and subsidy. So in territories as diverse as early modern Austria, Languedoc, the Aragonese kingdoms and Sicily supply was conditional upon redress, although the effectiveness of that bargaining advantage varied. When the Languedoc estates met it was normal to devise both the terms of a tax grant and a list of grievances. But it was not unknown for a monarch to decide on a tax before making a request to the assembly. In Aragon too monarchs did not invariably accept the imposing formal rights of the assembly. Grievances had to be approved by unanimous vote, presented and redressed before a *servicio* was granted. Spanish kings were constantly vexed at the time consumed by grievances, though many of them were not abuses by royal officials but complaints between social orders, localities, interests and individuals. In the sixteenth and seventeenth centuries they frequently attempted to speed up the process by prompt responses to petitions or using pressure and patronage to persuade *procuradores* into action. In the Cortes of the 1592 crisis *nemine discrepante* was replaced by the principle that 'the majority of the estate makes the estate' (except in relation to Aragonese penal laws and assent to taxes). Yet in the following century the business priorities of the Aragonese Cortes remained unchanged. Redress of grievances was equally important in the assemblies of Valencia and Catalonia. There too it was also unpopular with the Habsburgs, as illustrated by Philip II's annoyance at the Monzon meeting of the Cortes of the Aragonese kingdoms in 1585 and the hostile response of Philip IV and Olivares to the deluge of Catalan grievances in 1626. Even in the Castilian Cortes, for long depicted as the crown's pliable tool, *procuradores* were capable of firmly-stated complaints and criticisms: for example, objections to non-parliamentary taxes in 1566–67 and demands for government actions and solutions to the serious economic problems from the 1580s onwards. In the Cortes of 1576 the *procuradores* actually achieved a reduction in the *encabezamiento* before granting the normal *servicios*. The advent of the *millones* tax arrangement and the conditions attached to it then established as a regular procedure what had previously been absent, the conditional nature of supply.[24]

Other assemblies were more dependent on royal goodwill for the satisfaction of their complaints. The right of petitioning was one of the three main functions of the Cortes of Portugal. Hundreds of local *capitulos* (petitions) were handed in at each meeting, whilst members also raised complaints which often provoked debate. Yet most grievances were not satisfied and Cardim describes petitioning as just 'a stereotyped way of expressing complaint' and 'a kind of ritual protest'.[25] In Sicily too 'redress before supply' did not in practice operate, although grants of money were theoretically conditional. Royal replies to petitions returned from Spain long after taxes had been granted the standing committee was ineffective; many petitions were rejected and some others were not put into effect. In parliaments as diverse as the English Parliament, the French Estates-general and the Diet of the German principality of Hesse the right to present grievances was unquestioned, but it was not linked to supply and so redress depended on royal goodwill. Moreover, the presentation of *gravamina* or *petita* to the landgrave of Hesse did not become a formally acknowledged right until 1764.[26] The Swedish *Riksdag* certainly acquired the right to present grievances and sometimes, as in 1650, the estates seized the opportunity to make specific demands on other issues. On a number of occasions during the seventeenth century they even attempted to secure redress before responding to the propositions.[27] That all ended, however, with the establishment of Karl XI's absolute rule in the 1680s. The *Riksdag* lost its effective role in legislation and taxation, whilst free speech was restricted.

Parliaments' other purposes and functions

Some parliaments were also high courts, another curial extension, or they acquired judicial functions over the course of time. Judicial process was also a first step on the road to legislation. Wherever one looks, from the British Isles to Scandinavia, Germany, Poland, Aragon and Italy, one will find early modern assemblies which made law and dispensed justice.[28] In some cases they also performed other important law-related functions, especially concerning the succession. The Swedish *Riksdag* flexed adolescent political muscles and gradually acquired status as it deposed and elected kings during the sixteenth century. Parliaments also came to the fore as they attempted to resolve conflict or provide a modicum of stability during the uncertainties of royal minorities, interregna and succession disputes where partible inheritance was the norm, especially in Germany.[29] Parliamentary effectiveness was, of course, dependent on a number of variables, such as royal approval or acquiescence and a broad-ranging agreement on the steps to be taken. So by a combination of persuasion and management Henry VIII secured from loyal English Parliaments a series of succession acts. They accommodated the changes in the legal status of his wives and children, laid down the order of succession at the time of enactment and gave statutory authority to his will as the final determinant of that succession. Elizabeth I would not tolerate parliamentary 'trespass' on such matters. But in 1701 the act of settlement determined the succession for centuries to come as it passed over fifty-seven Roman catholic Stuart claimants in order to guarantee a protestant dynasty after Queen Anne's demise.

One very important function of parliaments, so far as the prince was concerned, was information. This was the one occasion when the ruler came together with not only his spiritual and lay elites, but also those who knew the state of play in the cities and ports, trade and industry, the law, countryside and farming sector. It gave him the opportunity to discover and make the appropriate response to problems and threats, actual or potential, in his kingdom. It was also a point of contact which enabled rulers to patronise and fraternise with the elites, reinforce the bonds of loyalty with their subjects and dazzle the lesser with the might and majesty of kingship. The early modern Portuguese Cortes offers an outstanding example of the way in which rulers exploited the occasion of parliament to several ends: not only *auxilium* but political interaction and, in the elaborate symbolism of the parliamentary ceremonial, a public 'ritual manifestation of the bond between king and kingdom'.[30]

As Julian Goodare points out in the case of the Scottish Parliament, an assembly could also fulfil a dual political role: it continuously reaffirmed the legitimacy of royal government and its actions; and its meetings enabled the political elite both to satisfy themselves as to the legitimacy of government actions and to give out warning signals if it found some of those actions unacceptable. In the violent politics which characterised Scotland until James VI created a more stable polity in the 1580s and 1590s it had an additional political role. It could not prevent civil war (as in 1570–73), feuds (as between Maxwells and Johnstones) or rebellion, but James used it to arbitrate in political disputes, settle feuds, resolve civil conflicts and patch up relations after the event.[31]

Affirmation of legitimacy was a common function of European parliaments. At the beginning of a new reign an assembly would confirm the new ruler's accession and in elaborate ceremonial give allegiance to him, often in return for promises on oath: in the conditional and contractual Aragonese oath; the *joyeuse entrée* of Brabant; the *grand privilège* imposed on rulers of the Low Countries from 1477 onwards; and in Portugal not only the acclamation of the new ruler but also the swearing in of his heir, the crown prince. Other dynastic matters were also subject to parliamentary approval. Such were the marriage of the Portuguese crown prince and, from 1576, of the king of Poland. So far as Elizabeth I was concerned, royal marriage was entirely a matter of the royal prerogative. Nevertheless her half-sister Mary had secured parliamentary ratification of the treaty for her marriage to Philip of Spain in 1554, whilst her father had resorted to statute to clean up his marital messes.[32]

Beyond this point generalisation about parliamentary functions becomes very difficult, because of the diversity in the formal powers and political muscle of assemblies, their relations with the rulers who summoned them and the strengths, weaknesses and stresses in a ruling dynasty at any given moment. Although foreign policy was generally recognised to be the ruler's preserve, an active foreign policy involving war required *auxilium* and so, by implication, parliamentary approval. It could also become a matter of consequence if that policy imperilled trading interests or offended religious loyalties. In 1621 a committee of the English house of commons petitioned James I that his heir should be 'timely and happily married to one of our own religion'. They trod on sensitive ground because, in questioning the wisdom of James's desire for an Anglo-Spanish match, they were touching on both foreign policy and dynastic matters. James's outrage at this invasion in turn raised the issue of parliamentary free speech.[33] In contrast, some European monarchs were much less sensitive and actively involved parliaments in foreign affairs. French kings sometimes sought the ratification of treaties by provincial estates; Duke Ulrich of Württemberg promised to consult the Diet before declaring war; and, in their succession charters, the seventeenth-century Swedish kings Gustav II Adolf, Karl X Gustav and Karl XI swore not to undertake military campaigns without the *Riksdag's* consent. Furthermore, as in the charter of 1611, the monarch acknowledged the estates' right of assent to alliances, truces or peace treaties. At various times and in various places parliaments influenced or controlled appointments to offices (e.g. in Poland), management of territorial administration (as in Württemberg), and the quality and devaluation of the currency (e.g. in the Low Countries and Poland). The *Bundestage*, which carried out public policy in the name of 'our lords', the communes of the Grisons (or Gray Leagues) in the Valtelline, made policy decisions, heard judicial appeals in civil matters, supervised the territorial administration and defence, appointed administrative and judicial officers, legislated, taxed, and regulated the religious life of the community.[34] The list of parliamentary activities is seemingly endless and always fascinating.

The lives of parliaments: frequency of meetings and permanent committees

The relative frequency and regularity of parliamentary meetings was largely determined by the needs of the rulers who called them. Apart from a few assemblies, such as the States-general of the Low Countries, which acquired the right to meet without being summoned, the occasion, duration and termination of meetings were government initiatives. Such initiatives were, in turn, responses to a wide variety of political circumstances, which tended to be fluid and changeable rather than static. Summonses were also prompted by the relative strength or weakness of dynastic governments and political elites, by the varying functions of parliaments and sometimes by their capacity to give political support to the ruler or conversely to challenge the direction of his policies. So the rhythms of parliamentary life varied from one dynastic state to another.

The variations tell us little about the relative strength of rulers and assemblies. The French monarchy called the Estates-general only eight times between 1484 and 1614, and all but three of those meetings were held when the crown was weak and under pressure during the wars of religion. Its preference was frequent meetings of the tax-voting provincial assemblies. Spanish kings rarely summoned the strong particularist Aragonese Cortes because it was not worth the time, cost and effort for such modest financial returns. German emperors could expect little, so the *Reichstag* met only forty-one times between 1492 and 1654. In contrast, the Polish *Sejm*, monopolised by a powerful nobility, met over 150 times between the end of the fifteenth century and 1661; in the Netherlands there were sixty-two meetings of the strong States-general between 1499 and 1576; and, if the Addled Parliament is included, there were forty-four English parliaments meeting in eighty-two sessions between 1497 and 1660. Circumstantial changes sometimes altered the regularity of assemblies. During the turbulent years of reformation and political conflict, followed by James VI's reassertion of royal authority, all between 1560 and 1603, some thirty Scottish Parliaments and seventy-seven conventions met. But from the regal union in 1603 until 1689 absentee monarchs called only seventeen and twelve respectively. Between 1499 and 1547 there were twelve Irish Parliaments but, as consensus politics were replaced by conflict, only eight in the following 90 years. In Castile the reverse occurred. Certainly the frequency of Cortes declined: from thirty-six between 1505 and 1598 (93 years) to fourteen between 1598 and 1665 (67 years). These figures, however, are deceptive. As Thompson shows, from the middle of Philip II's reign it changed from an occasional assembly to 'a more or less permanent part of the political scene'. Between 1539 and 1572 it was in session for under two months a year on average; then, between 1573 and 1665, that figure was eight. For all but 20 months it sat continuously between 1656 and 1665. This was not because kings confidently applied to a weak assembly for more and more money. It was because, from the later sixteenth century, the Cortes acquired 'a far more active role . . . a new vitality and a new functional importance'.[35]

In one respect, however, it is possible to generalise. From the fourteenth century many continental assemblies established what the English Parliaments lacked: permanent committees.[36] The previously cited figures refer only to meetings of full assemblies. Between such sessions permanent committees performed a variety of functions. In addition to their role as constitutional watchdogs and protectors of parliamentary, local and social liberties and privileges,[37] many – in Germany, the Aragonese kingdoms, Sardinia, Sicily, Franche-Comté and Friuli – collected and administered taxes and in some cases even controlled appropriation. The syndics and other bureaucrats in *pays d'états* such as Béarn, Dauphiné and Provence had important administrative and financial functions. In Friuli the parliament and committees, especially the *consiglio* or standing committee of twelve members, eventually acquired an important role in the government of the principality until it was absorbed into the Venetian Republic. The Polish *Sejm* developed important permanent bodies, notably the constitutional deputation and the treasury affairs committee. In Sweden the Secret Committee (formed in 1627) dealt with confidential government matters such as foreign policy and it became of central importance in the *Riksdag*, whilst the Committee on the Bank (given permanent status in 1672) reviewed the state of the Bank of Sweden. Both were recruited from the estates of clergy, nobles and burghers, but excluded the peasantry. Some parliaments became dependent on their committees. Early modern German *Landtage* tended to work through such permanent bodies rather than full parliaments. In Württemberg (from 1521) committees not only exercised fiscal and administrative responsibilities, but they also participated in important decisions about government and the economy, without the need to summon a full parliament. The Dutch parliamentary system was fully operated by standing and special committees. For centuries the Scottish Parliaments had, in effect, handed over business and authority to the committee of the articles. This was not a permanent committee. But in 1640 the covenanters dismantled its power and replaced it with a network of committees, one of which – the permanent committee of estates – exercised full parliamentary authority and sat between parliaments and sessions in 1640–51.[38]

Standing committees gave continuity and permanence to parliaments. Two weaknesses, however, could and sometimes did diminish their effectiveness. It is an eternal commonplace that a proportion of the money gathered in for public service slips through official fingers into private purses. Parliamentary committees, which collected and managed tax revenue, were no exception. The powerful *diputació* of the Catalan Corts, for example, 'had turned into an enormous racket run for the benefit of the ruling few'. Indeed Philip III and Philip IV regarded it as the villain primarily responsible for the deteriorating political relations between the crown and Catalonia. The estates' committee of nine in Franche-Comté was similarly corrupt. And one has to ask questions about the financial integrity of the Swedish Committee on the Bank, when the governors of the Bank of Sweden took part in the committee's review of their financial management. Furthermore, standing committees were vulnerable to royal influence and management, even manipulation and control. The classic case of course is the Scottish committee of the articles, which James VI transformed into the vital mechanism for ensuring productive Parliaments in the royal interest – he even sat on the committee and voted. There was, however, a common princely preference for committees, the membership of which was relatively small and so could be persuaded or pressurised into compliance, especially between sessions. The Valencian *Deputación* was weak; so too was its Castilian counterpart, established during a brief noble victory over royal authority in 1469 but subordinated to the council of finance in the sixteenth century. Spanish viceroys even controlled the composition of the Sicilian *Deputazione del Regno* and the Neapolitan *Deputazione delle grazie*. Committees were at their weakest when, as in Bavaria, the dukes coerced the standing committee rather than call a full assembly of the estates for a tax grant.[39]

Ceremony and ritual: the importance of hierarchy, deference and precedence

Parliaments were occasions not only to parade the majesty of kingship but also to demonstrate that society was based on rank, order and degree. The state openings of English Parliaments were grand affairs and popular public occasions as crowds turned out to see the monarch, peers and bishops, richly attired and in dignified procession from Whitehall Palace to Westminster. Everything was conducted with due solemnity: the church service; the procession with peers in order of degree and antiquity of title; and the state opening in the lords' chamber, when monarch, bishops and nobles in their robes were seated and the commons were summoned to stand below the bar at the lower end of the house, in order to hear the lord chancellor's speech. In 1604 very few commons' members heard their new king, James I, address the assembly, because their summons was forgotten. Yet that did not hold up a ceremony in which their presence was peripheral rather than central.

In the opening ceremonies, processions and seating arrangements of continental assemblies too pomp and circumstance combined with important statements about each person's place in the pecking order. With some variations, most assemblies adopted a similar scenario, which involved a religious service or a sermon at some point and then a meeting between ruler and estates. At that meeting the reasons why he had called the assembly were formally delivered: for example, the *propositio* in Friuli, Sardinia and Sicily and the chancellor's address in England, France and Poland. These were often admired as works of art. Vincent Fabricius described Prince Ossolinski's speech at the *Sejm* in 1647 as 'so crafted by nature, so arranged, that next to all the rest it ought to be assessed as incomparable, and as nearly divine in merit'.

Some opening ceremonies were particularly grand. When a new Habsburg king visited Aragon he promised the Cortes that he would uphold the kingdom's *fueros* and liberties and the estates swore allegiance. The inaugural session of the Aragonese Cortes (at which the protonotary stated the government's needs) and the closing *solio* were, as in England, occasions of splendour and the only ones when the various component parts of the assembly came together. The Catalan assemblies too were called to celebrate a new reign and do homage and fealty to a new king. By all accounts, the opening of the medieval and early modern Portuguese Cortes, 'a moment of great emotional and symbolic intensity', was even more elaborate. And when it acclaimed a new king (including the rebel duke of Braganza in 1640) and swore in a crown prince, the occasion was designed to project an image of the monarch as leader of the kingdom and father of his people. Although it was a secular state ceremony, the reading of the opening address by a member of the clergy illustrates, in Cardim's words, 'a crucial liturgic element and a divine touch'. After 1539, however, the Cortes of Castile lacked a noble presence and so it was a relatively dull and colourless occasion. With this exception, meetings of the Iberian Cortes were opportunities to demonstrate the power and majesty of the crown in ceremonies which were elaborate and splendid. However, in Portugal the ritual and ceremonial changed over time from a statement of royal strength to a way of masking royal weakness.[40]

Even a relatively small and politically unimportant state such as Württemberg promoted the commencement of the *Landtag* as an important state occasion, though it was a mixture of pageantry, informality and affability. There were the usual ceremonies: a stately procession, a solemn opening in which the president of the privy council read the *propositionen* or reasons for calling parliament, and a sermon in the castle church. There were in addition, however, a preliminary lecture to the estates on the etiquette to be observed, a concert of organ music and singing, and a banquet at which the duke was present for six hours. At the beginning and end of the opening ceremony he shook hands with every member and he drank a toast to them all at the banquet. The whole day was designed to express the bonding between the duke and the estates.[41]

All opening ceremonies were intended as statements of royal authority, order, political harmony, loyalty and stability, qualities which would then characterise the session. Unfortunately such worthy intentions were sometimes frustrated. Lack of organisation could be the culprit. Oxenstierna's criticism to the Swedish *Riksdag* in 1617 related to the conduct of business, but the recommended reforms which followed began with the procedures and seating arrangements for the opening ceremony. Order had to be imposed at the very beginning. A similar concern was shown in Württemberg, where the etiquette lecture was designed to prevent uncouth elected provincial yokels from disgracing themselves or offending the duke at the banquet.[42]

This, however, was not the only problem. Precedence in processions and seating arrangements could cause much stress. The opening of the Scottish Parliament was colourful and majestic, especially from James VI's reign. In 1587 an act of Parliament regulated the procession known as the 'riding of the Parliament', in an attempt to reverse the 'decay of the forme, honour and majestie' of the institution. James was very conscious of the public impact of a carefully staged opening. So he laid down the dress requirements for the brilliant riding to the 'Red Parliament' of 1606, when members of the estates wore silk of crimson and scarlet, trimmed with ermine and velvet. But confrontation and violence were always a danger, as a proclamation of 1578 indicated, when it warned members to come 'in quyett maner without armour'. In 1567 the burgesses of Dundee and Perth brawled on a point of precedence; when the privy council ruled on three precedence disputes between rival nobles in 1587 the losers withdrew from Parliament and one even issued a challenge to a duel. There were more clashes in 1600 and, despite the issue of a table of rankings in 1606, disputes continued.[43]

There were other necessary formalities which required action at the beginning of a parliament, such as the examination of titles and nomination of committees (as in Sardinia), the presentation of instructions and powers by delegates to the Dutch States-general, the scrutiny of credentials and proxies and, in post-Reformation England, the ministering of the oath of supremacy. As the redress of grievances was a legitimate and, to deputies, a very important parliamentary function, complaints procedures were often put in motion at the beginning of some assemblies. This might involve the appointment of scrutineers to sort petitions and assess their validity. Estates in France and Sweden, for example, had to compile composite schedules or *cahiers* of grievances for presentation to the government. This was no formality as the Swedish estate of peasants discovered in 1634, when the council reprimanded it for 'so ill-considered a memorandum, with its threat to go home immediately if they did not get their business despatched without delay'.[44] So far as governments were concerned these were the sometimes irksome preliminaries to the main business of the session.

Parliamentary proceedings: transaction of business

That 'main' business was the fulfilment of the purposes for which parliaments had been called. It was accepted that members had priorities of their own. These included redress of grievances which, as we have seen, had their allotted procedural slot. But taxes and possibly new laws had primacy of place. Royal needs, stated in the opening addresses, constituted an appeal. So the Castilian propositions emphasised the king's piety and his 'deserving goodness'.[45] Those needs were then considered and, with varying degrees of managerial guidance, responded to and fulfilled. This basic function of parliament is nowhere more clearly set out than in the Swedish *Riksdagsordning* of 1617. After the opening ceremonies each estate, sitting apart, considered the king's proposition. The king would then visit them in turn and accept or question their response. If the estates disagreed, a representative of each one would meet and discuss their differences in the king's presence. '[I]n the end the divergences are reconciled, or His Majesty takes that which appears best'. This degree of royal involvement is rare in early modern Europe. The characteristics of discussion and resolution by each estate, however, was a common characteristic. The Swedish government's attitude, that the estates' responses should be confined to matters contained in the propositions, was also a common view amongst monarchs and indeed many politicians. The English commons' discussions of foreign policy stirred James I to fury in 1621 and elicited an angry riposte from Charles II's government in 1677: 'The people cannot consider it: that is proper only for the royal breast'. When in 1650 the Swedish commoner estates made proposals which were not related to the propositions, the outraged response was that they discussed 'such matters as came into their own heads . . . which in most other countries is wont to be accounted intolerable'. The royal propositions, however, were usually broad enough to allow the Swedish estates to introduce their own proposals into their answer. Furthermore, even when transacting the king's business, members of the English Parliament, the Swedish *Riksdag*, the French Estates-general and others were prepared to raise sensitive issues when the occasion seemed to justify or allow it.[46]

The *auxilium* for which parliaments were usually called was normally secured by legislative enactment, which required the approval of crown and estates (and in the Aragonese Cortes all members of each estate): so new laws and taxes were confirmed at the closing *solio* in Aragon, by the English king's pronouncement of *le roy la veult* and by the signing and sealing of the '*Riksdag* decision'.[47] Legislation, however, also benefited the monarchs' subjects. It was a widespread and customary practice, for example, as already observed in German principalities such as Bavaria, Hesse and Württemberg, Habsburg German lands (e.g. Lower Austria) and Iberian states, to present petitions. In the case of harmless, unexceptional requests, this might be the first step to the enactment of beneficial laws. Grievance petitions, however, were often neglected or rejected. They could be seen as an irritating distraction from significant business or, as in Portugal, they could lead to violence and riots by frustrated petitioners. Over the course of time, however, petitions to some parliaments were transformed into bills which underwent parliamentary scrutiny and were either rejected or enacted into parliamentary law. Late medieval and early modern English Parliaments developed and refined the classic bicameral three-reading procedure, which included committee scrutiny in each house. Proceeding by bill, however, was not a uniquely English development. It was standard practice in the other British parliaments. Although their procedures were less well-developed than those of the English Parliament, new Scottish procedural rules were made under James VI, whilst the English antiquary, John Hooker, wrote *The Order and Usage* to assist James Stanihurst, the speaker of the Irish commons. On the continent too, in territories as diverse as Hesse and (from the later seventeenth century) Sweden, private bills were or became a way of obtaining remedies or benefits.[48]

In order to facilitate the transaction of legislative and other business, parliaments developed appropriate procedures of debate and by the early modern period these were often well established and very precise. In the English Parliament, for example, 'For all that commeth in consultation, either in the upper house or in the neather house . . . he that will, riseth up and speaketh with it or against it: and so one after another so long as they shall thinke good'. Some, however, were slow to regularise the order of business, as we have seen in the case of Sweden. Until the law of 1690 there were few regulations about debate in the Polish *Sejm*, apart from a ban on discussion after dark and allocation of the session's last days for summing up debate. That law, however, did incorporate older usages which had been accepted parliamentary practice since the early sixteenth century.

Communication of opinion and the process of debate were not without their problems in early modern parliaments. Secrecy, or at least privacy of debate, was regarded as a desirable circumstance, even a prerequisite for open and honest debate in which members could freely express their views. The English commons was particularly sensitive to discussion of its affairs outside the house. Whereas, however, the presence of royal councillors or observers was often regarded as inhibiting, indeed intimidating, that was not the case in England, where elected privy councillors normally acted as a managerial team. The Castilian *Comuneros* in 1520 complained about the presence of a chairman appointed by the king to preside over the deliberations of the *procuradores*. On the other hand, lack of effective control could frustrate the best of intentions. This was clear in the Polish *Sejm* at the time Vincent Fabricius described the Chamber's procedure in 1647. The marshal (or speaker) had little authority; topics were not discussed in accordance with importance; and those who wished to disrupt had every opportunity to do so, especially during the sixteenth century 'execution of the laws' campaign. There was no pre-arranged agenda and 'there is no method of handling arguments here . . . whoever has already begun to speak is shouted down by the rest, and the Marshal is nearly torn to pieces' by others clamouring to speak. In this 'admirable conclave', where 'a prudent and ingenious Nobility rise there out of merit', sabres were on occasions unsheathed and violence threatened. Certainly, the *Sejm* did not have an enviable reputation amongst Poland's neighbours. Chancellor Oxenstierna of Sweden said of it that 'one says "write this", and another gets up and says "write that", and so one after another until at last somebody says "tear the whole thing up", and they depart no better than they came'.[49]

Differences of opinion might occur not only within a chamber, but also between the houses or estates of a parliament. In this respect at least developments in the Polish *Sejm* held out prospects of a more harmonious relationship. By the beginning of the sixteenth century *colloquia* of senators and deputies for discussion about a range of matters were already taking place. In bicameral or multi-cameral institutions such liaison was a natural development, indeed a necessary one in the interest of productivity. It did, however, have certain limitations. If one English member is to be believed, the commons' joint-conferences with the lords could result in the 'terrefienge of men's opinions', because deputies at such meetings would note their lordships' inclinations and 'knowinge that in the comon howse nothing is secret' they followed their wishes.[50] And, despite such frequent inter-cameral communication in the Aragonese Cortes, it was difficult to achieve effective co-ordination. 'Each estate was a world unto itself, and its priorities and interests could not be shared by the others.'[51]

Parliamentary productivity required discussion to be followed by decision, which in practical terms meant a vote. It could be very formal: one by one each bishop and peer in the English lords pronounced 'Content' or 'Not content', whereas in the commons acclamation was the first option before a division. Voting could be open or secret – in the Sicilian *Parlamento* both were used. A majority vote sufficed there as it did, for example, in the British parliaments. Some parliaments, however, required unanimity: for example, in all *brazos* of the Aragonese Cortes, the Valencian noble *brazo* and the Dutch States-general. This would have made decisions very difficult to achieve, if the assemblies had not adopted a flexible approach in practice. So the Aragonese *brazos* referred contested matters to a small committee with powers to make decisions; on one occasion the Valencian nobles ejected a solitary dissenter before voting; and the Dutch did not rigidly enforce it. In contrast, the roles of *unanimity* and *unity*, which developed in the Polish *Sejm*, imposed increasing constraints and a consequent lack of productivity.

At the end of parliaments in some European states, princes and assemblies came together in elaborate, often splendid, closing ceremonies. There the monarch assented to legislation passed by the houses (as in England) or, as in Aragon, together they would proclaim the new laws and taxes. In contrast to the Polish *Sejm*, and of course those assemblies left in abeyance by autocratic or disillusioned princes, most early modern parliaments had reason to celebrate their continued service to community and government in solemn closing rituals.

Notes

1   See above, pp. 28–9, 77–8, 97; D.L. Smith, *The Stuart Parliaments, 1603–1689* (Oxford, 1999), p.175.

2   José I. Fortea Pérez, 'The Cortes of Castile and Philip II's fiscal policy' *PER* 11, 2 (Dec. 1991), pp. 117, 138; I.A.A. Thompson, 'Castile: absolutism, constitutionalism and liberty', in P.T. Hoffman and K. Norberg, eds, *Fiscal Crises, Liberty, and Representative Government, 1450–1789* (Stanford, CA, 1994), pp. 193, 195, 217–22; see above, pp. 73, 89–92.

3   In 52.4 per cent of France, according to J. Russell Major, *From Renaissance Monarchy to Absolute Monarchy. French Kings, Nobles and Estates* (London, 1994), p. 41.

4   P.T. Hoffman, 'Early modern France, 1450–1700', in Hoffman and Norberg, eds, *Fiscal Crises*, pp. 247–9.

5   Myers, *Parliaments and Estates*, p. 29.

6   K. Krüger, 'Regional representation in Schleswig and Holstein: a special type of early modern political participation' *PER* 7, 1 (June 1987), pp. 34–6; J.A. Vann, *The Making of a State. Württemberg, 1593–1793* (London, 1984), pp. 45, 112–14; see above, pp. 96–100; V. Press, 'The system of estates in the Austrian hereditary lands and . . . Empire. A comparison', in R.J.W. Evans and T.V. Thomas, eds, *Crown, Church and Estates. Central European Politics in the Sixteenth and Seventeenth Centuries* (London, 1991), pp. 3, 9; R.J.W. Evans, 'The Habsburg Monarchy and Bohemia, 1526–1848', in M. Greengrass, ed., *Conquest and Coalescence* (London, 1991), pp. 143–4.

7   *Stats Realm*, vol. III, pp. 813, 939; vol. V, p. 11. J.M. Goodare, 'Parliamentary taxation in Scotland, 1560–1603' *SHR* 68, 1 (April 1989), pp. 45–7; ibid., 'Parliament and society in Scotland, 1560–1603' PhD, University of Edinburgh, 1989, pp. 212–24, 277–80, 509–17; ibid., 'The Scottish Parliament of 1621' *HJ* 38, 1 (1995), pp. 29, 33–5; J.R. Young, 'The Scottish Parliament, 1639–1661' PhD, University of Glasgow, 1993, p. 511; see above, pp. 108–9.

8   M. Roberts, ed., *Sweden as a Great Power, 1611–1697* (London, 1968), p. 9; M.F. Metcalf, ed., *The Riksdag: A History of the Swedish Parliament* (Stockholm, 1987), pp. 102–4.

9   J. Miller, ed., *Absolutism in Seventeenth Century Europe* (London, 1990), pp. 76–7.

10 The viceroy himself was constrained, however, because he could not alter the ancient laws without the approval of the *Parlamento*. A. Marongiu, *Medieval Parliaments. A Comparative Study* (London, 1968), pp. 167–8.

11 See above, p. 93; X. Gil, 'Crown and Cortes in early modern Aragon: reassessing revisionisms' *PER* 13, 2 (Dec. 1993), pp. 110, 119–20.

12 S.G. Ellis, 'Parliament and community in Yorkist and Tudor Ireland', in A. Cosgrove and J.I. McGuire, eds, *Parliament and Community, Historical Studies* XIV (Belfast, 1983), pp. 47–8, 50; see above, pp. 48–9.

13 Unlike some encompassing English laws such as the acts concerning Wales (1534 and 1543), franchises (1536) and artificers (1563). Goodare, 'Parliament and society', p. 77.

14 Ibid., pp. 281–472; J. Wormald, *Court, Kirk and Community: Scotland 1470–1625*

(London, 1981), p. 21; J. Cameron, *James V. The Personal Rule, 1528–1542* (East Lothian, 1998), p. 339.

15 Goodare, 'Parliament and society', pp. 492, 495, 498; T. Thomson and C. Innes, eds, *The Acts of the Parliaments of Scotland* 12 vols (Edinburgh, 1814–75) vol.IV, pp. 14–17, 18–20.

16 G. Donaldson, *The Scottish Reformation* (Cambridge, 1960), pp. 211–13; Goodare, 'Parliament and society', pp. 16–17, 36–7, 78–9; Young, 'Scottish Parliament', pp. 506–11.

17 See above, pp. 104–5. Grace bills bearing the sign manual, and so more likely to be enacted into law by the two houses, became a token of royal favour and a form of patronage under the Tudors. M.A.R. Graves and C.R. Kyle, '"The Kinges most excellent majestie out of his gracious disposicion": the evolution of the grace bills in English parliaments, 1547–1642' *PER* 18 (Nov. 1998), pp. 27–43.

18 E.g. the most productive English parliaments in each reign between Henry VIII and Charles I (to 1629) were: 1540 (80 acts), 1548/49 (60), 1553 (33), 1563 (52), 1624 (75) and 1628 (27).

19 See above, pp. 103, 125–6; Metcalf, ed., *The Riksdag*, pp. 104–5; A. Upton, 'Absolutism and the rule of the law: the case of Karl XI of Sweden' *PER* 8, 1 (June 1988), pp. 35–7; M. Roberts, *Gustavus Adolphus* (2nd edn, London, 1992), p. 89.

20 See above, p. 51; H.G. Koenigsberger, 'Why did the States General of the Netherlands become revolutionary in the sixteenth century?' *PER* 2, 2 (Dec. 1982), p. 103.

21 A.F. Upton, 'The Swedish *Riksdag* and the English Parliament in the seventeenth century – some comparisons', in N. Stjernquist, ed., *The Swedish Riksdag in an International Perspective* (Stockholm, 1989), pp. 121, 123, 125.

22 E.g. in Aragon and in England, especially with the revival of parliamentary impeachment in James I's reign.

23 Metcalf, ed., *The Riksdag*, p. 100; A. Marongiu, *Medieval Parliaments. A Comparative Study* (London, 1968), pp. 143–4, 151, 197, 199.

24 G. Griffiths, *Representative Government in Western Europe in the Sixteenth Century* (Oxford, 1968), pp. 234–6, 239–40, 242–9; P. Sanz, 'The cities in the Aragonese Cortes in the medieval and early modern periods' *PER* 14, 2 (Dec. 1994), pp. 99, 106–8; X. Gil, 'Crown and Cortes in early modern Aragon: reassessing revisionisms' *PER* 13, 2 (Dec. 1993), pp. 115–22; J.L. Palos, 'The Habsburg Monarchy and the Catalan Corts: the failure of a relationship' *PER* 13, 2 (Dec. 1993), pp. 140–1; I.A.A. Thompson and Bartolomé Yun Casalilla, eds, *The Castilian Crisis of the Seventeenth Century* (Cambridge, 1994), p. 28; C. Jago, 'Philip II and the Cortes of Castile: the case of the Cortes of 1576', *P&P* 109 (Nov. 1985), pp. 26–7.

25 P. Cardim, 'Ceremonial and ritual in the Cortes of Portugal (1581–1698)' *PER* 12, 1 (June 1992), pp. 12–13; ibid., 'Politics and power relations in Portugal (sixteenth–eighteenth centuries)' *PER* 13, 2 (Dec. 1993), p. 107.

26 B. Kümin and A. Würgler, 'Petitions, *Gravamina* and the early modern state: local influence on central legislation in England and Germany (Hesse)' *PER* 17 (1997), pp. 41–2, 44, 47.

27 Metcalf, ed., *The Riksdag*, pp. 98–101.

28 See above, pp. 28, 48–9.

29 See above, pp. 23–4, 29, 35–9, 52–3, 103–4.

30 R. Holinshed, *Chronicles of England, Scotland and Ireland* 6 vols (London, 1807/8), vol.3, p. 826; Cardim, 'Politics and power relations', pp. 95, 107.

31 Goodare, 'Parliament and society', pp. 10–15.

32 See above, pp. 20–1, 31, 38; H.G. Koenigsberger, 'Parliaments and estates', in R.W. Davis, ed., *The Origins of Modern Freedom in the West* (Stanford, CA, 1995), pp. 174–5; Cardim, 'Ceremonial and ritual', p. 4; H. Olszewski, 'Reflections on the theory and practice of Sejm debate in Poland from the 16th to the 18th centuries' *APH* 48 (1983), p. 65.

33 S.J. Houston, *James I* (2nd edn, London, 1995), pp. 82–4.

34 R.C. Head, *Early Modern Democracy in the Grisons* (Cambridge, 1995), pp. 95–7, 106–8.

35 R. Bonney, *The European Dynastic States, 1494–1660* (Oxford, 1992), pp. 317–18; I.A.A. Thompson, *Crown and Cortes* (Aldershot, 1993), VI, pp. 30–1; K.M. Brown, *Kingdom or Province? Scotland and the Regal Union, 1603–1715* (New York, 1992), p. 13.

36 This does not apply during the 1640s when the English and Scottish parliaments had virtually continuous existence.

37 They were, however, susceptible to royal pressure, persuasion and favours.

38 See above, pp. 30, 147; H.G. Koenigsberger, 'The Italian parliaments from their origins to the end of the 18th century', in *Politicians and Virtuosi* (London, 1986), pp. 42, 46, 52; Olszewski, 'Sejm debate', p. 68; Metcalf, ed., *The Riksdag*, pp. 101–2; Young, 'Scottish Parliament', pp. 9, 11–16, 29–33; J. Scally, 'Constitutional revolution, party and faction in the Scottish parliaments of Charles I', in C. Jones, ed., *The Scots and Parliament* (Edinburgh, 1996), pp. 59–61, 71–2; Gil, 'Crown and Cortes', pp. 120–1; J.H. Grever, 'Committees and deputations in the assemblies of the Dutch Republic, 1660–1668' *PER* 1, 1 (June 1981), pp. 14–17; J. Russell Major, *Representative Government in Early Modern France* (Yale, New Haven, 1980), pp. 166–8.

39 J. Wormald, 'James VI and I: Two kings or one?' *History* 68 (1983), p. 195; J.H. Elliott, *The Revolt of the Catalans, 1598–1640* (Cambridge, 1984), pp. 134–7; Metcalf, ed., *The Riksdag*, p. 102.

40 A.B. Pernal and R.P. Gasse, 'Procedure in the diets of the Polish-Lithuanian commonwealth: a description by Vincent Fabricius in 1647' *PER* 12, 2 (Dec. 1992), pp. 113–15; P. Croft and I.A.A. Thompson, 'Aristocracy and representative government in unicameral and bicameral institutions. The role of the peers in the Castilian Cortes and the English Parliament, 1529–1664', in H.W. Blom, W.P. Blockmans, H. de Schepper, eds, *Bicameralisme* (The Hague, 1992), pp. 67–9; E.R. Foster, 'Staging a parliament in early Stuart England', in P. Clark, A.G.R. Smith, N. Tyacke, eds, *The English Commonwealth, 1547–1640* (Leicester, 1979), pp. 129–31; Gil, 'Crown and Cortes', p. 113; Cardim, 'Ceremonial and ritual', pp. 4–6, 7, 9–11.

41 This summarises the account of the 1672 opening in Vann, *The Making of a State*, pp. 128–32.

42 See above, p. 183; M. Roberts, ed., *Sweden as a Great Power 1611–1697* (London, 1968), pp. 11–13; Vann, *The Making of a State*, p. 130.

43 Goodare, 'Parliament and society', pp. 518–23; Wormald, *Court, Kirk and Community*, p. 156; R.S. Rait, *The Parliaments of Scotland* (Glasgow, 1924), pp. 531–2.

44 Roberts, ed., *Sweden as a Great Power*, pp. 30–1.

45 Miller, ed., *Absolutism*, p. 74.

46 Metcalf, ed., *The Riksdag*, pp. 98–9; Upton, 'Riksdag and parliament', in Stjernquist, ed., *Swedish Riksdag*, pp. 120–2; Roberts, *Sweden as a Great Power*, p. 13.

47 Metcalf, ed., *The Riksdag*, pp. 98–9.

48 Kümin and Würgler, 'Petitions, *Gravamina* and the early modern state', pp. 42, 44; Cardim, 'Ceremonial and ritual', p. 12; V.F. Snow, ed., *Parliament in Elizabethan England. John Hooker's Order and Usage* (Yale, New Haven, 1977), pp. 14–15.

49 Sir Thomas Smith, *De Republica Anglorum*, ed. Mary Dewar (Cambridge, 1982), p. 81; Olszewski, 'Sejm debate', pp. 65–6, 69–71; W. Uruszczak, 'The implementation of domestic policy in Poland under the last two Jagellonian kings, 1506– 1572' *PER* 7, 2 (Dec. 1987), pp. 136–7; Pernal and Gasse, 'Diets of the Polish-Lithuanian commonwealth', pp. 115–17; A. Mączak, 'Executio Bonorum and Reduktion: two essays in solutions of the domain–state dilemma', in Stjernquist, ed., *Swedish Riksdag*, p. 98.

50 Olszewski, 'Sejm debate', pp. 67–8; B.L. Harl. MS 253, fol.35v.

51 Gil, 'Crown and Cortes', p. 113.

8

Reflections on Counsel and Consent

ONE OF THE original and prime functions of medieval and representative assemblies, to which little attention was given in the
previous chapter, was *consilium*. That apparent neglect is in itself a
reflection of developments and changes in the role and functions of early
modern parliaments. Early medieval rulers 'were counselled by their
curia, their court of magnates, lay and ecclesiastical'.[1] As governments
developed, their functions and responsibilities became more diverse,
complex and demanding. They needed advice not only from the
traditional ecclesiastical and noble counsellors but also from those rural
and urban sub-noble elites who represented the wider community. And,
when parliaments emerged, from the thirteenth century onwards,
princes sought both *consent* and *counsel* from them. So, in 1295, Edward I
summoned each peer to the English parliament 'to treat with us [on]
certain important matters touching ourself and our realm . . . and to
give us your counsel'.[2]

Counsel could be expressed in a number of ways:

1   As parliaments were extensions of royal *curia*, advice was one of
    their initial purposes and duties. Over time that duty also became a
    parliamentary right.
2   As parliaments were 'points of contact', monarchs used these
    occasions to seek information on the current state of affairs in the
    kingdom. Members could respond with accompanying advice on
    remedies for current problems.
3   Monarchs sought advice and might even call parliaments to counsel
    them on specific issues. Emperor Maximilian I (1493–1519) in-
    structed his son Philip that 'for the conduct and execution of your
    great affairs . . . never give authority over yourself to those who live
    under your rule . . . [but] I advise you . . . always to ask their
    counsel and help'.[3]

4   In addition, as previously considered, parliaments acquired the right to present petitions and seek redress of grievances. In practice, this embodied advice on what needed to be addressed, accompanied sometimes by warnings of what might happen if it was not.

Such expressions of counsel were common to many late medieval European parliaments. Early modern monarchs, however, often became less interested in *consilium* and much more in *auxilium* – with the usual qualification that all such generalisations about European parliaments carry a quota of exceptions. Sixteenth- and seventeenth-century rulers increasingly saw the primary, even exclusive, function of parliaments as *auxilium*. Above all, this meant money to meet the fiscal imperative of war-driven governments, especially those of composite monarchies with a range of defensive commitments. If parliaments could not or would not deliver, their future was liable to be bleak. Many, though not including the French Estates-general and Castilian Cortes, also serviced states with new laws, especially in times of crisis. Co-operative parliaments enacted a sequence of religious changes for successive English monarchs between 1529 and 1559, whilst Gustav Vasa secured his crown, its hereditary succession within the ruling dynasty, the Church's wealth and a Lutheran Reformation by appeals to the Swedish *Riksdag* in 1527 and 1544. According to James I, Elizabeth's chief minister, Burghley, once said that there was nothing that an act of parliament could not do.[4]

That was certainly borne out in the early modern English parliaments.

So the old parliamentary function of *consilium* lost its importance, value and even relevance to many early modern monarchs. As the French national assembly neither granted taxes nor made laws, its *raison d'être* was counsel. And when it could not even offer constructive and effective counsel, as in 1560–61 and 1614–15, it ceased to be called. French kings turned to alternatives, such as the assembly of notables for advice and assistance on reforms. Advice, however, was often and to a growing extent unwanted. On all but three occasions during her reign Queen Elizabeth I summoned English Parliaments specifically for money. The three exceptions were: in 1559, when it was called for 'consultacion, advise and contentacion [by assente] . . . [on] the well making of lawes for the . . . unitinge of the people of this realme into an uniforme order of religion';[5] and in 1572 and 1586 the publicly declared reasons for their meeting were to devise laws for Elizabeth's safety and to counsel her on the fate of Mary Stuart. Once the new Church had been established, however, it became a prohibited topic in future Parliaments. In 1572 she called the assembly reluctantly and under pressure whilst in September 1586 her chief minister, Lord Burghley, wrote that 'We stick upon Parliament which her Majesty mislikes to have'.[6] It did not prevent her from using the opportunity to obtain a tax grant. In brief, Elizabeth did not welcome advice. Three generations of Stuarts – James VI and I, Charles I and Charles II – all resented criticism and counsel on foreign policy as unwarranted interference in a perceived prerogative matter.

These British monarchs were not exceptional. They simply expressed what amounted to a common and growing impatience and sensitivity amongst early modern rulers. Such attitudes were generally fuelled by relentless financial pressures, reinforced in some cases by autocratic inclinations. The anger expressed by Philip IV and his withdrawal from the 1626 Aragonese Cortes, because it was more concerned with its grievances than with royal tax needs, illustrate the trend. Spanish kings, from Charles I onwards, were willing to use pressure, intimidation and bribery to achieve their parliamentary ends. Even weaker rulers such as the Polish kings, whose national diets met for a set period of six weeks and so could not be rushed to conclude business, sought priority for their proposals over consideration of the grievances of the estates. When Vincent Fabricius wrote his account of the king's attempt to achieve this in 1647, King Wladyslaw IV was under such desperate military pressure from the Turks that he had raised an army and gone to war without the *Sejm*'s required approval. And he needed prompt parliamentary support, rather than time spent on complaints and remedies.[7]

Of course there were exceptions. There was still room for counsel, both in the parliaments of republics, where decisions were reached by collective discussion, and in those which grew in political strength and whose voiced complaints and advices had to be heeded by rulers.[8] Generally, however, early modern parliaments were called for practical assistance. For most of the time and in most cases monarchs were not in search of counsel. And when a ruler publicly announced that a parliament had been called for consultation with his loyal subjects, the real purpose, more often than not, was to drum up support for policies already adopted or decisions already made. Such decisions were often potentially controversial and might involve costly actions. In other words, they sought to justify themselves and so obtain parliamentary support of a practical (especially financial) kind. It was an operation orchestrated by monarchy and one which involved appeals to loyalty, persuasive arguments of the benefits which would accrue, the seductive skills of the patron and, sometimes, the selective use of pressure and intimidation. It is an irony that Simon de Montfort's enlarged assembly of 1264, the prototype of English medieval Parliaments, was called to rally political support for his position against the current monarch, Henry III. In the sixteenth century Gustav Vasa proved to be a parliamentary stage manager *par excellence* when he informed the *Riksdag* at Vasteras in 1627 that he regretted having been elected king by ungrateful Swedes, that he could not effectively govern on the crown's income which was pathetically small compared to that of the Church, that he was accused of favouring heresy and that, in consequence, he intended to abdicate. As observed previously, in a state of panic the *Riksdag* limited the Church's political power and wealth and transferred much of that wealth to the crown.[9]

For those of Gustav's contemporaries who ruled composite monarchies, the task of drumming-up support was a more complex one. Charles V had to consider the needs of his entire empire. These, however, were of little concern to the parliaments of individual territories. Charles had to persuade the States-general of the Netherlands, for example, 'to support an imperial policy which was for them always remote and often incomprehensible'.[10] At a critical moment in his reign another contemporary, Henry VIII, lacked either the confident skills of Gustav Vasa or Charles's knowledge of what he wanted in his parliamentary dealings. When Henry called Parliament in 1529, after his failure to secure the annulment of his first marriage, he presented no specific policies or proposed solutions. Lehmberg suggests that he called the assembly 'in the vague hope that its members might suggest a solution'. If so, this was an example of a ruler utterly dependent on counsel at that moment.[11]

Here, as in so many other respects, variety and change are qualities which are repeatedly displayed in the colourful tapestry of European parliamentary history. Simple personality differences or eccentricities can disturb or mock the carefully constructed propositions or theories about parliamentary developments. Whilst so many parliaments were under intense pressure, contention was common and some even disappeared, in the early and middle years of the seventeenth century the *Riksdag* under Gustav Adolf grew in strength and confidence. To a considerable extent this was a consequence of the parliamentary skills, even artistry, of the king and his chancellor, Oxenstierna. The *Riksdag* was more effectively organised, and collaboration was its characteristic feature. The *Riksdag* ordinance of 1617 incorporated a remarkable degree of personal contact: after the estates' consideration of the royal proposals, the king would personally receive each one's answer, give a written or oral reply and hear differences between the estates discussed 'until in the end the divergences are reconciled'. This parliamentary rapport is exemplified in Gustav Adolf's farewell to the estates in 1630, desiring the nobility to display 'manliness and knightly qualities', exhorting the clergy to set an example of righteousness to their flocks, wishing the burghers 'that your little cabins may become great mansions' and the peasants 'that their barns be full' so that 'without sighing' they could fulfil their 'duties and obligations'. The following reigns, however, were characterised by conflict between estates rather than by such communication and co-operation. In any case it all ended in 1680 with Karl XI and the establishment of absolutism. This may cause us to reflect once more on a common, albeit by no means comprehensive, drift of affairs in early modern European states. The value of consent to rulers declined as the need for increased resources and freedom of action, with or without consent, became paramount. It was expressed in a shift of attitude: from the co-operative to the coercive and exploitative. At worst, parliaments were not called again. They were not, however, suppressed, but simply left in abeyance. They could be recalled at any time, as the French Estates-general was in 1789.

Notes

1   H.G. Koenigsberger, 'Parliaments and estates', in R.W. Davis, ed., *The Origins of Modern Freedom in the West* (Stanford, CA, 1995), p. 151.

2   J.E. Powell and K. Wallis, *The House of Lords in the Middle Ages* (London, 1968), p. 222.

3   Koenigsberger, 'Parliaments and estates', p. 176.

4   J.P. Somerville, *King James VI and I: Political Writings* (Cambridge, 1994), p. 209.

5   T.E. Hartley, ed., *Proceedings in the Parliaments of Elizabeth I*, vol.I, *1558–1581* (Leicester, 1981), pp. 33–4.

6   M.A.R. Graves, *Burghley* (London, 1998), pp. 75–6.

7   A.B. Pernal and R.P. Gasse, 'Procedure in the diets of the Polish-Lithuanian Commonwealth: a description by Vincent Fabricius in 1647' *PER* 12, 2 (Dec. 1992), pp. 111–12 and n.20.

8 In the case of the Polish *Sejm*, however, the principles of unity and unanimity and the *liberum veto* could have the reverse effect by annulling the legislative end-products of discussion and petition.

9 M. Roberts, *The Early Vasas. A History of Sweden, 1523–1611* (Cambridge, 1968), pp. 75–6.

10 H.G. Koenigsberger, 'Parliaments in the sixteenth century and beyond', in Davis, ed., *Origins of Modern Freedom*, p. 291.

11 S.E. Lehmberg, *The Reformation Parliament, 1529–1536* (Cambridge, 1970), pp. 2–3.

Index